VALLEY FORGE

THE MACMILLAN COMPANY
NEW YORK · BOSTON · CHICAGO · DALLAS
ATLANTA · SAN FRANCISCO

MACMILLAN AND CO., Limited
LONDON · BOMBAY · CALCUTTA · MADRAS
MELBOURNE

THE MACMILLAN COMPANY
OF CANADA, Limited
TORONTO

GENERAL GEORGE WASHINGTON

Portrait by Rembrandt Peale in Chester County Historical Society, West Chester, Pa.

Valley Forge

By

HARRY EMERSON WILDES

"Naked and starving as they are, we cannot
enough admire the incomparable patience
and fidelity of the soldiery."

NEW YORK : The Macmillan Company : *1938*

E
234
W55

Feb. '39

NᴇN 2.34

17237

To Kiki

PREFACE

VALLEY FORGE has never had its due. Though the Nation was born in Boston and in Philadelphia, and though every one of the Thirteen Colonies and of the thirty-five States which have since been added to the Union has shared in the development of these United States, the country was preserved through the inspiration of the Valley Forge winter. The army came there in defeat; the troops left to win their victory.

Not for eighty years has Valley Forge had a full-length history. In 1850 Henry Woodman, born at Valley Forge, set down in letters to newspapers of Philadelphia and Doylestown, the reminiscences of his soldier father and other surviving veterans. Most of our present knowledge of the encampment is based on these letters, later gathered into book form. Woodman, however, was no scholar; his dates and facts and deductions were frequently in error.

The author, who lives at Valley Forge and who long maintained an office address at Independence Square, looking out upon Independence Hall, has sought to remedy this lack of a complete account of Valley Forge in its full historical setting. He has seen the encampment as the central feature of the Revolution; he has looked upon the camp site as the place where American democracy first grew to manhood. The wintry ordeal at Valley Forge was the Nation's great sacrifice for freedom.

Material on the sufferings at Valley Forge is not readily discoverable. The soldiers did not whine over their hardships. More often, they glossed over their hardships as did New York's Richard Wheeler who reassured his mother, "We are very comfortable and are living on the fat of the land." Yonkers' George Ewing modestly entered in his Journal: "Were I to describe the hardships and the difficulties we underwent, no person but those who were with us would credit my relation. Therefore I chuse to pass it over in silence."

Family traditions, legends, diaries, and a few letters piece out the gaps. Old folk in the Valley Forge neighborhood have been generous in their reminiscences. Incredible as it seems, some of them have actually known survivors of the camp! Two old ladies, Rachel Peck Posey and Mary McDonald, children at the time of the encampment, lived more than a century after Washington's departure. Half a dozen old soldiers survived to tell their tales to young lads whose lives spanned the nineteenth century.

Traditions, however, require careful checking. In providing such corroborative detail the files of the Historical Society of Pennsylvania and of the Chester and Montgomery County historical societies have been carefully combed. The curators of the Chester County Historical Society, at West Chester, have been particularly gracious in their assistance.

Especial thanks are due to the devoted friends who labored so hard to keep this book free of the more glaring errors. Dr. Henry Pleasants, Jr., of West Chester, gave lavishly of his learning in matters concerning the military aspects of the war, and particularly concerning Brandywine and the Battle of the Clouds. Robert Ferree Brinton, also of West Chester, was assiduous in suggesting new ideas. Much of the plan of the book is due to his thoughtful assistance. Jerome

J. Sheas, for more than a quarter of a century the Superintendent of Valley Forge Park, and Gilbert S. Jones, his capable successor, have been kind in their coöperation and have checked the chapters dealing with the Park. Jerold O'Connell, long postmaster at Valley Forge and now chief of the guide service at the Park, has been a helpful and inspiring critic. Mrs. W. Herbert Burk, widow of the energetic rector who created, at the Washington Memorial Chapel, an inspiring and beautiful memorial, made generous suggestions. George W. Schultz, of Reading, assisted greatly in clarifying details of old forges and iron-making methods. The contributions of Julius F. Sachse, formerly of Berwyn, on early Chester County history, particularly on matters concerning old inns along Lancaster Road, must be gratefully credited. A particular debt is due to the author's friend, the late Ellis Paxson Oberholtzer, for the use of manuscript notes and memoranda collected during Dr. Oberholtzer's service on the Valley Forge Park Commission. The late Francis M. Brooke's collections have been similarly drawn upon.

The writer is exceedingly grateful to the Valley Forge Park Commission, to Mrs. Burk, and to Dan J. Voorhees, of Valley Forge, for permission to use illustrations originally published in their popular booklets.

The author is deeply indebted to Katharine Elizabeth Dealy, indefatigable worker and assistant, for her many criticisms and for her untiring helpfulness. Last, but not least of all thanks are due the author's wife, Helen Jaquette Wildes, for her enthusiastic interest and assistance. The volume, it is only fair to say, was first suggested by Mrs. Wildes and has been largely shaped by her ideas.

HARRY EMERSON WILDES

Valley Forge

CONTENTS

ILLUSTRATIONS

xiii

CHAPTER ONE

Where Dogwoods Bloom

THE Revolution was won at Valley Forge. A defeated, dispirited, and tattered array came here hungry, cold, and broken; Washington led away the same men, drilled and disciplined into a confident army, in pride to victory.

Valley Forge was more, however, than a camp. Within its shadow were fought two major battles: a bloody bayonet attack broke down the American morale; an unfought battle might, save for the accident of cloudburst, have brought victory to the Continentals five years before the final peace was signed. Near here, too, Washington had three other important camping grounds; from this vicinity, he drew his most essential war supplies.

The area was, however, a land of peace. Within a radius of twenty miles from Washington's Headquarters were settlements more famed for spiritual and material culture, prior to the Revolution, than any similar section of America. The first American beginnings in art, science, and invention, in steel-making, music, and scientific agriculture were essayed within sight of the encampment grounds. The people were as remarkable as their achievements: saints and spiritual leaders dominated the vicinity. But, above all else, Valley Forge was famous for its beauty.

Valley Forge is lovely in the spring. The rich meadows bordering Valley Creek are gleaming green as the morning sun drinks up their early dew. The slowly sloping hills which billow upward from the creek-side hollow where the Washington Headquarters nestle are delicately fragrant with spring bloom of honeysuckle and azalea. Upstream, the narrow creek, winding gracefully through the high protecting wooded walls that line its banks, ripples peacefully in its sharp-cut canyon. Migrant wild ducks float here, with kingfishers and blue herons to bear them company.

Summer, too, is lovely. Bright scorching suns may parch the Great Valley that stretches twenty miles into the west, but the hills of Valley Forge are cool and pleasant. The wooded groves that dot the wide expanse of open rolling country are dense enough to offer cooling shade, yet not so thick as to cut off the soft south breezes. The Schuylkill's crescent bend adds to the picture of calm peace. The crickets chirp incessantly.

Valley Forge is lovely in the autumn when lavishly the woods display their brown and golden colorings. Scarlet maples and bright-hued gums turn it into a flaming forest. The wide Park plains are deeper, darker green, speckled by the blowing leaves; the tree boles are more individual; on rainy evenings the trunks, shown suddenly by headlights, glisten with a shining blackness. The skies, when storms have passed, are deeper blue.

So, too, is Valley Forge lovely in the winter. Smooth, unbroken snows spread outward, soft sometimes as cotton; crystalline again when gray, cold sunlight freezes a surface into crust. The tall, thin trees stand slender, unprotected save by each other. Now that the katydids have gone, and now that all the sounds are stilled, Valley Forge is silent in contented quietude. Only the flight of juncos indicates that Valley Forge is living.

The picture is of Valley Forge today, after art has come to make a Park of hills and meadows, streams and gently rising fields. For fully half a century, Pennsylvania's landscape artists have lavished their best skill in transforming Valley Forge into a lasting monument worthy of the heroes who suffered there. But, after all allowance has been made for artificial aid devoted to this shrine of beauty, there still remains a recognition that the site itself is fraught with loveliness. For the glory is not alone within the fairly narrow limits of the Park itself. Eastward across the Schuylkill, in the rich plains and well farmed hills that stretch to distant bluish mountains, lies a scene of less sophisticated beauty. Southward across the Great Valley rise the high South Valley hills, sharply cut to let small brooks flow to the Schuylkill, folding closely where the mountains meet. A long and forested expanse, green with its hemlocks even in the winter, golden brown and brightly crimson in the fall, runs along the south horizon.

Westward indefinitely stretches the Great Valley, its evergreen pastures threaded by the winding Valley Creek, its smooth, rich, fertile land patterned by the dogwoods and the cherry trees that bloom so snowily in spring. Far in the distance, before the Great Valley curves to find its way through the twin mountain ranges that protect its isolation, the land begins to rise in swelling grassy terraces. From the hills of Valley Forge, the watershed is visible where streams flow either to the Schuylkill or to the distant Brandywine.

Rounding the roadways through the Park, charming views

3

spring suddenly to sight. A quick glimpse through the forest shows a silver stream slashed through the deep green meadows; another passing flash allows a rapid sight of stony-shelved Mount Misery, standing its wooded guard at the rear of Washington's old camp. The visitor who comes to Valley Forge over the slowly rising farm lands is suddenly struck silent by an unexpected sight of the Schuylkill, looking like a mountain lake almost at his feet. On almost every pathway through the Park such scenes of loveliness abound.

Valley Forge was quite as lovely in the difficult days when Washington's eight thousand men camped here. From December, 1777, until the following June, while he and his foreign assistants were molding a force of brave individual soldiers into an invincible, disciplined army, the camp ground was quite as beautiful, in its wild, rugged, natural disorder, as it has since become through the artistry of landscape experts. Man has tamed the lavish exuberance of Valley Forge just as efficiently as Washington and Steuben drilled the Continental soldiers into their smooth efficiency.

The hills were forested when Washington came here, and they are forested today; but the trees themselves have changed. None of the great white oaks which towered a hundred feet or more above the camp have lived until today. That bitter winter of 1777–1778 was much too cold for ill clad, half-starved soldiers to endure without the roaring camp-fires which such trees could make. Great oaks, five feet or more in diameter, were felled for fuel or shelter. Smaller hickories, slim black oaks and poplars, low-growing gums and wide-branching unkempt locusts fed the fires or were cut down to pile before the breastworks.

Four trees now remain from the time of the encampment, but only two stand within the Valley Forge Park grounds.

WHERE DOGWOODS BLOOM

An old white ash, once tall and graceful in its delicate contours, throws now a feeble shade across the entrance to the Washington Inn, the site of ancient camp ovens. It is the only living thing at the encampment proper which was alive when Washington arrived at his Headquarters; and undoubtedly it owes its life to its small size at the time, for when troops were quartered on this ground the ten-year trunk was too thin for good fires, too thick to make a pike for officers. Washington must have stood beneath the slender limbs.

At the southern limit of the camp, in the little village of Port Kennedy (famous once for its exports of limestone), is the only other Park tree surviving from the encampment days. An elmlike hackberry, rare in Pennsylvania, struggles in a sheltered hollow. Filmy with flowers in the spring, dark purple with its sweetish, almondlike fruit in fall, the hackberry has battled earnestly to free itself from the parasitic witches'-broom that kills so many of its species. The trunk is bolted now; the limbs are guyed to brace them from the winds; the Park Commission labors to preserve its life. This, too, was a sapling, barely five years old when soldiers came to draw water at the spring close to its roots.

Two other trees, more ancient, were adult when Washington's bleeding soldiers passed on their historic march through wintry snows. Three miles from the Headquarters, near the crossroads at the King of Prussia Inn, a great white oak, now nearly twenty feet in girth, has been made a Pennsylvania state memorial. Already two centuries old when the tattered army passed beneath its branches, the oak has survived a stroke of lightning which gashed it almost asunder; it has suffered from the vandalism of road builders who cut its largest roots; it has been mutilated, too, by ruthless linemen who lopped its magnificent branches; but the tree, show-

5

ing the same determination as did the Continental army, indomitably lives on.

Almost equally aged is the Rehobeth sycamore, southeast of the Park grounds, shading a stone building once used as General Nathanael Greene's quarters. This ancient tree, whose hundred-foot spread is equaled by its height, links the memories of the first white settlement in the Great Valley to the present time. Under its shade, the first pioneer to wander seeking game in lands known only to the Indians, dug out a rude cave shelter. Later he built here the first house near Valley Forge.

Though these four trees alone remain from the thousands seen by Washington, much of the area around Valley Forge remains a forest. The woods that once were called the "Hundred Mile Forest" because they reached unbroken from Philadelphia to the Susquehanna are still extensive. Westward of the campground lie more than two hundred thousand tree-clad acres. Mount Misery is covered with black birch, poplar, beech and hickory, ash and maple, chestnut oaks and, here and there, a cedar. Toward the far horizon are mountain forests where unbroken blocks of woodland lie almost untraversed.

Even these trees of today are not, however, direct successors to the woods that the Continental troops cut down. The chestnut blight that swept across the land killed off the myriads of chestnut trees which once flourished on the hills. And here again, the spirit of the soldiers seems to survive for, year after year, the roots of ancient chestnuts, whose trunks have long since died, put forth new shoots to struggle bravely upward. The new shoots, growing fanlike to a height of four or five feet, die in their turn, but still the chestnuts struggle to reëstablish their supremacy. Valley Forge imbues

6

its creatures with unquenchable determination. On such a campground, freedom could not die.

In Washington's day, as well as in our own, the dogwoods edged the forests. The spectacular pink blossoms, which now so admirably set off the common waxy, white variety, were not in evidence, for these resplendent trees are recently developed "sports" artificially created by careful budding; but the small white dogwoods, bending forward from beneath the shadows of the larger oaks, were a familiar sight.

The choice of dogwoods, hardiest and longest-lived of flowering native trees, was a happy thought as a memorial to the Continental camp. Distinctively American, these great white blossoms typify the spirit of the Park. Enduring unharmed the swift changes of temperature which mark a Pennsylvania spring, standing unscathed when high winds and drenching rains strip the blossoms from the more delicate cherries, and growing again when careless scything cuts off tender shoots, the dogwoods seem almost deathless. So heavy are their blooms that ancient trees seem often bowed down by drifts of heavy snow.

At Valley Forge, the dogwoods have been blooming in their present splendor for more than forty years. When, in 1895, the newly created Valley Forge Park Commission set to work to clear away the tangled underbrush, a score of flourishing young trees were blooming. These were kept, and were allowed to grow unhampered by ranker vegetation; new dogwoods were set out. Background masses of laurel, with here and there a Judas tree, were placed behind the dogwoods.

Each year in May, on Dogwood Sunday, the display of blooming trees now holds the interest of a nation. No other floral offering, not even the magnificent Japanese cherry blossoms of the Washington Tidal Basin, draws so large a throng. Thousands of motorcars, slowly climbing the steep grade that leads to the hill where Maxwell's New Jersey troops encamped, bear visitors to marvel at the beauty. Neither the Shenandoah apple-blossom festival nor the south Jersey peach displays, neither the lilacs of Rochester nor the azaleas of the South present so glorious a spectacle as the dogwoods that glow so pink and white upon the slopes of Valley Forge.

The dogwoods offer an additional delight because they are so natural to Valley Forge. The famous Dogwood Grove presents the largest massed display; but on the edges of the forests, in open glades in every near-by woods, along the fences of the farms, the dogwoods bloom. They lean forward from the taller poplars, oaks, and hickories; they grow irregularly along the borders of the meadows; they gleam in every unexpected spot where sunlight penetrates. The roads are lined with dogwood trees that blossom each spring, and give gay touches to the autumn, with their clusters of red berries. If Valley Forge had no other claim to national attention, the Dogwood Grove and the thousands of accompanying dogwood trees would merit a high place for beauty.

The scene has been changed since Washington was here. The Park land is today a place of restful peace, of well kept woods, of graceful, rolling lawns, of landscaped beauty. When Continentals were building their small log huts under the shelter of the hills, and digging their double line of breastworks as a safeguard against surprise attack, the little settlement was desolate. A tiny town, once throbbing with industrial activity, had been destroyed. The acrid smell of rain on fresh-charred timbers still hung heavy at the crossroads where William Dewees' Mount Joy Forge had stood. A hundred workmen who had labored at munition making fourteen hours daily throughout the tropic summer now tried to put the ruined forge again into operation; but, without heavy machinery, they were unable to restore the ironworks to its full efficiency.

The sawmills and the gristmill, which stood along the creek bank in front of what is now the Washington Headquarters, had been raided, too, before Washington arrived. Their stone walls were smirched by the smoke from fires which redcoats had kindled. Not even private houses had been spared. Raiders had thrust their bayonets into chests of drawers to pry loose the locks; they broke the furniture, threw mirrors and paintings on the wide-board oaken floors, and set fire to the piles. Some homes were used for slaughterhouses for farm animals captured in the barnyards. When Washington arrived at Valley Forge, the stains of the slaughtering were still visible in the few houses which had not been burned.

None of this desolation is now visible. Valley Forge is not a place where rancor has been kept alive. The Park is not a propaganda agency to fire the hatreds of a later generation. Rather is it a patriotic shrine to stir the modern mind to recollect the glories of the past, to inspire contemporaries to remember the heroic sacrifices of the men who made the nation, to cause a rebirth of the ancient virtues. The hardihood of Continental troops, their courage and devotion, their unending faith in freedom, their confidence and ceaseless perseverance, and their resolution to create an independent country, are the qualities for which Valley Forge stands sponsor.

CHAPTER TWO

Wrangles and Witches

VALLEY FORGE was slow of settlement. Twenty miles from the capital, the site in early days seemed remote and dangerously isolated. Farmers, preferring the abundant fertile land closer to deep water, were disinclined to venture over the stony, forested South Valley hills. Not for a quarter-century after the founding of Philadelphia were efforts made to take up the Great Valley territory.

Then, almost simultaneously, three streams of colonists flowed into the isolated upcountry valley. Northward upon the Schuylkill's treacherous channels and through the untracked forest, people poured to take up land. Welshmen, Swedes, and English Quakers, each wary of the others, ventured into the rich, unoccupied acres. Once in possession, they remained, in happy enjoyment of the abundant yield of crops. Families in their eighth generation of direct descent today till lands deeded to their pioneering ancestors by William Penn. Seldom had any of these early settlers felt inclined to wander aimlessly away to distant homesteads in the west. The family names which Penn once knew are still dominating names in the Valley Forge community.

WRANGLES AND WITCHES

Pleasing legends tell of the settlement of these lands at Valley Forge. In the early days of Pennsylvania's development, William Penn, traveling inland to view the land he had acquired, came to the present site of Valley Forge. Fording the Valley Creek, he climbed the western hillsides and pressed onward into the interior. He struggled through the heavy timber that even then clothed the mountaintops, he cut his way through grapevines and through thickets until, toward nightfall, he gave up his progress in despair. He looked about but could not see the Schuylkill, which had been his guide; despondently, he named the hill Mount Misery. Then, retracing his steps and fording the creek again, he climbed the hill where the observatory now stands and regained his bearings. In consequence, the hill was called Mount Joy. At a later day, he gave much of the land in this vicinity to his daughter Letitia Aubrey, who, in memory of her father's explorations, called her land the Manor of Mount Joy.

More firmly grounded in historic fact is Lewis Walker's story. One of Penn's companions on the *Welcome,* Walker took up in 1708 a homestead in the rich, untilled Great Valley which he was the first to cultivate. Under the old sycamore on the hillside, near a strongly flowing spring, he built a small log hut for himself and the girl whom he had met and courted on the voyage. When his little house of barked, hand-hewn timbers, with its pounded earth floor and its ladder to the second-story sleeping chamber, was finished, Walker undertook the cultivation of his acres. He carried seed corn from the Philadelphia water-front to his farm land, planted it, and, when the crop matured, sold the grain for cash enough to buy a horse and cow. These he tethered, by grapevine ropes, to stakes driven into the ground; he pastured them on the abundant grass, and harnessed them to pull his homemade wooden plow. Still later, as his crops returned him profit, Walker built the great stone house Rehobeth, which still stands, protected by the ancient sycamore.

Not all the Welshmen were, however, as fortunate as Lewis Walker. Some believed that they had come to Pennsylvania under false promises. When their agent had first talked to William Penn there was an understanding that the Welsh might buy an uninterrupted tract of thirty thousand acres, to be a barony "within which all causes, quarrels, crimes and disputes might be tried and wholly determined by officers, magistrates and juries of our language and our choosing." It was cheap land, too, for Penn asked but ten cents an acre cash, together with an annual rental of twenty-five cents per hundred acres forever after. As an added inducement, Penn offered bonuses of city lots in Philadelphia and of land just beyond the city limits.

The terms seemed good; perhaps they were too good. When the Welshmen arrived in Pennsylvania, after a terrible passage of seven months during which they were half starved, caught in storms, wrecked, and driven down to Barbados, they heard that they were the victims of a mistake.

The land was not to be in one continuous estate; a small part was in Merion, then northwest Philadelphia; the rest, far off in "the wild woods where there were none to welcome them." There was to be no barony; the Welshmen could not choose their own officials; they could not even live as neighbors, for their lands were scattered far and wide through six sparsely settled townships. As for the rent, Penn's agent said, the Welshmen were already in serious default. Those rents should have been paid a year ago; if all the money were not paid at once, the rights of ownership would revert to William Penn.

WRANGLES AND WITCHES

Of course there was a protest, a wordy, violent objection such as only Welshmen could have voiced. Penn's agents asked for written proof that William Penn had ever made specific promises; and when the Welshmen said that no documents existed, and that they relied only on the Quaker's word, the cases were thrown out of court. To keep further quarrels from arising, the agents showed their power; certain of the Welsh grants were flatly canceled, and the lands awarded to English claimants. Unless the arguments were dropped, the agents said, all Welsh land would be confiscated.

There was further trouble. The Welshmen, finding that neither cows nor horses were now purchasable at any price, and that wheeled vehicles were entirely absent, carried their crude plows and hoes, their saws and scythes and grindstones, their spades and axes and their iron bars upcountry on their backs. They grubbed out little fields to plant their crops of wheat. They had been told by Penn that any man who came with a hundred pounds in cash could buy five hundred acres, hire two men, live comfortably for a year, with four pounds left over for emergency, and that when the year was past his money profit, over and above the costs, would net him 44 per cent return. But there was a flaw which Penn forgot to mention.

The crop could not be milled unless a heavy fee was paid. The Proprietor retained complete monopoly over sawmills, gristmills, bridges, boats, and ferries. All grain was compelled by law to go to Penn's mill on the distant Chester Creek. Penn, it seems, had failed to mention that he intended to retain this most important right.

If official records were not available to certify the curious events that followed, the aftermath would be incredible.

13

At their own expense the Welshmen built a road; the Surveyor General promptly set up milestones, marked with the three plates that were Penn's arms, and charged the Welshmen taxes for the cost of building. They built a raft to cross the Schuylkill but the first man to attempt a passage was arrested. They sought to pay the taxes, even those which Welshmen thought unfairly laid, but could not secure surveys to show them for what property they were assessed. Then they were threatened with ejection unless they tilled efficiently all the lands that could not be located.

The crowning indignity appeared when Penn's administrator expelled the Welshmen from the city. By a secret Council meeting, which no Welshman was permitted to attend, new boundaries were drawn which put the Merion settlements outside Philadelphia limits. Philadelphia taxes were, nevertheless, assessed against them, and when a Welshman entered protest he was ejected from the Council chamber. "He annoyed the Governor by his presence," the formal report complained.

By two successive votes, even the Philadelphia English Quaker electorate rejected their officials. Each time the Governor refused to recognize the verdict of the election he had authorized. Then at last he was recalled to London. It was a relief to all concerned. Standing on the deck of the ship that was to take him home, the Governor proclaimed his happiness, for, said he, "I am sick of this Pennsylvania mess."

Things went more smoothly thereafter. The enterprising Welshmen gained fortune, power, and prestige. They did not, however, forget their wrongs. Though William Penn back in England stoutly insisted that he had been misrepresented and that the Welshmen had misunderstood his statements, they continued to oppose his rule. When John Penn fell heir to the province, they shifted their antagonism to the new Proprietor. And, since John Penn was thought to hold Tory principles, the unreconciled Welshmen were, if only for this one cause, sympathetic to the Revolution.

The Swedes, who settled somewhat south of Valley Forge, had a happier experience than their Welsh neighbors. In 1712, thirty years after the founding of Philadelphia, Matts Holstein, whose ancestors had lived in Delaware for more than half a century, canoed up the Schuylkill to find good farming land remote from the developing city. Portaging around the Schuylkill Falls, paddling past the Welsh settlements of Merion, carrying his canoe and all his small store of household goods around the shallows and the stony rifts, he came to the hills opposite the present site of Norristown. Here, on the west bank of the stream, where Bridgeport now stands, he found thick woods of heavy oak, in which bears and wildcats roamed and Indians were believed to dwell. Beyond the woods, upon a sharply rising knoll, were open fields, well watered and covered with dense grass that proved the soil's fertility. High hills cut the region off from the inland Welsh settlements.

Holstein settled here. Three years later, when the Indian fears were well known to be groundless, he cleared the forests to the water's edge, and gave himself the easy river crossing that ever since has borne the name Swedes' ford. Soon he set up a flatboat ferry, guiding his boat across the stream by a rope stretched from shore to shore. The Holstein ferry became an important factor in establishing a highway from New York and the Jerseys westward into the interior of Pennsylvania. On both sides of the Schuylkill, the road that led to Holstein's plantation was long known as the Swedesford Road; it bears the same name to the present day.

Following the Holstein settlement, more Swedes moved up the river. Many of them settled near Swedes' ford; some took possession, through grant of Penn and his successors, of other lands along the river bank. Long before the Revolutionary War, the west shore of the Schuylkill was dotted by small Swedish communities. At what is now the town of Conshohocken, three miles south of Holstein's farm, Peter Mattson set up an estate. He, too, had a favorable location, for two large creeks wound through his lands, one of which, the Arrowmink, sweeping through rocky ravines into the river, gave him an ample guard against a possible encroachment by his Welsh neighbors, while the slower-moving Fox Creek afforded him fertile and well watered pasturage for cattle.

The little Swedish settlement prospered. On the picturesque knoll overlooking the ford, the pioneers built a church to serve as a community center. Before the days of the Revolutionary encampment, settlers from as far up the Schuylkill as Morlattan, near Reading, canoed downstream past Valley Forge, to hear the ringing Swedish sermons of their pastors. From as far south as Philadelphia itself, women, riding horseback in their "safety petticoats," dismounted under the tall, solitary pine shading the corner of the old churchyard. There they doffed their flowing underskirts and hung them over the picket fence like banners while they went indoors. The service was an all-day affair, with a noonday interval during which the worshipers picnicked on the grass.

To some degree, however, certain of the Swedes were suspect. Whispers ran through the little congregation that the Mattsons were bewitched. One of their remote ancestors in the early settlements south of Philadelphia, Dame Margaret Mattson, had been tried before William Penn and the Provincial Council for putting spells upon the cattle. Penn and his

16

councilors had heard the evidence. Puzzled by her strange admission that she might have bewitched calves and geese, but that oxen were beyond her power, the court had refused to hand down a definite decision. Margaret Mattson was found "guilty of having the common fame of a witch, but not guilty in the manner and form as she stands indicted."

The Swedes and their Finnish cousins, to whom sailors have always imputed magic power over winds, were feared in the community, but they were courted, too. When Valley Forge girls suddenly "shivered and agitated, scratching the walls and floor," witch doctors were called from the Swedesford settlement. A strange black liquid, forced down the throats of sufferers, for none would drink it willingly, was the only known curative medicine. Boys, wasting with mysterious maladies, were told by Swedish witch doctors to stand upon the bed until the next woman caller came. The visitor would unquestionably be the wicked witch, but if a sufferer's parents were careful not to give or lend the caller any article whatever, the child would at once recover. Otherwise the boy would surely die.

Not every Swede was thought a witch, but the Great Valley people long refused to run the risk of close association with the Swedish people. Not until a few years before the Revolution were the Welsh and English Quakers reassured that all the Swedes were safe neighbors.

Valley Forge itself began with an elopement. The story, following traditional romantic patterns, richly merits novelistic treatment, for a poor indentured servant, bought by a crusty miller, won the daughter of the rich, conservative, Welsh Quaker family, ran off with her to break hitherto untilled farm land, built a home in the wilderness, achieved success, and gained eventual forgiveness.

In 1713, the year following Holstein's arrival at Swedesford, Thomas Jerman, Quaker preacher who was nicknamed "The Thrifty Miller," went into Philadelphia to buy a sleigh. There he found a ship just arrived from England, bringing, among other passengers, a redheaded, twenty-year old Scotch boy. The man to whom this James Anderson was indentured desired to sell the lad's services, and Jerman, attracted by his bright personality, bought the boy for little more than the five pounds' transportation cost. The Thrifty Miller took James Anderson upcountry to his Great Valley Mill, the first inland gristmill to be licensed after Penn gave up his mill monopoly.

Quick-witted and pleasant-spoken, laughing Jim Anderson worked faithfully and hard, though the serious Welsh Quakers thought him frivolous. Elizabeth, the elder daughter of the Jermans, was captivated by his charm. A few months after his arrival, the two were deep in love. Jerman was disappointed; he had intended Elizabeth for Enoch Walker, son of the pioneer of Rehobeth, hoping that thus Rehobeth and the Great Valley Mill might be united into one great property.

Anderson and Elizabeth found no encouragement. As soon as Jim's service had expired, they fled in the moonlight down the trail that led toward Holstein's Swedes' ford, past Walker's farm, and over the fields that now comprise the Valley Forge Park reservation. Once safely through the narrow pass beyond the present site of Valley Forge, they took up three hundred acres of unbroken hilly land.

Only the Indians lived near by, but these, charmed by the friendliness of the young Scot and of his bride, befriended the elopers. "Sky," their young Lenni Lenape neighbor, married them by Indian rites and showed them how to make a hut. It was a log house with one room, one door, and a window, and it was in a dangerous position, for each night the wolves prowled in the neighborhood. Even later, when Anderson had bought sheep, the snow about the tight-walled sheepfold was trampled nightly by packs of hungry wolves. For long months, Jim Anderson slept with a loaded gun by his bedside to protect his flocks against unusual attack.

Sky gave fluent counsel on how to care for crops, but Anderson preferred to follow better and more modern methods. When Sky showed how the Indians cleared ground by kindling fires to kill the tree roots, Anderson urged that the roots be grubbed out before seed was sown. The cost of repairing one plow broken on a stump, he said, was greater than the added cost of complete clearing. By so caring for the land, moreover, the fields would be immediately as fit for cultivation as they would be after twenty years of inefficient Indian practices. Sky's advice that children should be thrown into the creek daily before dawn to make them hardy was likewise disregarded, though Elizabeth left the young Andersons in Indian care whenever she rode back to see her people.

The families were friendly again, for after Elizabeth's elopement, the Thrifty Miller had married her younger sister Mary to the favored Enoch Walker. When the harvests were gathered, therefore, and the grain was flailed, Elizabeth rode back into the Great Valley to take the wheat to be ground.

Following the Andersons, other Quaker families settled close to Valley Forge. By 1742, the first of the forges was established, by Lewis Evans, Daniel Walker, and Joseph Williams, descendants of Welsh settlers. Later this Mount Joy Forge, with some four hundred acres of charcoal-producing woodland on both sides of the creek, was sold to John Potts, whose iron-working family had already built a prosperous forge and furnace industry farther up the Schuylkill.

19

Potts brought prosperity to Valley Forge. Carting pig-iron over rough roads in clumsy carts, he turned it into finished goods. Negro slaves and white redemptioners, the latter bought for thirty pounds each, turned the crude pig-iron into wrought-iron blooms. From these the blacksmiths made excellent hardware, nails, hinges, latches, and small tools. Negro Strephon, chief of the slaves, Thomas Connor, and Henry Seligman, the best of the redemptioners, directed the activities so efficiently that, at times, more than four tons of finished goods were ready to be hauled away to Philadelphia markets. The Mount Joy, or Valley, Forge was famous through the wide community that now stretched far west into the Great Valley, south almost to Philadelphia, eastward, across the river, for twenty miles.

During fourteen years, John Potts gave personal attention to the Mount Joy Forge. To his iron interests, he added a gristmill, a feed-chopping mill, a cooperage, two charcoal houses, a sawmill, and a store. These he erected either on the shores of Valley Creek between the river and his forge, or along the road that led into the iron country. He built himself a stone mansion of unusual design. Later occupied by Washington during the encampment, this house is now carefully preserved as a patriotic shrine.

In 1771, however, Potts retired from active management. Colonel William Dewees, his son-in-law, took over the direction of the works and, two years later, almost on the day when his father was elected sheriff of Philadelphia, the county in which most of Valley Forge was then located, Colonel Dewees purchased the estate. He anticipated a long career of profitable service as head of a prosperous industrial community.

CHAPTER THREE

Prosperity and Peace

THE old disputes had long since subsided when Colonel Dewees assumed the management of Valley Forge. The bitter arguments between the Welshmen and the Proprietor had lessened in intensity. Each realized that there had been too quick a readiness to make unfounded charges; each understood that greedy go-betweens, by misunderstanding statement and by distorting fact, had angered innocent parties. Neither William Penn nor the Welsh settlers had been deliberately unfair.

Living as close neighbors, with a more accurate appreciation of each other's qualities, Englishmen and Welshmen alike saw that justice was a common aspiration. Intermarriages added to the understanding. United by a common religion, interested in identical community problems, the Welsh and English Quakers drew closer in their friendships.

It was a short step, thereafter, to solve the less difficult controversies between the Quakers and the Swedes, and between the Quakers and the adherents of other faiths. Long before the Revolution, the Great Valley folk were enjoying prosperity and peace.

Prosperity, however, failed to dim their sense of justice. When they believed that wealthy aristocrats were conspiring with Governor William Denny to strip the popularly chosen Assembly of its rights, and when they thought that rich absentee landlords were urging the King toward a more tyrannical rule, these Great Valley farmers complained against their provincial governments.

Unluckily for the democratic cause, the chief official in the neighborhood was the haughty, harsh, and testy Judge William Moore, a wealthy slaveholding dictator whose luxurious mansion at Moore Hall, three miles above Valley Forge, was the center of the aristocratic faction. A wordy war ensued. From the thronelike easy-chair to which the gouty judge was frequently confined, he sent out vituperative manifestoes accusing his opponents of drunkenness, ignorance, and rascality. They retorted with violent attacks upon his wickedness, corruption, usurpations, and extortions.

The Whig Assembly took the offensive but was checked by Tory administrators. The Assembly ordered Moore to come before it for impeachment, but Governor Denny refused to enforce the order. The Whigs then arrested both Moore and his sharp-tongued son-in-law, the Reverend William Smith, provost of the University of Pennsylvania, charging them both with criminal libel; but the Governor at once pardoned the prisoners. Next the Assembly charged all three Tories with "an apparent design to overthrow the Constitution and enslave the People"; but Denny produced a royal decree expressing the King's "high displeasure at the Assembly's unwarranted behavior." Each subsequent step taken by the Assembly was similarly checkmated. Moore remained as judge until the actual outbreak of the Revolution. Even after Independence had been proclaimed, he continued to hold his Tory court at Moore Hall until rebel soldiers took possession of the mansion.

FIREPLACE AT THE VARNUM QUARTERS

(Photograph by Dr. William A. Jaquette)

WASHINGTON'S HEADQUARTERS

(Courtesy Mrs. W. Herbert Burk)

WASHINGTON'S BEDROOM

(Courtesy Mrs. W. Herbert Burk)

PROSPERITY AND PEACE

The Revolutionary crisis was particularly serious for the Pennsylvania pacifists. Neither the slender-framed blond Welshmen nor the broader-faced English Quakers wanted war. Save for a few hothead dissenters from the sedate Quaker discipline, the prosperous planters of the Great Valley prayed for peace.

Their quiet dignity was evidenced by their simple, tasteful houses. Scorning the elaborate carvings and the baroque decorations of the homeland, they erected homes noteworthy for beauty of proportion and for charm of style. Whether the buildings were of brown native field stone or of home-kilned brick, they were designed for comfort.

The great brick-paved kitchens, truly the living rooms of most Great Valley homes, were pleasant places even in the winter. Great, wide fireplaces, large enough to burn enormous logs, blazed cheerfully. Sometimes, on gusty nights, they puffed wood smoke into the room, adding more blackness to the hand-hewn beams; but the occasional choking clouds were a small price to pay for the blankets of heat that usually poured forth. Some of the eight- and ten-foot fireplaces had tiny windows under which the old grandmother sat, away from draughts, cozily warm, twinkling her busy fingers with unending knitting and watching for signs of life on the roads along the snow-clad fields.

Fastened to the left wall of the kitchen fireplace was a swinging black iron crane from which, by pothooks, portly cooking kettles hung. Before the fire, on brackets, a long iron spit extended horizontally. Meat was speared on this, and then the rod was slowly turned so that it might roast on all sides equally. Usually the turning was a job for small boys, but more progressive houses had a clockworks arranged to keep the spit revolving. An iron pan beneath the spit caught drippings. Heavy, closely covered baking kettles, banked about with glowing embers, stood upon the fireplace floor.

Most of the baking was, however, done by great bake-ovens built behind the fireplace. A small opening, closed by an iron door, led from the rear wall into a square brick space, whose special flue was connected with the chimney. When there was baking to be done, a fire was kindled in the oven with short lengths of carefully dried wood. An hour later, when the bricks were hot, the wood and ashes were cleared away, the special flue was shut, and bread dough was pushed into the bake-oven by the long-handled peel. After another hour, the baking was brought out.

These folks fed on plain but wholesome fare. The substantial, though by modern standards improperly balanced, meals were admirably suited for the hard-working, outdoor life followed by the masses. For special treats, there might be battercake desserts of flour, eggs, and milk, baked with lard and sprinkled with crumbs of sugar; there might be puddings, rich with beef suet and with drippings; there might be chocolate, boiled with sausage and eaten with a spoon. A generation before the Revolution, there had been a fleeting fashion of buttering boiled tea leaves as a vegetable. This fad had been short-lived, nor had a later practice continued of simmering the sour home-brewed beer with bread crusts and molasses. Most Great Valley homes ate mush and milk for breakfast.

The great kitchens had but simple furnishings. A line of sadware pewter trays and platters, gleaming bluish gray because of their high lead content, stood on the cupboard shelves. Tankards, bowls and plates, a garnish of assorted porringers, a series of long, wide-bowled spoons, a bit or two of blue Canton chinaware, occasionally a silver teapot or a creamer, completed the table service. Save these and the huge copper kettles, standing brightly burnished by the fireside, there was slight beauty to attract the eye. A few hickory chairs, a dough trough, a pine table, and a water bench on which to rest the pails brought dripping from the springhouse supplied all necessary furniture. Small wooden tubs, filled with hot water from the fireplace kettles, served for washing and rinsing dishes.

In homes of greater wealth, the living rooms were more comfortably arranged. The mansions of the richer folk were well supplied with simply carved, brass-handled highboys and with mahogany chests of drawers. Chair seats of needle-point upholstery, tall, gilt-framed mirrors and translucent china vases, bearing the initials of the owner, bespoke prosperity. Some Great Valley folk preferred the slat-back, rush-bottomed chairs, which even in the Revolutionary days seemed slightly old-fashioned; others boasted Windsor chairs, whose curving backs had been steamed until the wood was pliable enough to bend to fit the figure. Drop-leaf and gate-legged tables, and a simple but commodious sideboard, were common possessions. The fireplaces were smaller than in the great kitchens; shining brass fire sets replaced the kitchen's iron tools.

In the great halls, often on the stair landings, a tall grandfather's clock ticked slowly. A table stood here, too, with a pair of high-backed chairs, but the chief beauty of the halls was usually the wide and graceful flight of stairs, glistening with snowy paint on which the candlelight threw flickering flame shadows. The halls were cool and popular in summer days; in winter they were passed through quickly for, remote from all the fires, they were often almost freezing-cold.

Valley Forge did not yet know the newly popular horse-hair furniture which Mrs. Deborah Franklin believed superior to the finest Italian silk upholstery. Damask and morocco leather still remained the favored covering for the graceful, solid bowlegged chairs. The luxurious silk patterns were more suited to the elaborately carved mahogany; the flicker of the firelight gave them a warmer, much more friendly, glow than could be lent to the austerely smooth black horsehair. The damask, too, blended better with the candles in their silver sticks against the waxed wood wainscoting, and with the hardwood floors, smoothed by the holystone and sanded in geometric patterns. Under a carved mantel-board, in front of pictured tiles that lined the big fireplace, the father of the family, dressed in his silver-buttoned coat, his smallclothes, and his embroidered waistcoat, with silver-buckled shoes and well fitted stockings, could feel indeed at home. It was a formal age when people spoke in rounded periods.

The silk-gowned wives and daughters, proud of their Irish linens and their fabric gloves, tucked away their finery in lovely painted chests, made mostly by the Pennsylvania Germans, marked by conventionalized tulip designs and colored garishly in many hues. Huge wooden hatboxes, covered with blue and white paper, hid the Sunday hats. On weekdays, the ladies, sewing patiently in their second-story guest bedrooms, wore needlework caps to keep their hair from disarray.

The other furniture of Revolutionary time lagged somewhat in artistry, though some pieces, like the beds brought out by William Savery in the year before Independence was proclaimed, were bamboo-fluted and well carved. More attention was devoted to the fishnet canopy, or to the bedspreads of quilted patchwork or of tufted candlewick. On Washington's bed at Valley Forge, a magnificent bedspread with an eight-pointed star, surrounded by a circle which in turn was enclosed within a square, and with a huge conventionalized tree spreading upwards from the footboard, gives indication of the elaboration which might be lavished on such decoration. This, however, is exceptional; in most houses the spreads were parti-colored patchwork, more befitting the feather mattresses and rope networks that stretched beneath.

In spring and summer and autumn, the beautiful old houses, often standing on a creekside knoll, commanded delightful views of flowering gardens. From their wide window seats the housewives could look out, past the scarlet trumpet vines clinging to the walls, over rolling fields to the blue summits of the distant mountains. Below them, sometimes in formal gardens bordered by clipped hedges, more often in more friendly, intimate plantings, were tall hollyhocks and gleaming marigolds, sturdy Dutch tulips of uncompromising reds and solid yellows, blue iris and more delicate sweet peas, great double larkspurs, lilacs, hyacinths and daffodils, snapdragons and hepaticas. Roses and honeysuckle, sweet shrub and aromatic pink perfumed the soft airs of late spring mornings.

Farmers might have difficulties with other less valued growths. Even in colonial times, the buxom double dandelion, the broad-leaved dock, Scotch thistle and the all-pervading garlic thrived. Some could be plowed out, or hoed away; others, like the odorous yellow linaria, then called the ranstead weed, or the glossy-green poison ivy, flourished against all human effort.

Then, as now, the gardeners were troubled by the insect pests, particularly as the knowledge of efficient deterrents was less general. Sometimes the caterpillars stripped the forest so completely that the midsummer woods were wintry bare. Often "measles" attacked the cherries, pears, and peaches;

destructive cankerworms killed the orchard trees. Regularly, at seventeen-year intervals, a locust plague had kept up a loud, unending, ringing din, but, since their last arrival in 1766, few had been heard in the Great Valley.

These troubles were, however, minor in comparison to the rich annual returns from fields and orchards. Wheat and rye and corn grew abundantly; the fair blue-blossomed flax yielded ample fiber for the good country linen which the housewives spun and wove; apples, grapes, and cherries were plentiful. The limestone soil of the Great Valley produced more bountiful crops per acre than did the land of any other part of Pennsylvania. Even tobacco flourished here, though Great Valley farmers preferred crops that required less labor and made fewer demands upon the soil.

Autumn found the barns of Pennsylvania filled with wheat and corn, the springhouses full of fresh-made cheese, the root-cellars well stocked with fruits and vegetables. It was the season when fat hogs and corn-fed steers were slaughtered, and when smokehouses were made ready for their yearly tasks of preserving hams and bacon. Fodder, at such a time, seemed inexhaustible in the rich farm lands of the Great Valley.

At just such a juncture, news arrived that British troops were on their way to Pennsylvania. Few residents of Valley Forge had thought that military operations would disturb their peace. Many of their boys, volunteering for service, had been sent away to help the rebel army in New England or in the New York neighborhood; Colonel Dewees' powder mills along the creek were active; the ironworks were casting guns and molding cannonballs, but all the fighting, Valley Forge believed, would take place in distant regions.

The shock was sudden, then, late in August, 1777, when

couriers arrived to say that a great British fleet was sailing southward from New York to bring the war to Philadelphia. The Valley Forge folk were confident, however, that even if the capital should fall, the inland settlements would remain unscathed. Nowhere as yet had redcoats ventured far from the deep water. General Sir William Howe's great armada was not expected to wreak much harm on Quaker Pennsylvania.

CHAPTER FOUR

War Comes to Pennsylvania

P ENNSYLVANIA'S peaceful-
ness was suddenly shattered. Without warning, the British
transferred the fighting from the lower Hudson River valley
to the rolling farm lands of southeastern Pennsylvania.

The move was the result of treachery. The British-born
General Charles Lee, who had given up a post in the British
army to take a higher position with the Americans, and who
had been granted a $30,000 subsidy by Congress in the hope
of assuring his loyalty, had turned traitor to the Continentals.
Captured by the British in December, 1776, he had amused
himself during his internment by drawing up a plan to show
how easily the rebels could be beaten. If, the cynical soldier
of fortune told Howe, the British should take an army up the
Chesapeake, Maryland, Delaware, and the Quaker counties
of Pennsylvania would either help the British or, at the worst,
stay neutral. England could end the rebellion by thus di-
viding the Continental forces.

Lee's plan was not made public. Few people, other than
the highest British generals, had an inkling of the intended
movements. Even the invading army was astonished when, in
mid-July, 1777, the entire royalist force was ordered to board

30

transports. Two hundred and sixty-six ships, ranging in size from frigates to small sloops, lay waiting in New York harbor. Speculation buzzed throughout the ranks. Some guessed that an attack was planned upon the South; others thought a descent would be made upon the rebel capital at Philadelphia; a few hoped wildly that the embarkation meant a journey homeward.

During a full week the armada lay in New York harbor waiting for a wind. The men, penned aboard the crowded ships, grumbled because they could not go ashore. Restless for lack of useful exercise, idle, and irritable, they spent their days in gambling, in grumbling, and in petty plottings against the discipline to which they were subjected. Then at last, on July 23, a faint puff of breeze led the Admiral, Earl Howe, to hope that the weather was about to change. He ordered the anchors weighed. Two hundred and sixty-six ships, close-packed with eighteen thousand soldiers, drifted slowly south along the Jersey coast. Daily thunderstorms rained down; lightning struck the masts of one or two of the ships; but the storms did not clear the atmosphere. The winds were so light that another week went by before the fleet arrived off the mouth of Delaware Bay. The ships had scarcely logged twenty miles a day.

Tory sympathizers rowing off from shore brought word here that the Delaware River route to Philadelphia was so closely guarded that no hostile ships could ascend the stream. Lines of spiked barriers had been sunk in the channel above Wilmington; strategic forts commanded the sharp bends where sailing ships, tacking against the wind, would be exposed to rebel cross fire; a fleet of gunboats lay above the forts and barriers.

The Admiral and his brother, General Sir William Howe,

31

changed their plans. They continued down the coast to the Chesapeake Bay, planning to follow Lee's suggestion that troops be landed in the Tory country southwest of Philadelphia. From the head of the Elk River, in the extreme northeastern part of the bay, they could then march overland across the Pennsylvania plains to take the capital. Thus, avoiding the strong defenses of the Delaware, they could catch the city in the undefended rear. Philadelphia would thus fall almost without a battle.

The scheme was excellent in theory, but the weather worked against the British. Tropic suns burned down from cloudless skies upon a glassy sea. An almost perfect calm prevailed. The great fleet made but a knot or two each hour. After nine days and nights of idle drifting, the ships had scarcely stirred from the Delaware estuary. Then came a somewhat better breeze; the transports moved more rapidly; but two full weeks went by before the troopships rounded the capes to enter Chesapeake Bay. There was still the long upstream voyage to complete.

By this time, both water and provisions were becoming dangerously low. Longboats were rowed from ship to ship to ask for the loan of fresh vegetables, of sweet water, and of untainted meat. The men were hungry. The livestock was in even more serious straits. Scores of horses died of thirst; others went mad. Many were thrown overboard, but in the calm sea the carcasses bobbed about the ships for hours.

The trip was torture for the men. For endless hours, through the sultry days and breathless nights, they milled aimlessly about the decks. The heat was stifling, and they could not breathe easily in their cramped and badly-ventilated quarters; nor could they, in their massed throngs, take proper exercise. Five hundred fell sick. For the others, sweltering in their heavy woolen, winter-weight uniforms, even drill might have been a welcome diversion, but the decks were much too jammed. Some of the men tried to catch crabs from the almost motionless ships; others leaned over the rails to fish; most of the soldiers, torpid in the tropic heat, idled for four long, sweaty weeks. It was the hottest August ever known in America.

So long as Howe's men were off the coast, their passage was as smooth as though they were on some small inland lake, but no sooner did they approach their destination than violent thunderstorms again broke suddenly. The overcrowded ships, packed with men whose nerves were badly shattered, moved slowly up the small tortuous Elk River. The British pilots, ignorant of the proper channels, ran the ships aground; the vessels collided with one another; sweating, swearing men pushed with long poles against soft, oozy mud banks until the ships were again afloat. For three days, heavy rains poured down.

Finally, on August 25th, the men were landed near the present town of Elkton; but their baggage was not set ashore. The soldiers, tentless in the storm, huddled about fence-rail campfires, snatching bits of sleep on corn-shuck beds. Their heavy uniforms were soggy; their cartridge boxes were flooded. Thousands of rounds of ammunition had been ruined. Essential stores, they then discovered, had been left behind at New York. Howe was obliged to replenish his supplies by raiding the countryside.

Three days later, in clear weather, the clay-surfaced trails dried out sufficiently for the British to begin their march toward Philadelphia. Baron Wilhelm Knyphausen's Hessians, scouring the countryside for livestock, found a hundred draft horses. These, added to the animals surviving the sea trip, were enough to haul the artillery, though the wagons had to be left behind under guard until more farm horses could be commandeered.

Knyphausen's raiders found abundant food. The grassy pasturages of Maryland and of southern Pennsylvania were filled with livestock. More than five hundred roan-colored shorthorn cattle were commandeered for British use, yielding upwards of a hundred and twenty-five tons of fresh beef. A thousand fat sheep were taken, too, and were driven forward on the march. The everlasting salt-meat rations of the tedious sea voyage now gave way to ample distributions of fresh beef and mutton.

Stocks of corn and flour, of molasses and coffee, of rum and cured tobacco fell into British hands. Nearly three hundred army wagons, each loaded with half a ton of stores, rumbled onward toward Philadelphia.

To this British force of eighteen thousand men, the American advance guard could offer only slight resistance. Washington had sent some six hundred Delaware militiamen, with a few of General William Maxwell's light infantry, to act as outpost, but many of these were ill armed. Some of Delaware's boys, called "Blue Hen's Chickens" because their mascot was a gamecock, had only their homemade "spontoons"—a sort of spear-knife fastened to a stout pole. They were helpless against the British cannon.

The "Blue Hen's Chickens," nevertheless, met the enemy, on September 3, at Cooch's Bridge, near Newark, Delaware. The skirmish was noteworthy because here, for the first time in history, the Americans flew their newly adopted Stars and Stripes at the head of an army column. Maxwell's six hundred men, however, were powerless to resist the British army. After thirty Americans had been killed by the British artillery

THE BLUE HEN'S CHICKENS

*From a painting, by Stanley M. Arthurs, of Caesar Rodney's
Delaware recruits*

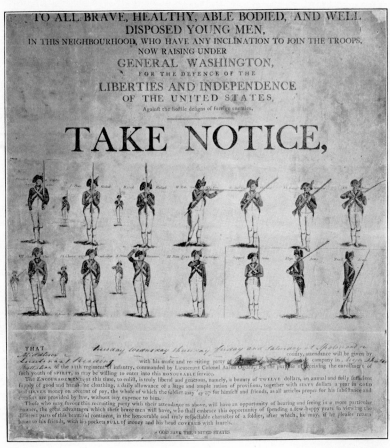

RECRUITING POSTER FOR THE CONTINENTAL
ARMY

(Courtesy the Historical Society of Pennsylvania)

and by a sharp bayonet attack, the rest of the small American detachment retreated in good order.

The way seemed clear for Howe's advance on Philadelphia. Washington's main army, tired after a long march through Philadelphia to meet the invaders, was posted on the steep banks of the swiftly flowing Brandywine Creek; but the rebel army was small and poorly equipped. Howe anticipated little difficulty in dislodging Washington from the strong position astride the highway to Philadelphia. Confidently, the British veterans tramped forward, in brisk, cool weather, through the undefended narrow valleys, toward the little town of Chadds Ford on the Brandywine. A remarkable borealis early in the morning seemed an omen of success.

Victory was not, however, to be as easy as the omens promised. The narrow, wooded Brandywine, with its marshes and its steep hills rising abruptly from the lowland shores, was a greater barrier than Howe anticipated. Misinformed by his scouts concerning both the rebel strength and the American determination to resist, Howe found an enemy strongly placed behind a natural glacis on well protected hills. Led to believe that the Americans were weak in ordnance and that their positions could be carried at the point of the bayonet, Howe discovered that the fords were few, and that the rebels could not be dislodged by direct attack. Many of the Continental cannon were obsolete French guns; some were rebored guns captured from the Hessians; all were of small caliber; but the artillery was formidably located.

Although Howe had been misled concerning the American strength, he was admirably informed about the terrain. Efficient scouting services had reported that the American munition making centers were at Warwick and Coventry north of Chadds Ford, and that, at almost any cost, it would

35

be most desirable to cut off a rebel retreat toward these iron-works or into the food-producing areas of the Great Valley.

Early in the foggy morning of Thursday, September 11, therefore, Howe undertook an unconventional maneuver. Seemingly in violation of sound military strategy, he ordered Knyphausen to feint continual attacks upon the American center, while he and his aide, Earl Cornwallis, set out upon a seventeen-mile march over rough country to cross the Brandywine by unprotected upper fords. To divide an army on the eve of a major engagement is frowned upon by military tacticians as suicidal, but Howe trusted that the surprise would be sufficiently successful to justify the daring move. If the enterprise should accomplish its purpose, Washington not only would be caught upon an unprotected flank, but would be compelled to retreat farther from his supply base at Warwick.

The division of the forces proved to be a brilliant plan. Throughout the misty morning, Knyphausen kept up a furious cannonading "to amuse the Americans." Washington was certain that Howe was attempting a direct assault upon Chadds Ford. When, therefore, the firing temporarily ceased, the Americans leaped to the conclusion that the British had been beaten and that they were withdrawing. A few of the Continentals forded the stream to pursue the supposedly re-treating royalists. To their surprise, they met an advancing Hessian wave and were compelled to rush back across the Brandywine to shelter. Knyphausen continued the pretense of attack.

Without an adequate detachment of light horse, Washington was unable to scout the British movements. Receiving his information chiefly from casual, nonmilitary sources, he was singularly at the mercy of bearers of false rumors. Report reached him about noon that Howe and Cornwallis were marching toward the upper fords, but a more detailed message, arriving somewhat later, assured him that the flank report was unfounded. Washington, deceived by the second message, ordered back Nathanael Greene, whom he had sent to support the threatened flank. When Howe and Cornwallis suddenly descended, therefore, the Americans were taken by surprise.

The mysterious character of the second message has given rise to suspicion that a British spy deliberately misled Washington. A New Jersey militia major, whose identity has never been satisfactorily explained, bore a message, purportedly from General John Sullivan, assuring Washington that all was well and denying that the British had crossed the creek. After he had talked with Washington, the supposed major returned to Sullivan's command bearing orders which Sullivan failed to receive in the form in which they had been sent. Sullivan's delay in carrying out the orders contributed greatly to the inefficiency of the American resistance. It is quite possible that Howe had made use of a British officer dressed in a New Jersey uniform to confuse the American troops.

The spy's activity served also to discredit for a time the testimony of Squire Thomas Cheyney, young, conservative slaveholding farmer, who galloped to tell Sullivan that the British troops were marching by the upper fords. Sullivan, reassured by the mysterious major, disbelieved the breathless Squire, but he allowed the horseman to ride downstream to consult with General Washington. The Commander-in-chief, likewise, doubted Cheyney's story, but he asked the Squire to dismount and to draw in the dirt a map of the roads over which the enemy was advancing. When one or two of Washington's green-ribboned aides-de-camp scoffed openly at the farmer's news, Cheyney indignantly cried:

"If you doubt my word, put me under guard until you can ask Anthony Wayne or Colonel Persie Frazer if I am a man to be believed." Then, turning to the scoffing aides, he added, "I would have you know that I have this day's work as much at heart as ever a blood of you."

Washington was at last convinced that Cheyney's warning was correct, especially as sounds of heavy firing were now heard in the distance. He again ordered Greene to support Sullivan's troops and so stressed the need for haste that Greene's men rushed four miles over bad roads in less than forty-five minutes. Washington himself spurred to the threatened front.

Squire Cheyney and Joseph Brown, an elderly farmer, were his guides. Years afterwards, Brown would tell how Washington, galloping at the head of his staff, spurred his horse to leap the fences while he kept shouting: "Push along, old man! Push along, old man!"

Washington had but narrowly escaped death earlier in the day. A British major, commanding the riflemen stationed in front of Knyphausen's Hessians, reported that a French hussar and a rebel officer, the latter dressed in dark green and blue, mounted on a good bay horse, and wearing a remarkably large cocked hat, had passed within easy range of the English sharp-shooters. "I ordered three good shots to stear near to them and fire at them," the Englishman reported, "but the idea disgusted me and I recalled the order. The hussar made a circuit but the other passed within a hundred yards of me, upon which I advanced from the woods towards him. Upon my calling, he stopped, but then he slowly continued his way. As I was within that distance at which, in the quickest firing, I could have lodged half a dozen balls in or about him before he was out of my reach, I had only to determine; but it was not pleasant to fire at the back of an unoffending individual who was acquitting himself very coolly of his duty, so I let him alone." The next day the British major was informed by wounded Americans that Washington, dressed exactly according to the major's description, and attended only by a French hussar officer, had been the man who so narrowly escaped death.

Howe, meanwhile, had been marching through the fog. By two o'clock in the afternoon, after a ten-hour march, his troops were across the creek. Then they turned downstream, well in the rear of the American defenders. Two hours later, Washington suddenly found himself caught between two powerful converging armies, each almost as large as his own. Retreat to the north was impossible. There was grave fear that the Americans would be penned between Howe's troops and the marshy creek.

The discovery caused a sudden shifting of the American plans. The Continental generals, quickly ordered their commands to abandon the creekside positions and, by a complicated maneuver, to take new positions on the hills. The Americans, unused to intricate mass movements and handicapped by the wooded hills, became confused. A half-mile gap separated two divisions of the rebel force. Through this the British poured, bringing sixteen heavy field pieces to bear upon the defensive works. Further complications came when one of the newly arrived French officers, jealous of his seniority privileges, sought to assume command of the Continentals over the heads of three American generals. Confusion was increased when the excited, usurping general lost control over his English and issued conflicting orders which

39

hopelessly entangled the defending troops. The young Marquis de Lafayette, hitherto the butt of brother French officers for his unofficial status as a personal adventurer, rallied the men so well as to earn the commendation of the observant British officers, but he could not stem the royalist advance. By five o'clock in the hot afternoon, after the hill on which the American defense centered had changed hands five times within an hour, the Americans were compelled to withdraw.

Three hundred Americans were killed; twice that number were wounded; four hundred soldiers were taken prisoner. Young Lafayette was wounded by a musket ball which, as he explained, "went through and through my left foot." His boot was filled with blood. After a quick first-aid attention, he attempted to renew the fighting but felt himself growing fainter, and rode off to safety before he collapsed completely.

The British remained masters of the field. If daylight had lasted longer, they insisted, they could have utterly destroyed the rebel army. As it was, they captured ten American cannon at the cost of about a hundred dead and about four hundred wounded.

The Americans were in no mood to place blame for the defeat, nor to congratulate themselves upon their luck in escaping the British pincer movement, until they were safely out of danger. Dusk had begun to fall before the firing ceased. Before the Continentals were in full retreat from the battlefield of Brandywine, night had closed in. Luckily, the time was a week before the full September harvest moon, and the growing moon gave ample light for marching. Washington led his tired and beaten army ten miles in the bright moonlight over steep hills and through three swift-flowing creeks before he reached a satisfactory camping ground. It was close to midnight when his men halted.

Lafayette had preceded the main body of the army. He too had ridden far; but, before he reached the town of Chester near which the men encamped, he had become unconscious. Carried to the Plow and Harrow Tavern, his wound was again dressed, this time by Mary Gorman, a practical neighborhood nurse, who stanched the flow of blood, retied a tourniquet about the leg, and performed the other surgical services of the time. Lafayette was later sent to the army hospital at Bethlehem, where he remained for more than a month.

Washington slept little on the night after Brandywine was lost. He spent most of the time trying to assess the losses suffered by the Continentals. Knowing that rich farm areas were now in British possession, and that the invaders would have ample food, he was concerned over the probable loss of even more important regions. At Warwick and Coventry, in the hills, thirty miles north of Chadds Ford, were iron mines, munition works, and storage houses. Great stocks of flour, powder, intrenching tools, and cannon balls lay exposed to capture. If the British were to move northward, over the two good roads that linked Chadds Ford with the Great Valley, they could take virtually all the American reserves of food and ammunition. They could, moreover, by marching ten miles from the battlefield of Brandywine, capture the great road that led from Philadelphia to Lancaster, and so could deprive the Continentals of help from the interior of Pennsylvania. In comparison with these losses, the falling of Philadelphia into British hands would be a minor calamity.

Washington resolved, therefore, to outmaneuver Howe. By an early start, he thought, the Americans, racing along the road to Philadelphia, might march out on the Lancaster road and so place themselves between the vital stores and the victorious British army. The march would be extraordinarily difficult and would entail great hardships; but unless the attempt were successful, the cause of independence might be wholly lost. He issued orders, therefore, for an almost immediate resumption of the march.

CHAPTER FIVE

Retreat to White Horse

INSUFFICIENTLY rested after the all-day battle, still weary from the hard night march to camp, the army struggled to its feet before the daylight came. A quick inspection showed conclusively that the troops were in no condition to renew the fighting. The guns were foul; cartridge pouches were entirely empty; confidence was weakened. The immediate need was to withdraw to some secluded spot where ranks could be re-formed and new supplies secured.

Washington believed that a sudden British onslaught might bring the Revolution to a dismal close. In the absence of an efficient intelligence service, he had no means of knowing that Howe and Cornwallis were in almost as desperate a plight as were the Continentals. Not until four days had passed was he to know that, in the words of Wayne, "the enemy lay in a supine state" unable to advance.

The rebel retreat led through picturesque and pleasant country. In happier days, the rolling pastures fattened cattle for the Philadelphia market; the streams gave water power to a score of mills; the countryside was rich in forage. An army less intent on haste could have found rest and happiness among the Whig communities nestling in the hollows.

VALLEY FORGE

The Americans, however, had no time to enjoy this charming scenery. Long lines of stragglers, marching in the frontier custom, trudged in double file along the winding, narrow road, through bogs and quicksands, climbing steep and rocky slopes. Still powder-stained and battle-grimed, the men splashed through the swollen creeks without delaying long enough to wash the caked sweat from their faces. It was no impressive array of well drilled troops in beautiful alignment for, as the Frenchmen were continually complaining, these Continentals had never learned the proper way to march. It was a rough, irregular retreat.

The men moved heavily, grousing at the lack of sleep, grumbling because of the innumerable stony hills, complaining of their weariness, criticizing, in the familiar fashion of every army in the world, the tactics of their leaders. There were bitter words because of reinforcements which had failed to reach the firing line in time, because of generals who drank too much, because of colonels who were too stupid to understand their orders, because of men who would not listen to commands, and, above all others, because of presumptuous foreigners who superseded good American commanders. Lafayette, alone among the Frenchmen, was singled out for commendation.

There was, however, little real discouragement. Brandywine had been fought; the battle had been lost; but the men were proud of their achievements. Howe's mighty force of veterans had been temporarily successful, to be sure, but the Americans had proved their prowess. Most of them were eager now to find some food, to get a thorough washing, and to refill the ammunition pouches. Then, after a good rest, they could resume the war.

Close to noon, after an exhausting march since dawn, the

men were cheered by a glimpse of the river. The Middle Ferry loomed ahead; the house of the caretaker was visible through the trees. The men were looking forward to a restful stay in Philadelphia. The talk turned toward anticipated pleasure. Surely the route would not again lead straight through the town; this time they hoped to play on Society Hill, to call upon the belles of Second Street, to savor the fine foods of the famous taverns by the waterfront. The soldiers, tired as they were, strayed to the roadside to pick wild asters and goldenrod and give themselves a gay appearance when they came into the capital.

Their happiness was short-lived. Orders came for the army to divide. The larger portion did cross the river; but, instead of marching into town, the line turned north along the river bank. Washington was returning to his base at Falls of Schuylkill, five miles above the city, to recruit more troops, and to replenish his ammunition. The smaller portion under Wayne was ordered to swing northwest through Blockley and Welsh Merion on outpost duty.

Wayne's route lay approximately along the present Lincoln Highway, but the road bore no resemblance to the existing six-lane boulevard that serves the famous Main Line suburbs. The way was little better than a trail, though dignified by being called the Great Road to the West. Commissioners had, indeed, been named in 1770, to lay out a public highway sixty feet wide from Philadelphia's Market Street to Lancaster; but virtually nothing had as yet been done.

The road was crooked and narrow, full of ruts and thank-you-ma'ams, miry in wet weather, dusty in the droughts. Tavern loungers were accustomed to sudden calls from teamsters to help haul heavy wagons from the mud. Innkeepers told of numerous occasions when the bright blue

45

Conestoga wagons froze fast in the ruts until the January thaws, or even until spring. The cedar trees which once had flourished on these hills had long since been cut as levers to pry the wagons loose.

Much of the march was now along the ridges, and this was fortunate, for heavy rains had softened lowland trails. Even on the heights, the narrow-tired wagons cut hub-deep into the mud. The monotony of the march was interrupted by the scrambling of soldiers over fences to gather corn shocks to fill in wet places. Then the tired men plodded on again. The army kept moving steadily.

Wayne's soldiers marched with some misgivings. Word had reached the troops that Merion and Blockley were afire with indignation. Twoscore of the most prominent citizens, including the principal innkeepers, had recently petitioned the newborn Commonwealth of Pennsylvania to take away all rebel troops from their vicinity. They complained that certain militiamen, welcomed as friends, had proved to be not only thieves but downright traitors.

"It is notorious that from the first day of their incamping," the angry letter read, "they began to shew their aversion for all Law, Divine or Human, abusing travellers, Robbing the Neighborhood of everything they could lay their hands on, pillaging their dwelling houses, Spring Houses and Barns, burning their Fence rails, Cutting down their Timber, Robbing Orchards and Gardens, Stealing their Piggs, Poultry and Lambs, and sometimes killing them through wantonness and bravado, and when complaints were made, they with the most unparralelled impudence, would threaten the lives of the Complainants or their Houses with fire, frequently damning the Congress, and Swearing they will never fight against King George."

Soldier gossip magnified this complaint into a violent pro-Tory sentiment. To their surprise, the Continentals learned that the scattered residents were fervent patriots. Though the retreating army was by no means presentable in its appearance, the inhabitants welcomed its arrival. Housewives hastened to distribute the small supplies of bread and pies that still remained on pantry shelves. It was unfortunate that hungry men should have come to Blockley on Friday afternoon just when the weekly bakings were almost exhausted. Saturday was the favored baking day in Pennsylvania.

At Eaglefield, a mile above the Middle Ferry, a real proof of sympathy was shown. "Governor" Samuel Morris, of the famous State-in-Schuylkill, officially offered hospitality to Wayne and his military "family."

To the great majority of the troops, the gesture carried slight significance other than as giving a momentary pause to marching; but to those familiar with the social life of Pennsylvania, the offer was extraordinarily gracious. The State-in-Schuylkill, as the élite well knew, was a fishing club which prided itself on its exclusiveness. Half jestingly, half seriously, the members had long since declared their independence from the British Crown. For half a century, the State had professed allegiance only to its own mimic democratic commonwealth. The members rented the land on which their "Castle" stood for one fresh perch a year, paid to "Baron" William Warner, their professed proprietor and feudal lord.

To Wayne and his staff, after an all-day battle and a thirty mile march, the offer of a State-in-Schuylkill dinner was attractive. Thoughts of barbecued pig, of broiled beefsteaks, and of the planked fish for which the State was internationally renowned, raced through their minds; the fish-house punch and the State's excellent Madeira were almost irresistible. But

47

Wayne was a soldier, and his detachment was under strict orders to push on to Merion. The State's offer was reluctantly declined.

Past the swinging sign in the open fields at the top of a high hill that announced Bill Stadleman's Black Horse Tavern was not far distant, past the inn itself, where Stadleman vainly beckoned for custom to men who had no time to stop to drink his flip and punch and cider, past Merion meeting-house, the most ancient of Quaker establishments and one which, because of its quaint T-shaped design, seemed to conservative Welshmen too closely kin to cruciform, Wayne's tired men plodded. They came at last, toward dusk, to the hospitable Tunis' Ordinary, now named in honor of the occasion, the General Wayne Inn.

Standing in the open doorway, the taproom behind him alight with candles, was the host himself, his broad face smiling, his jovial voice offering the soldiers eggs and ham, salt beef and fowl, with rum and water as their drink. The split slab tables, supported by round pegs stuck into auger holes, were bountifully decked out with wooden bowls and pewter plates, with wood trenchers, and with hard gourd shells. Pewter mugs would be filled with rum from huge stone jugs for those with pence to pay. This night, the meal which Tunis offered officers was not of pork and mush and milk, nor of the everlasting "hog and hominy" which was the customary fare, but rather of a generous potpie, with beet tops, corn and beans, and, as a special treat, mugs of good, hot coffee.

Here the tired troops rested, after two long days of battle and of marching. The men camped for the night in the open moonlit fields; the officers stretched flat upon the sanded tap-room floor, in wide circles round the stove, each man on his straw sack, covered with his coat. They waited comfortably for the arrival of the larger army.

Long before Wayne came to Merion, Washington had reached his Falls of Schuylkill base. His troops were busy scrubbing off the powder grime of Brandywine and scraping caked mud from their uniforms. They cleaned their guns and filled their cartridge pouches. They carried water to wash out their linen and, though the hard north winds blowing across the hills made river bathing cold and disagreeable, the men found great relief in cleanliness. New supplies were issued from the stores; the remainder of the goods was packed in wagons to be shipped away to the new base at Valley Forge.

March was resumed on Sunday morning, three days after Brandywine. Soon after breakfast, the bugles called the soldiers into ranks, and the men headed into the strong, chilly, north wind to make the rendezvous with Wayne at Merion. They were to cross the Schuylkill by three fords, the two more distant crossings separated by about five miles. They waded waist-deep across the swollen stream, holding their freshly cleaned rifles and their powder horns high above their heads.

Tragedy accompanied the fording of the river. Ten French officers, headed by the impetuous General Du Coudray, clattered to the bank, demanding that a flatboat be assigned them for the passage. All but Du Coudray dismounted while they were being ferried overstream, allowing their horses to be led across by soldiers. Not so the proud Du Coudray, who foolishly insisted on remaining mounted while the soldiers poled the flatboat to the western shore. His horse took fright and leaped overboard. Du Coudray was stunned, by striking his head against the rocks. He drowned in comparatively shallow water.

VALLEY FORGE

It was a stupid accident, particularly as it seems incredible that his escort could not have pulled the general from the river. The incident did, however, clear an impasse that had threatened to disrupt the high command. Du Coudray was a fresh arrival, bearing promises of preferment made in the name of the United States by the acting American envoy to France. A careless Congress, honoring the promise, had appointed the Parisian to a generalship that ranked several native-born Americans. Greene, Henry Knox, and Sullivan, angry because too many foreigners had already been accepted at their boastful self-appraisals, threatened to resign if Du Coudray continued to receive high rank. Congress, not daring to lose face by yielding to the American generals' ultimatum, had asked Washington to reprimand his officers. John Adams, too, had privately advised them to apologize to Congress, but the generals had refused to withdraw their resignations. Du Coudray's death lessened the tension and prevented the loss of three of Washington's best officers. The internal jealousies in the American army were not, however, ended.

Seldom was the American intelligence division so inefficient as it was during the three days after Brandywine. Testy William Smallwood's Marylanders, supposedly watching Howe's movements from a safe observation post far to the British rear, failed to forward their dispatches to the Commander-in-chief. Having too few horsemen for scouting purposes, not daring to detail his few light troops for reconnaissance, and being himself too far away from Howe to receive deserters, Washington was unaware of what his enemy was doing. Sure, however, that sound strategy required the British to move northward into the Great Valley, Washington hurried forward to block the British march. By moving westward along the Lancaster road, the Continentals could protect their stores at Reading and at Valley Forge, and could command the roads to Coventry and Warwick.

The Sunday march of September 14, however, was not long, since the immediate objective was merely to reunite the two divisions of the army. The officers spent the night at Philip Syng's palatial country seat, the former St. George's Inn, where huge stone barns, four enormous stables, and a gigantic storehouse at the bottom of a hollow promised ample food. The massive chimneys, the inviting stone terrace, the smooth lawn, mown close by Syng's specially made grass clippers, and the fruitful orchards gave St. George's an attractive appearance.

Washington, however, pressed on to hold a consultation with his generals. Anthony Wayne, restless and impatient, eager to rejoin battle with an enemy whom he considered as badly battered as the Americans themselves, was clamoring for an attack. Mad Anthony had spurred six miles ahead to scout the situation, and had returned with news that redcoats were not visible. After a long excited argument, decision was reached, late in the afternoon of September 15. The men were to march westward in the moonlight thirteen miles to White Horse, near the Warren tavern, close to the point where the best roads from the battlefield of Brandywine intersected the highway to Lancaster. Their route would take them through friendly, fertile country.

Washington was marching through a land of rich estates. Only in the New York patroon settlements, or in the great plantations of tidewater Virginia, were farms so wide-flung and so fertile. Most of the grain had now been harvested, for wheat ripens early in July in southeast Pennsylvania; but corn was in the shock, standing like irregular tepees amid the ragged rows of cut stalks. The meadows had been freshened by the recent rains, and though most of the stock had been driven off for safety against foragers, there yet remained herds large enough to yield the army food.

From the highest hills, Washington could see the site of Valley Forge; but between him and his future camp there lay long miles of marching, a major battle, and sufferings of unimaginable intensity. He had no anticipation of the hardships that would almost overwhelm his army in the weeks to come. Had he been able to foresee that Valley Forge would be his winter quarters, he might have gathered provisions from the food that lay in plenty about him. By December, when he returned, all these provisions had been commandeered by the British, or destroyed, or sent away for safety.

The younger Pennsylvanians cheered at the sight of the Spread Eagle. It was a patriot resort, and was Wayne's favorite tavern. Only the day before the main body of the troops arrived, Mad Anthony had tarried here to write Washington a letter, begging that he give battle to the British; and when Washington had seemed to give the letter insufficient heed Wayne had ridden back from the Spread Eagle to urge the Commander to take action. This very march in which the army was now engaged was the result of Wayne's insistence.

The soldiers' friendliness to the Spread Eagle was, however, due rather to their past pleasure at the low, stone inn than to the tavern's political associations. This Spread Eagle had been one of Pennsylvania's gayest rendezvous. Kept by Adam Ramsower, formerly host at the fashionable Yellow Springs, the inn stood at the crossroads of travel. For eight years, Ramsower had managed a place of entertainment where young folk might dance and drink and dine, and where "other Vices and unlawful Games" could be conducted. Outraged neighbors, by protesting to the courts, had closed down Ramsower's resort, and by the time the Continental troops appeared the Spread Eagle was run by a more staid boniface; but the Pennsylvanians were mindful of the past. They waved cheerful salutes as they passed by into the rolling Tredyffrin hills that lay ahead.

Dusk had not yet fallen when Washington came to the crossroads. Marking the presence of a chestnut tree which stood upon a knoll, he sent a scout into the topmost branches to see if there was any sign of British pursuit. The soldier saw no enemy, though he could look far down the road. Northward the view extended over the Great Valley to Valley Forge; southward, the scout's keen eye followed the creekside paths but could detect no hostile movement. Washington marched forward, knowing that his long retreat had proved wholly successful. He was again between the British and the munition centers. The army could relax; a few Pennsylvania leaders might even pay fleeting visits to their families.

Meanwhile the men moved forward through Cocklestown, named for the long-leafed purplish red flower that grows weedlike in the wheat fields, to the old Blue Ball, the earliest established tavern of inland Pennsylvania. Wayne, who knew the tavern well, remembered how an enterprising landlord, seeking to draw trade, had changed the inn's name to King of Prussia, to honor Britain's ally in the French and Indian War. But now the inn had changed its name again, and the King of Prussia sign swung at the doorway of another tavern halfway between the Blue Ball and Valley Forge.

The men were tired of marching. Ten miles over a difficult trail had brought them here long after nightfall. Some preferred to stay and rest at the Blue Ball, though rumors were current that travelers were murdered here. Others hoped

to stop to get some dinner, even though the Blue Ball offered little but salt pork and turnip tops. Even the bread
was bad. The wheat fields in this neighborhood produced
grain of excellent quality, but the people spoiled it by raising it with a leaven of boiled hops. The loaves so made
with "sots" were heavy and sour.

The soldiers, undismayed by the Blue Ball's reputation,
and its small accommodation for travelers, would willingly
have stayed. They were accustomed to sleeping on the floor,
and they were confident that when the meal was set upon
the table they could more than hold their own in the great
game of reaching across their neighbors for whatever food
might be available. They knew the tavern rule that it was
each man's duty to see that he secured his meat even if he
had to hack it from the joint with his own knife. But the
officers were in haste to push on to the west.

The clear skies were clouding as the men marched on
beyond the Blue Ball. The moon was obscured, the long
black shadows of the trees no longer reached across the road
as on the night of the retreat from Brandywine. Rain was
undoubtedly coming before the night was over.

A mile or so beyond the Blue Ball, the Frenchmen suffered sudden shock. A large, brightly lighted tavern, bearing a swinging sign with the name and figure of General
Pasquale Paoli, stood at a crossroads. Some of the Americans set up a shout of greeting, but the Frenchmen were
stunned to silence.

To Frenchmen, the General Paoli inn presented a dilemma.
All of them were in America ardent republicans and stanch
advocates of freedom; all struggled for the rights of oppressed
colonists to gain self-government. Yet they were French patriots and they were loyal to their king. The rebellious Paoli,

leader of a few hundred Corsicans, had fought armies of five thousand French veterans and had won a few successes before being driven into exile. Here in America, the rebel was a hero. Out of loyalty to Louis, the French volunteers dared not cheer their former foe, yet they dared not condemn a man who, to the Americans, seemed to typify the same cause as did Washington himself. The French were glad when the army was instructed to press on to White Horse.

They passed the General Warren Tavern on their way and this, too, awakened unpleasant memories. The name celebrated the valor of Sir Peter Warren who, with American volunteers, had taken Louisburg from France. By popular repute, the name also honored New England's Joseph Warren who had died at Bunker Hill. The French, however, knew little of the latter; they still winced at the memory of their Louisburg defeat.

With such backgrounds, the Warren should have been a strongly patriotic hostel; but in reality the inn was a redcoat rendezvous. Its owner, royalist John Penn, had installed as host Tory Peter Mather, and Mather had devoted the Warren to the entertainment of British prisoners on parole. Held captive at Lancaster, they were allowed to wander at will to points within thirty miles of Philadelphia, and they had been frequent visitors at Mather's inn. It was at Warren Tavern that Captain John André, one of the paroled prisoners, had drawn maps of the Great Valley area, and where he had completed plans approving the traitor Lee's suggestion that the British move by way of the Chesapeake to capture Philadelphia.

Here at last, after what must have seemed an endless day of marching, the army halted. Washington walked in the rainy night to his new quarters near the White Horse. He had

55

reached his objective. Now, he was confident that the Continentals lay safely between the British and the vital stores. Howe was believed to be far distant. With Americans safely occupying the hills, he could wait with equanimity any future British advance. All was safe. He and his soldiers sought sound sleep.

CHAPTER SIX

Battle of the Clouds

Howe's strategy is inexplicable. He might have crushed the Revolution had he followed up his victory. His unconventionality in splitting his force during a major battle proved a daring maneuver, but he threw away his gains. Had he renewed the fight the morning after Brandywine, he would have caught the Continentals helplessly unprepared. They could have retreated only into greater danger. But instead of marching forward, Howe stood still. He permitted Washington to withdraw to safety.

To one who stands upon the hills of Valley Forge, the proper British plan is glaringly apparent. Northwest from Valley Forge, beyond the distant mountain passes, were scores of munition works. Washington's most pressing need, after his defeat at Brandywine, was to replenish his supplies. Howe's main army was astride the great high roads that led across the Great Valley through the passes to the iron regions.

For four days, Howe did nothing. His army, in Wayne's picturesque phrase, "lay in a supine state," recovering from the battle. Some regiments had gone south to Wilmington to turn that thriving little mill town into a British base of operations. Well below the Delaware River forts, easily accessible by British warships, transports, and provision vessels, Wilmington was twenty miles closer to the capital than was the head of Chesapeake Bay. The communication lines were much easier for Howe to guard.

Though most of the army was lying idle, Howe was making friends. Understanding that an invading general must defeat the enemy but must not act in so Draconian a fashion as to terrify civilians, he set himself to win the confidence of the populace. Warning his troops to be considerate of noncombatants, ordering them to pay in gold for all the requisitioned goods, holding his soldiers under strict restraint, he tried by courtesy and gold to gain the friendship of the Quaker farmers.

Knowing that hardheaded business men would infinitely prefer good golden guineas to depreciated Continental paper, Howe paid generously for what his army ate and for the abundance that it carted off in wagons. He had, indeed, much more provision offered than could possibly be used. Entering the richest farm lands of the Americans just as the harvest was complete, he found the barns filled with wheat, corn, fruit, and vegetables. Fodder seemed inexhaustible, for though the summer had been unusually hot, the crop had not been parched by drought. Livestock were less plentiful, for, after Knyphausen's early raids, the canny farmers had driven off their herds and sheep to safer pasture in the hills; but there was still an abundant meat supply. The well fed and well supplied invaders wrote home that the land was "more beautiful than can be conceived."

The British skimmed the cream for their own use and burned the surplus, lest it fall into Continental hands. So thorough was the devastation that "the path of Howe's army was like that of a tornado." Washington had nothing but the scantiest of leavings. For these, he offered payment in poor paper, in due bills payable at some future date, or in orders drawn upon a migratory treasurer who, when found, could offer only Continental currency. The most extreme patriots could maintain their love of independence under such conditions; for many of the others Howe's golden guineas were persuasive propagandists.

There were, of course, innumerable violations of his rules requiring that foragers remain polite, that they take only actual necessities for themselves, and that they always pay liberally for what they took. The British soldiers, after Brandywine, were stripping the countryside. The rural folk whom Howe was hoping to win back to loyalty could not be reassured by mere verbal protestations that the looting was entirely against orders; they demanded restoration of their valuables. Some, whose pacifism was less deep, insisted that marauders be severely punished. Howe and Cornwallis, realizing that they must make an example of some culprit, lingered in the neighborhood of Brandywine to mete out stiff punishment against the first proved violator.

Actual identifications were not easy. When seventy-year-old widow Jane Gibbons, whose father-in-law had been a juryman in the Mattson witchcraft trial, stormed into Howe's presence to demand the return of her favorite cow, Howe was unable to discover who had taken the animal. The aged "Queen of the county," whom Howe accused justly of loving her cow more than her king, insisted, however, that the cow be found, and that she be indemnified for the loss of milk during its captivity. Howe yielded to her demands. He was to meet her at a later day in an even stormier mood.

Howe's opportunity to execute a proved offender came soon after the call from Mrs. Gibbons. On Monday morning, four days after Brandywine, while Howe and Cornwallis were smoking breakfast pipes and wondering where more flour supplies might be stored, they heard a loud commotion in the hall. The sharp metallic bark of the commander's sentry shouted, "You can't go in there." A high-pitched soprano, shrill with excitement, scolded: "Don't you dare touch us. We're here to see the general. We won't take orders from a common soldier."

Howe and Cornwallis, starting from their seats, turned to face the door. It flew open suddenly. Two girls in their late teens flounced into the room, their faces flushed, their eyes snapping angrily. Behind them rushed a worried sentry.

"General, I tried to stop them. They pushed past me. I hope—"

"Silence," ordered Howe. "Get back to your post. I'll take care of this."

"Never knew you to turn young ladies over to another man," drawled Earl Cornwallis. "This seems interesting. I think I'll let that flour business wait."

Both officers were handsome, polished, and urbane, and both had eager eyes for pretty girls. But neither Mary Martin nor Martha Cox was in flirtatious mood. They paid no heed to Howe's polite invitation to be seated. Mary stared intently at each man, guessed quickly which was Howe, and taking three steps toward him, shook her finger in his face, and demanded that he restore the jewelry stolen from her by three British soldiers.

Cornwallis, whom the soldiers called "Old Corncob," enjoyed his chief's discomfiture. His left eye blinked badly as it always did in moments of excitement. Nervously, he continued poking the hair back from his temple as he was wont to do when he was thinking rapidly.

BATTLE OF THE CLOUDS

Dandy Sir Billy Howe, who liked "his lass, his glass, and his game of cards" as well as any man in His Majesty's armed forces, was somewhat perturbed, but now that he had recovered from his first surprise he hoped to cool the temper of the angry girl. The matter might, he thought, give him the awaited opportunity to show the rebels that he could be kind and reasonable, and that his offers of amnesty were genuine.

Cornwallis suggested that the troops be paraded, and that the girls be given a chance to identify the robbers. Howe, in full uniform, flanked on either side by a determined girl, slowly stalked the lines. Mary picked out three soldiers. Then, to make identification more certain, Howe ordered the regiments to parade again in different arrangement. This time, the troops marched by while Howe and the two girls stood still. Again Mary picked out the culprits. In still a third test, she was once more successful. The men were searched and portions of the stolen property were found in their possession.

This was Howe's opportunity. By drumhead court-martial, in the presence of the troops, the three were tried, were found guilty, and were sentenced to death. Lots were drawn; two of the three were chosen to be hanged by the third, and then, when the hangings were completed, the third man was shot. Mary's stormy eyes watched the whole proceedings, although Martha broke down in tears. Two other Britishers were later hanged for other pillaging; many were lashed; some were ordered to be jailed. Then, considering that he had proved his good faith, Howe marched northward to meet Washington again.

He was four days too late, though possibly the psychologic value of his punishments was sufficient reward for his delaying. A ten-mile British march on the morning after Brandywine would have crippled the Continentals by cutting them off from their supplies. If Howe had gone to Valley Forge, fortifying the near-by hills, Washington would have been compelled, in utter desperation, to storm Howe's armed position or else give up the war for lack of guns and powder.

Washington, however, taking full advantage of British inaction, had rushed his tired men sixty miles in a half-circle around the idle British army. He had thus won by walking what he had lost in battle; he was again between the British and the Warwick and Coventry munition centers. Howe's splendid strategy had gone for naught.

The Americans, moreover, had a mounting morale. Only ill fortune and the want of good light horse, as it now seemed to the rebel leaders, had prevented victory at Brandywine. The loss of that engagement had, it is true, somewhat weakened American confidence for the moment, but the recovery of the way to Warwick had canceled the effects of the disaster. Anthony Wayne and his fellow leaders were convinced that in another trial of strength the British would be badly beaten.

Now that Washington was camped on the South Valley hill, on heights that Howe must scale before he could attack, the odds seemed even more favorable for rebel victory. The Continentals could rest while waiting for the British to advance; they would be fresh while the enemy was tiring; they would have the great advantage of the upper position. Close to their munition centers, while the British were obliged to haul supplies from Wilmington over a long and vulnerable communication line, the Continentals were growing stronger with each hour of delay. Howe, realizing now that his inaction had destroyed his victory at Brandywine, was forced to undertake a new offensive.

Early on a gray and misty morning five days after Brandywine, when fog covered the floor of the Great Valley, Washington learned that the British were approaching. He was eager for an action. A thousand of his men were shoeless and many more were poorly clad, but their spirits were unbroken. His troops, well rested after their sixty-mile retreat, had ample artillery and were well supplied with small-arms ammunition. The thin rain was not unpleasant but served rather to lend an added zest to the exertions of the coming battle. The men waited confidently for the victory which would hurl back Howe's advance, and which, it was believed, would clear the British from the neighborhood.

The site is visible from Valley Forge. Washington encamped upon the hilltops, near the present site of Villa Maria, the large building which now dominates the South Valley hill. The line of American entrenchments stretched for three miles upon the heights, controlling the approaches. Behind the lines, in the Great Valley, were at least three good roads whereby, in the event of disaster, the rebels might retreat into the safety of the broken northern hills. Such a retreat was not expected, but, in case of need, the move would carry Washington into his munition centers and would permit a quick replenishment of his supplies. Howe could not follow without running an extraordinary risk of ambush and annihilation.

A light rain was falling when the first royalist advance made contact with the American outposts. Three British columns moved near by, ready to converge upon the strong American positions. The rain increased. A few British cannon were discharged; Washington lost perhaps a score of men. To the astonishment of the American commanders, a newly posted picket party of about three hundred men, "shamefully fled at the first fire." The British pursued. The rain was now pouring heavily. Washington, waiting on the rising ground at White Horse in the Great Valley, could not see through the low-lying clouds that veiled the hill-tops.

Soon the rain came down in floods. Neither British nor Americans could fire a single shot. The powder on both sides was drenched. Even the British cartouches, presumably water-tight, were dripping-wet. Neither side was able to glimpse the enemy in the dense fog that settled over hill and valley. This Battle of the Clouds was stopped at the outset.

The outcome was a disappointment for both sides. Washington had lost, by accident of weather, an opportunity to retrieve the Brandywine defeat; Howe had been unable to take advantage of the American outpost weakness. In better weather, he could have thrust forward with the bayonet; but, with visibility so poor and roads so soggy, his men would have been hopelessly confused. Howe, invariably considerate of his troops, refused to order an advance. He camped in the dripping woods at the foot of the South Valley hills in Tredy-ffrin until the weather cleared.

Washington, waiting on his hillock at White Horse, kept alert all day for the renewed attack that never came. By four o'clock, convinced that no more fighting would be possible, he signaled for retreat. He was desperately in need of dry munitions. He did not know that the British were quite as unprepared as he to carry on a battle.

Withdrawal seemed impossible. The Great Valley was a rain-soaked swamp. Its roads were marshes; rain swept down incessantly; the greater number of the horses had already been sent off with the baggage. Most of the soldiers were quite certain that all the cannon would be caught in quagmires. But, by commandeering all the draft beasts in the valley, by harnessing the soldiers to the guns, and by steady hauling through the night, Washington managed to draw off his army through the passes into the mountain country where the British dared not follow. Ten hours of steady labor carried the men a scant five miles from White Horse, but the distance was great enough for American security.

The Battle of the Clouds was indecisive. Howe held the road to Lancaster and was within easy distance of the Swedes' ford across the Schuylkill. He had possession of the fertile Great Valley and controlled an ample stock of food and fodder. He was, however, in grave danger. Smallwood's militiamen, known to be lurking in his rear, would have but little difficulty in cutting his long lines of communication. Washington, by yet another of his extraordinary marches, might swing through the hills toward Valley Forge. Then, if the Americans should establish cannon on the crests of the North Valley range, and if a rebel party could harass the British rear, Howe would be caught in a trap.

To form a trap was the counsel of Anthony Wayne. He had been the strongest advocate for renewing the attack after Brandywine; he had led the van on the long march to White Horse; he had taken the aggressive at the Battle of the Clouds. Now he renewed his demands for battle, urging Washington to pen Howe in the Great Valley.

Wayne snorted with impatience at his Commander's explanation that the men were too fatigued to move. He insisted that his fifteen hundred Pennsylvanians could rush to Warwick for dry powder and new guns, and be sufficiently fresh to return to the South Valley hill to fight the British. He hoped to cut off Howe's rear guard and to take possession of the British baggage. He might, indeed, drive the redcoats eastward. If Washington would hurry through the mountain regions to Valley Forge, Howe's army would be unable to escape. Though Washington had little confidence that the venture could succeed, he yielded to the insistence of Mad Anthony.

While Washington and Wayne were talking, Wayne's Pennsylvanians bivouacked in the woods. They had neither tents nor blankets to protect them against the driving rain, and they had come both barefooted and hungry, but they were cheerful once again. Their scouts had found a herd of forty shorthorn cows. These had been slaughtered, and though fires were difficult to keep alight in such a storm, the troops had managed to half-cook the beef. The butchering had been extraordinarily wasteful, but the men had been allotted almost ten pounds of meat apiece. Much of it they ate, in an impromptu banquet that lasted until dawn; the rest they stowed away in haversacks. Many of them marched away with huge chunks of cooked beef tied to their belts.

From the cowskin they hurriedly fashioned moccasins during that sleepless, drenching night. Great squares of rawhide bound about their feet and fastened by untanned leather thongs wrapped tightly about their calves gave them protection against the rocky roads. When the men rushed off at daylight to get the powder and the guns, these moccasins raised blisters; and when they turned almost immediately upon arrival at the Warwick arsenal, to dash ten miles back to the new positions on South Valley hill, the untanned cowskin shrank and pinched their feet until, in despair, many of the men preferred to march barefoot.

CHAPTER SEVEN

From Hell to Egypt

WASHINGTON moved more leisurely than the excited Wayne. The strain of hauling cannon through the mud had taken a heavy toll of strength; the troops, though rested by one night's good sleep at White Horse, had no great reserve of energy. If they were to swing through rugged mountain roads to intercept the British, the journey must be done by easy stages. Replenishing guns and ammunition, drying the uniforms, arranging for new supplies of food, required more time than Mad Anthony supposed.

The country was vastly different from the fertile farms through which the route had previously led. Washington had hitherto been fighting in garden communities, in pasture lands, and in fields of grain; he now was moving into oak and chestnut forests, into mining sections, and into the busiest heavy industry districts of Pennsylvania. He was leaving agricultural communities, where the populace was pacifist; he was entering an iron-making section where the people were almost unanimously Whig. Such centers as Coventry and Warwick had suffered severely from the rules that gave manufacturing monopolies to Englishmen. The ironmasters were

67

warring for their economic as well as their political independence.

For the first time in the war the Carolinians, Virginians, and Georgians felt at home. New England and the middle colonies had seemed like a foreign land. Houses, food, and modes of labor were strange; the people were peculiar. Quaker folk were broad in mental outlook and tolerant of divergent thought; perhaps, indeed, they were indifferent to new ideas; but, in the estimation of the Southerners, Quaker folk had no conception of the proper means of finding full pleasure in their wealth. Southerners complained that most of the cold North knew nothing of the gracious ways of life, knew nothing of the generous plantation hospitalities. But here in the iron regions there were theories very close to those so warmly cherished in Virginia's tidewater homes.

Here were self-sufficient manors presided over by veritable feudal lords; here were stately mansions, set in fragrant gardens, and equipped with costly furnishings; here were fine china and heavy plate; here were the wholly unofficial, but completely respected, communal courts, and here were the special servants who basked in the reflected glory of their masters. The homes of more important ironmasters were almost precise replicas, so far as culture was concerned, of the Big Houses of the slave states.

There was further similarity in that, beneath the shadow of the castle on the hill, there clustered villages of small log huts with whitewashed walls where workers dwelt. Few slaves lived here, though some few furnaces had experimented with forced labor of Indians, redemptioners, and Guinea Negroes. Such furnaces were likely to be inefficient. Northern communities seldom had the knack of close social relationships on a caste system.

The army saw, however, little of these labor difficulties. It saw, instead, the glare of furnaces in blast, the streams of scintillating sparks, the glow of white-hot metal passing under heavy hammers to create new guns and better ammunition for the Continental cause. It heard the cooling splash of falling water as the great wheels creaked about; it listened to the laboring of carts hauling iron ore, wood, and limestone along the rugged mountain roads; it stood startled at the sudden roar which burst like volcanic eruptions from the top of the great stacks. Proudly the ironmasters, looking on these fiery sights, nicknamed their region "Pennsylvania's Hell."

More than one among the officers regretted that boisterous, hot-tempered General Daniel Morgan was not now with Washington's command. The one-time wagoner who once had suffered five hundred lashes on the bare back for daring to strike a British officer was a son of just such iron-making country. He, too, had heard the horn that called the men to work at four o'clock on summer mornings, and he had breathed the heavy fumes that rose from charcoal pits. More than any other officer in Washington's army, he knew the practices of iron industries. But the ambitious, self-made Morgan was far distant in New York, leading his fringed-uniformed riflemen against Burgoyne's invasion.

There were novel sights in this black country, which the natives boasted was so close to hell. The iron stove plates which the Pennsylvania Germans liked to put behind their fires to reflect heat into the rooms were strange artistic gems. These firebacks were cast in such Bible patterns as the miracle at Cana, the slaying of Goliath, and Cain killing Abel. Together the series made an almost complete "Bible in Iron." Since the French and Indian War a new design had also become popular, which showed Justice and Virtue, while beneath the figures two swords crossed a plowshare and above their heads a pruning hook was surmounted by a long-handled spear. This pattern symbolized the text, "They shall beat their swords into plowshares, and their spears into pruning-hooks."

Strangest of all the plates, except to those well read in German lore, was the extremely popular Dance of Death, wherein a skeleton, brandishing a human leg, was interrupting a dispute between two persons clad in fifteenth century costume. Few but the German householders of the odd Schwenkfelder faith knew of the ancient "Basle Tagdentag" from which the legend was derived, but Germans of all sects delighted in the ownership of the strange plate. It had been popular among them, in their German homes, for more than two centuries.

These were, however, not now being cast, nor were the Franklin nor the tenplate Hopewell stoves among the present products of the forges. All energies were being turned to casting cannon and to making shot. Each ironmaster hoped to match the marvelous wrought-iron cannon built the year before by William Dunning of Carlisle. Two of these remarkable guns had gone through Washington's campaigns but one had been lost at Brandywine. Rumor, which swiftly spreads in any army through mysterious channels, was already busy with reports that Howe was planning to dispatch this gun to England with requests that British ironworks duplicate the piece in bulk. The men from upstate Pennsylvania also said that Dunning had desired to cast another and still larger cannon, but that no one in Carlisle was rash enough to face a furnace heat which, according to reports, was melting the lead buttons on Bill Dunning's coat.

The encamping place was famous for its hospitality. Coventry Hall, once the home of Robert Grace, a leading Philadelphia financier, stood as the show place among all the big estates. Built by the iron pioneers who, sixty years before had begun the first forges in the state, it had seen the industry develop from an isolated frontier work amid dense forests to a point where seers were wondering whether sufficient trees would be available to supply charcoal for the future fires. More than any of the rival mansions, Coventry Hall prided itself on its English manor mode of life.

Rebecca Nutt Grace, chatelaine of Coventry, heir to almost all the founders of the iron barony, was among the most outstanding women of colonial Pennsylvania. Brought up in the iron country, she and her able mother Anna Nutt had managed forge and furnace. Aggressive, enterprising, and, withal, strikingly beautiful, she had, by her second marriage, to Robert Grace, achieved a dominance in metropolitan Philadelphia society. For the quarter of a century before Grace died in 1766, she had ruled the intellectual salons of the province. But then she had gone back to her iron barony to resume the reins.

The handsome, white-haired dowager, once queen of Philadelphia social life, had lived in virtual retirement since Robert Grace, the friend of Franklin, died. Her spacious High Street house, built of imported black-end brick, was closed. The intellectuals no longer thronged to her salon, through that arched carriageway that led through Pewter Platter Alley, to talk about the latest London books. The leather-aproned young experimenters who played with chemistry and the electric tubes were grown men now, engrossed in serious pursuits. She never had forgiven them for their refusal to allow her to attend the memorable dinner where

71

"a turkey was to be killed by the electric shock, and roasted by the electrical jack before a fire kindled by the electrical bottle," particularly as she was never quite convinced that they had been successful in their enterprise. The beautiful, quick-minded widow, whom many thought more charming at fifty-eight than she had been as a demure young girl, had missed the alert exchange of wit to which she had become accustomed.

Washington's arrival with a staff of handsome officers gladdened Rebecca Grace's heart. Their uniforms were drenching-wet, and the green ribbons of the youthful aides-de-camp were crumpled into sodden strings; but their gayety was still infectious, and their spirits still ran high. The great mansion, built of the red sandstone quarried from her own estate, welcomed Washington and Madison and Hamilton as it, in former days, had welcomed Franklin.

Indeed it had not been long since Franklin had been there. Barely a year before, she told her dripping guests, the aged statesman had driven up to Coventry to pay a social call. She pointed out to Washington the room to the left of the great center hall where the very first of Franklin's patent stoves was standing; she told her visitors how Franklin and her husband had been friends and how the Junto that became the Philosophical Society had sung its club song at her house on Friday evenings. "Theirs was a motto," she told Washington, "that our patriots would do well to use as their own slogan. The Junto made each initiate swear to respect each fellow member, to love mankind, to believe in freedom of opinion, and to love truth for truth's sake."

She did not say that the Franklin journey had been moved by deeper motives than a superficial social call. Franklin had professed himself in love. The good doctor, almost bowed down by academic honors and by public praise, was lonely. His wife was dead; his only living child was married; he was about to sail for France.

According to Rebecca's version of the call, she would not hear of a third marriage. Recently she had been won to Methodism, then sweeping through the county in triumphant progress. The dancing wit of Robert Grace had wounded her when he had poked his endless puns at this new interest. She remembered how he came back home, after two weeks' unexplained absence, sending a scared lackey to her parlor with his hat. If she were amiable, he sent word, she might keep the hat and he would come in too; but if she sent the hat away, then he would make his absence longer. She recalled the day that she had gone to pay a call upon her minister and had come out to find, scrawled on the wall with soapstone:

> Your walls are thick, and your religion thin,
> The Devil is without, and Grace within.

Franklin, Rebecca thought, was too much of a piece with Robert Grace in his spiritual principles. She liked him, and she remembered gratefully the earnest interest he took in culture. His mind was not so quick as hers, his mood more sober, but his lack of serious religion seemed insurmountable. Gently she refused his marriage offer. By one tradition, current among her descendants, she went to him when he was old and sick and needed comfort; but there are other rumors, which the present generation holds to be in better keeping with Rebecca's character, that she refused to make the visit.

Of these matters, of course, Washington knew nothing. He was intrigued by the great bell of Warwick, hung here to summon the vicinity to bury cannon if the Hessians were to come. He chuckled in hearing how young Tom Potts, son-in-law of the dowager, had revived the ancient Coventry Steel Mill to circumvent a law prohibiting the erection of new steel mills and slitting works, and how he had then scrapped all the old machinery, keeping nothing but the Coventry good-will.

Washington lingered three days among the comforts of Coventry, Wayne had long since gone to take his post on the South Valley hill, where he might harass the British rear; the British had already left the site of the unfought Battle of the Clouds to move against Valley Forge and to take possession of the roads that led to Philadelphia. Now that the storms had passed, and the weather had again become as fine as only Pennsylvania knows it in mid-September, it was high time for Washington to march.

However, it was much too late for the Americans to move toward Valley Forge along the western shore of the Schuylkill. British advance parties were already camped along the north approach to Valley Forge; their scouts were ranging far inland along French Creek, looting homes and wrecking mills. If Washington now sought to follow Wayne's plan, he would be obliged to cross the river, to march down the eastern Schuylkill shore, and so to ford the river on the British flank.

On Friday September 19, the army passed the swollen river at Parkerford, almost midway between the present sites of Phoenixville and Pottstown. It was no easy crossing, for the men, lately so drenched by three days of northeast storm, declined again to wet their uniforms. As each detachment reached the river bank, the men delayed to strip. No amount of example from their officers, pointedly wading waist-deep in the coffee-colored water, could persuade the soldiers to plunge in until the men were naked. Then, with clothing rolled tight into bundles held above their heads, the companies picked their way across the ford. On the east bank of the river, they halted to dress again in leisure.

Eight hours thus elapsed, and there was yet a distance to be marched. Washington designed to move south toward the Fatland ford at Valley Forge, through the rich and fertile farming region which, for half a century, had borne the nickname of the Fatlands of Egypt. Toward this goal the men were now to march. It was to be an all-day journey, and was to continue late into the night. The common soldiers had been wiser than their leaders, for the troops, at least, were dry, while the officers were wearing dripping uniforms. All were hungry, tired, and thirsty, but when they came to Trappe, where they were to camp along the banks of little Perkiomen Creek, they found themselves among devoted friends of freedom.

CHAPTER EIGHT

Paoli Massacre

EXACTLY a week after Brandywine, on September 18, Wayne was ready to renew hostilities. Safely stationed in the woods, hiding in a secluded position some distance off the main highway, with artillery ready to be posted on advantageous hills, he was waiting for Washington to complete the long encircling movement through the hills to Valley Forge.

Success depended upon secrecy. Mad Anthony hoped that the enemy would not discover his proximity until both he and Washington were ready to attack. To prevent the British from learning that he was in their neighborhood, he carefully refrained from sending out sufficient scouts to learn all the movements of the British. To avoid all need of foraging for food, he ordered ten of his own fat prize cattle to be driven to the hiding place from his nearby Waynesborough farm.

Fifteen hundred men could not keep silent during the many waiting hours. Their cooking kettles clashed noisily; the soldiers shouted loudly to one another; some, finding their loadings jammed, fired their muskets to clear the guns. The campfire smoke rose from the hiding place to betray their presence. Detached as they were from the main body of the Continentals, without sufficient support until such time as Smallwood's slowly moving Marylanders should arrive from their rear-guard position back of Brandywine, the position of Wayne's men was becoming hourly more hazardous.

Howe was now well aware of Washington's probable intentions. Scouts had informed him of the Wayne position and of the Washington movements. The British leader, therefore, had already moved the bulk of his army eastward to secure the road along the Schuylkill River. Washington could now carry out the entrapment plan only by fording the river, marching down the east bank of the Schuylkill, and crossing back at either the Fatland or the Swedes' ford. More time would be required for this long encircling movement; meanwhile Wayne would be isolated. Letters in which Washington had tried to inform Mad Anthony of the situation had been captured by Howe's vigilant scouting parties.

Immediately upon the lifting of the fogs after the Battle of the Clouds, Howe had sent light infantry to capture Valley Forge. The large American magazines, insufficiently guarded since the transfer of the stores from the Falls of Schuylkill base, fell easily into British hands. Here were almost four thousand barrels of flour, enough to feed the regular Continental army for a month, huge stocks of essential camp supplies, thousands of axes, shovels, and entrenching tools, twenty-five barrels of horseshoes, and other needed commodities.

The capture of the stores, during the driving northeast storm of September 18, 1777, was a crushing blow to the Americans. The largest magazine south of Reading, relied upon to supply the army during the immediate campaign, was now in the hands of the enemy; the good Fatland ford across the Schuylkill gave Howe convenient access to the farm lands across the river where he could block the American advance. Washington was completely cut off from all contact with the sea; he could not readily communicate either with the capital or with the Continental forces in other sections of the United States.

Methodically, Howe now proceeded to destroy the American resources. Colonel William Dewees' mills and forge and storage houses were burned; his stone houses were looted. Leather bottom chairs were wantonly broken; good feather beds were ripped, together with the hangings; silver tankards, teapots and tablespoons were stolen. Two great mirrors, heirlooms from the Potts' family, were shattered. According to a statement "sworn upon the Holy Evangelists and Almighty God," Dewees suffered damages amounting to more than twenty thousand dollars.

Rumor swiftly spread that Valley Forge had been betrayed. The raid seemed linked to a disaster some months earlier when a near-by powder mill exploded. On that occasion, Peter de Haven, superintendent of the plant, denounced a former friend, charging that when the acquaintance had been "Sumwhat in Drink he Damned the Powder Mill, and told Colonel Dewese Let us Blow it to hell, which I thought Was a very odd exprestion when Colonel Deweese told me . . . So I remain, your Friend and Humble Servant." Nothing came of the accusation, for due investigation freed the loose-lipped friend, but the destruction of the Dewees forge seemed to many a coincidence too glaring to be accidental.

The Hessians, too, were now let loose. Partly as a compensation for compelling them to fight a war beyond their native boundaries; partly as a bribe to prevent them from openly rebelling as they had done prior to their departure from Germany, their officers gave them license to pillage and destroy. Taught to believe that the Americans, by revolt against a rightful king, had forfeited their fertile country, and that the acres were ready for division among Hessians once the war was won, the mercenaries put no bounds to greed. Destruction of scientific apparatus for the sake of brass, the treating of valuable books as though they were waste paper, the breaking and burning of paintings, furniture, and artistic treasures were common incidents of Hessian vandalism.

The very sight of brass-capped, long-mustached Hessians spread terror. The great, glum foreigners, muttering heavy gutturals, were relentless. Probably the feelings of the Valley Forge community were best expressed by little Betty Coates, who when a Hessian caught a goose by the neck and exultantly cried, "Dis bees goot for the poor Hessian mans," shouted angrily, "I hope you choke on it."

Again, Howe failed to follow up his advantage. Reading, chief storehouse for the Continentals, lay almost defenseless thirty miles to the north. A small British raiding party could have captured the American supplies and could have released the prisoners of war interned at that inland Pennsylvania German town. But Howe contented himself with the possession of Valley Forge and the Tredyffrin vicinity.

The British camp extended northward along the Schuylkill from Valley Forge to Tory Judge Moore's estate near the mouth of Pickering Creek. The high-spirited old man, edging toward his eightieth year, still smarting under the unfair accusations lodged against him by the Whigs, welcomed the invaders. When Howe commiserated with him on the injustice of the charges, Judge Moore's cracked voice quavered that he paid no attention to such ravings. "I am little solicitous," he said, "about the ravings of an ass whose particular talent and characteristics have been slander and obloquy."

Now that the west bank of the Schuylkill was in British hands, Washington could cross the river only by the distant Parkerford. Howe by feinting back and forth, first toward Reading and then toward Philadelphia, could keep the Americans in constant apprehension. Deliberately he proceeded to mystify Washington and thus to keep the rebels on the defensive. He could rest most of his own men while preparing for the main attack upon whichever objective he might choose.

Wayne, waiting two days in the woods for Smallwood to arrive, was open to British attack. Major General Sir Charles Grey was in command of the Black Watch, Howe's rear guard at Howellville, where the Swedesford road meets the highway from the south, approximately halfway between Valley Forge and Wayne's hidden camp. Knowing through his spies and from Washington's intercepted letter how serious was Wayne's situation, Grey planned attack before the Maryland militia could arrive.

In their temporary quarters in the stone tavern under a buttonwood tree at Howellville, John André and Grey elaborated a scheme to throw Wayne off his guard. Believing that Howellville farmers were carrying secret messages to Wayne, they let word leak through the camp that they planned to move eastward to the Swedesford at two o'clock in the morning. It was, as Grey and André knew through an intercepted message, the information for which Wayne was waiting. He intended to attack the British rear as soon as the force was under way, hoping thus to throw the army into confusion. If, as Grey and André reasoned, Wayne believed that the move would not occur until the early morning, he would let his soldiers sleep for the first half of the night. Then, having put Wayne off his guard, they arranged an earlier attack to strike the sleeping rebels.

Both British and Americans expected rain before the dawn. Wayne warned his men to wrap their coats about their cartouche boxes to keep their powder dry for the expected dawn attack upon the British rear; Grey ordered his own troops to use no guns whatever. The soldiers were forbidden to carry flints in their muskets, lest, in the heat of the encounter, they forget their strict injunctions. "No-Flint" Grey believed that bayonet attacks would be sufficiently successful against an unsuspecting enemy. He desired no repetition of the Battle of the Clouds.

The British attack was well planned. Lieutenant Colonel Thomas Musgrave took a force to guard the Lancaster road so that Wayne might not escape toward Philadelphia; a second, and smaller, party hurried to surround Waynesborough on the chance that Mad Anthony might be at home; Grey himself took the third, and largest, division along the Swedesford road to mount the steep hills to Wayne's secret camp. One road was inadvertently left unguarded by which Wayne might flee into the iron country to reunite with Washington. But Grey was hopeful that only a few Americans would be able to escape his bayonet attack.

The plan worked well. No civilians were on the roads at midnight to give warning to the rebels; an American mounted sentry was driven in. The vedette fired his gun and spurred back to the camp, but though the rebel sentries heard the shot, they paid no attention to the warning. American pickets were quick to fire at shadows; the sound of one lone rifle gave the camp no real alarm. A second shot from a closer sentinel caused more concern, but when this was reinforced by the arrival of a speeding vedette with warning that the enemy was advancing, the Americans were called to quarters.

There was ample time, it seemed, for Wayne to arrange his men in battle line. A horseman, hurrying over a well known road, could cover the intervening distance between Grey and the Wayne encampment in much less time than Grey's trudging Black Watch would require. Wayne had fully ten minutes' warning that he was to be attacked.

Evidently the Americans became confused in making their formations. Some men, wheeling in the wrong direction, passed directly in front of the campfires, thus silhouetting themselves clearly against the light. The British, pressing forward with the bayonet, killed two hundred rebels. They themselves lost but a dozen lives.

Because the night attack took place near the General Paoli Inn, though closer to the General Warren, the American rout has generally received the name of the Paoli Massacre. Around the incident, legends have since gathered. Revolutionary publicists, taking full advantage of the fact that cold-steel fighting was comparatively unknown in the Continental army, represented the affair as deliberate murder of sleeping men by cruel Hessians. Reports spread that the British, finding Wayne's sick and wounded lying helpless in the camp, set fire to the straw on which the men were resting. Rumors were current that Grey refused quarter to his prisoners.

None of these reports was true, nor were the counter rumors accurate. Enemies of Wayne told how Mad Anthony, warned in advance of the attack, was too much interested in a game of cards to protect his camp. A variation of the hostile story said that he had saved his life by turning his uniform coat inside out to display its red lining. Thus, it was said, he had escaped by passing himself off as a British officer. The more elaborate versions explained that Wayne, caught by the enemy, took command of the British and ordered the Black Watch to cease attacking. Still another popular yarn described Wayne as hiding in the big green boxbush at Waynesborough while the British searched the house in vain. These myths, like those which accused the British of deliberate massacre, were wholly false.

For years following the Paoli Massacre, however, neighbors believed that Peter Mather, keeper of the General Warren Inn, had betrayed Wayne to the enemy. Mather, a known Tory, operating the inn for John Penn, the loyalist owner, was said to have guided Grey's column to the camp. Mather, it was pointed out, was among the very few property owners in the Valley Forge area who had not suffered depredations from the British raiders. Though he strenuously denied his guilt, the popular opinion ran so strongly against him that neighbors avoided using the General Warren. Eventually he was obliged to give up his innkeeping and retire to Philadelphia.

"God frowned on him," the pious Americans later declared. "His stock died; his crops failed." Mather fell lower in status, became a teamster, later a wheelbarrow-huckster. Half a century after Paoli, small boys in the Philadelphia streets badgered him by following his barrow and calling out the rebel watchwords with the ominous addition, "Remember Paoli."

Wayne, however, escaped with the remainder of his men, dragging his artillery westward along the open road. He had not retraced his steps more than a mile before he met the laggard Smallwood Maryland militia. The Marylanders were twelve hours behind their schedule. Smallwood and Wayne

joined forces; the combined army of more than three thousand
soldiers crossed the Schuylkill at Parkerford a day after Washington's main army had passed over.

The British, jubilant at a victory won without having fired
a shot, now returned to Howellville. They raided Mary
Howell's tavern, stole her stock of liquor, refusing to pay because, they said, she ought to help celebrate the British
triumph. Then, breaking camp, the rear guard also moved
eastward to Valley Forge. They camped along the river bank,
waiting for an opportunity to cross the Schuylkill. Washington was in camp at Pottsgrove, northward in the Pennsylvania German country.

CHAPTER NINE

Lost Camp at Pottsgrove

WASHINGTON had now come into another land of plenty. The Fatlands of Egypt, lying along the eastern Schuylkill shores and stretching inland on both sides of the narrow Perkiomen Creek far into the distant Goshenhoppen hills, were rich storehouses. Wide fields of corn ready for the harvest, luxuriant meadows where full-fed herds of cattle pastured, peach and apple orchards heavy with ripe fruit, testified to the farming skill of the hardworking, frugal German settlers.

The folk who lived here in the Fatlands, directly across the river from Valley Forge, were pacifist by inclination. Descended from immigrants who had fled from Germany to escape the devastations of the Thirty Years' War, they well knew the havoc which conflicts caused. The old folks told how roots and grass and even leaves had been the only food available after the warring armies had laid waste the fertile German farms; tales were current of how, after the troops had gone, the wolves had roamed unchecked throughout the countryside; whispers ran that famine had been so extreme that cannibalism had been known. The Germans of the Fatlands, knowing what horrors would come of war, were peaceful people.

Though they were pacifists by inclination, yet the Pennsylvania Germans were patriots by conviction. Hating war, they were even more opposed to what they thought unjust. Firmly believing that the Continental cause was right, they bent every effort to give comfort to the troops.

Luckily the red-painted "Swisser" barns, built on hillsides so that heavy farm carts might drive directly into the upper story haylofts, were full of grain and fodder. During these late September days, the great four-horse teams, each hauling a ton of farm produce, were bringing from the fields huge mounds of yellow corn. The bows of bells, set in high arches above the collars of the harness, chimed in pleasant harmony as the big wagons bumped across the harvest fields. The light treble of the leader's bell blended gayly with the deep bass of the wheel-horse harness.

Bountiful harvests such as these, the Germans were sure, were due to strict observance of the occult rites handed down from pagan times. Seed had been sown when the waxing moon guaranteed that crops would prosper. Horoscopes cast by the astrologers had shown which days were favorable for planting. Then, when the seed was sown and all the formal incantations were performed, the Pennsylvania German farmers had gone to the highest near-by hills to build their magic fires. These, kindled in late June, on the eve of John the Baptist's Day, had aided, the Germans thought, in the growth of good crops. Into the brightly burning blaze they had thrown field flowers, pine boughs, and bones of sacrificed farm animals, muttering the proper magic formulas. When all the ceremonial had been performed and when the fires died down, the farmers rolled the embers down the hill. Thus, they knew, all pestilence would be averted, harvests would be large, and prosperity would be assured. Later, on Christmas

Eve, the German farmers would show their gratitude. Then they would build fires of resinous pine boughs which, by their wide circle of rising tongues of flame, would symbolize their thankfulness.

The Continental army had but little concern over the means whereby the vast stores of provision had been procured; the men were primarily interested in food. Within the thick-walled stone houses, there were ample rations for all. Each *Hausfrau* drew lavishly upon her stocks of rye-coffee, pork, beans, onions, and potatoes. Bake ovens roared to turn out fresh batches of the heavy, dark rye bread which, the soldiers said, was tough enough to screech when bread knives cut slices from the great round loaves. They drank huge draughts of the rich milk which Pennsylvania German cattle yielded so abundantly. Envious neighbors believed that the cows of frugal Germans gave twice the quantity of milk that other cows produced. But, again, the Pennsylvania Germans thanked their age-old superstitions for the bounty.

Hand in hand with traditional belief in pagan rites went a strong devotion to the classic culture. These Fatland settlements were famous for their learning. Many a backwoods farmhouse, the soldiers found, boasted a library of Pennsylvania German literature. The fifteen-hundred-page history of Christian martyrdom, written by Dielman Kolb and Bishop Heinrich Funck, and published at isolated Ephrata, was a favorite compendium from which these farmers learned the story of the past. Christopher Dock's handbook on education, the first American textbook of pedagogy, the German-language Bible printed in this neighborhood forty years before an English Bible was published in America, the Christopher Sower pamphlets on social reform, were popular Fatlands reading. Benjamin Franklin was so well aware of the desire of Pennsylvania Germans for solid classic reading that more than half the books that issued from his printing house were German volumes for the Fatlands homes.

Presiding over the welfare of this rural community was Henry Melchior Muhlenberg. A thin, straggly German, trained as a missioner, he had, since 1741, been educating the stolid German settlement. From his pulpit at Augustus Church at Trappe, his soft, dignified persuasive tenor voice had roused the patriotic emotions of his congregation. His example, and that of his six strapping preacher sons, each with "a temper like a fiery furnace," made of the Fatlands community a matchless center of revolutionary fervor.

Here at Fatlands the troops rested, camped on both sides of the road, their double line of fence-rail fires burning through the crisp, cool night. Washington himself rode on, to check the reports that the British were encamped across the river.

Riding over the old Perkiomen bridge, where the oldest inn of Pennsylvania is still standing, the Commander-in-chief went three miles to the crossroads where the highway met the trail to the Schuylkill fords. He wished to see for himself if Howe might, by a quick passage of the river, take the Continental army by surprise. From the river bank, he knew, he could scout the enemy position on the west bank of the stream, and he might glean knowledge of their intention.

At Pawling's ford, where the slender Perkiomen joins the curving Schuylkill, the water was too high for crossing. No sign of the British could be seen, though there was smoke to westward which Washington believed came from the British camp. No enemy patrols guarded the western Schuylkill bank; no pickets were in sight. Washington believed that Howe was unaware of the American position; he thought, too, that the enemy had no intention of crossing at this point. He rode,

"—AND A TIME TO FIGHT!"

John Peter Gabriel Muhlenberg, "Teufel Piet," reveals his Continental uniform beneath his preacher's gown (from a painting by Stanley M. Arthurs)

SENTRY OF THE CONTINENTAL LINE

therefore, through the low fields on the eastern side of Schuylkill to inspect Fatland ford, directly across the river from Valley Forge. This was the more probable crossing, for though the river was usually deeper here than at Pawling's the footing was more secure. But this ford, too, was now impassable. The heavy rains had swollen the stream greatly, and the water, though falling, was still too high for men to wade.

Washington now knew that, for at least a few hours, the British could not ford the Schuylkill to attack his army; he knew, too, that Wayne's plan of attack was no longer feasible. Wayne, he still believed, was hiding in the British rear, waiting for the major portion of the Continental army to cross at Valley Forge to catch Howe in the Tredyffrin trap. He had not yet heard of Wayne's defeat, but he could see that the British were safe from surprise. Probably, thought Washington, Howe would march on Reading, far up the Schuylkill, to destroy the Continental stores. Then the Americans must themselves turn back to meet the British and save the Reading storehouses.

Before returning to camp, Washington halted at Mill Grove Mansion, on the crest of the hill overlooking Valley Forge, to call upon James Vaux, the pioneer in scientific farming. The conversation at dinner was agreeable, for it turned on agriculture. Vaux explained his experiments with red clover as a fertilizer crop and urged Washington to introduce it at Mount Vernon after peace might be restored. Vaux told, too, of his success in burning black stone coal, which learned men called anthracite, and which was found a few miles up the river. The neighbors, Vaux chuckled, thought that the rock was incombustible, but he had made a special stove in which the stuff burned hot and smokelessly.

Washington was interested, too, to hear that John Penn,

Tory grandson of the founder, had bought the land adjacent to Mill Grove to build himself a country home when peace should be declared. The land, said Vaux, was growing much more valuable now, for though William Penn had purchased all the ground from Philadelphia to the Water Gap and from the Susquehanna to the Delaware for twelve guns, six coats, six blankets, and four kettles, John Penn had paid a goodly price for a scant three hundred acres. John Penn could not, however, take advantage of his purchase until the war was over; meanwhile he was renting the gristmill and the sawmill to the former owner.

After dinner, Washington rode back to Fatland to reexamine the ford and found that the water was dropping more rapidly. If this continued, he calculated, the stream would soon be fordable and the British might be able to cross the stream. Writing to General Alexander McDougall to bring sixteen hundred troops to guard the ford, he himself hurried back to Trappe.

He found the troops disheartened. Word had just come of Wayne's defeat. Couriers riding down from Parkerford, where Wayne, following his commander's march, had crossed the Schuylkill, told of the surprise. The soldiers, well fed but jittery because all night long their sleep had been disturbed by false rumors of impending attack, grumbled angrily when they were ordered to be on the march again at four o'clock Sunday morning. Knowing nothing of the facts, resentful of the endless marching back and forth, complaining because they had to leave their campfires in the middle of the night, they blamed Wayne for inefficiency, for carelessness, for failure to keep watch, and for every other military sin.

Washington, almost broken by the news of the disaster, hurried northward to meet Wayne. The march would serve several purposes. Not only could the main body come to Wayne's support, but, by marching toward Reading, the Americans would keep abreast of Howe. Thus the stores would be more easily protected and, meanwhile, the Americans would be moving into progressively more favorable country. The farther the Continentals penetrated into Pennsylvania German country, the more friendly the assistance that could be relied upon.

Staid Lutherans, riding down the road to attend Sunday service at Muhlenberg's beautiful Augustus Church, shook their heads in dismay at the sight of the retreating Continentals. There was no spring in the march; the men walked with drooping shoulders; the customary joking was not heard. Only the Pennsylvania German troops were smiling, for many of them were moving closer to their homes.

Past the German-rural Augustus Church, with its triangular apse, its gambrel roof and its strange gallery windows, past Limerick, seat of the Scotch-Irish, and past the road to Parkerford, the Americans plodded in retreat. Then, ten miles to the north of the temporary camp at Trappe, the road veered right, along the Manatawney Creek, through a narrow passageway. This was the entrance to the Falckner Swamp; the passage, a natural fortress, was well known as the "Old Swamp Tohr."

Here, in the Crooked Hills, Washington set up Camp Pottsgrove, where his men, safe against attack, might rest, re-form their lines, regain their confidence, and be refitted with equipment. The troops were now well armed and, for the moment, well fed; but there was need of clothes, of reorganization, and of drill. The plan of marching all the way to Reading was abandoned, for Washington believed that his Continentals were in no condition now to risk a major battle.

Wayne's disaster had disrupted the American morale; the shrieks of his wounded soldiers, suffering their operations without anesthetics on a tavern table, were audible to the camp.

Two miles from the "Old Swamp Tohr," in the old house of Henry Antes, at a site commanding an admirable view of distant mountains, Washington established his headquarters. The tiny town of Frederick was near by, but the surrounding fields were wholly rural.

The Swamp belied its name. It was no dreary marsh devoid of human habitation, but a friendly fertile valley, sheltered by high, wooded hills, and farmed by prosperous, contented Pennsylvania German patriots. The atmosphere was peaceful.

The peacefulness had not always been typical of Falckner Swamp. When first the Germans came, there had been innumerable quarrels over titles. William Penn had promised to deed his friends of the Palatinate a manor of twenty-five thousand acres "along some navigable stream." It was precisely the same offer that the Welsh had had, and there had been exactly the same misunderstanding. The Germans had come to Philadelphia anticipating the erection of a barony along the Wissahickon, but had found, like the Welsh, that Penn held different conceptions. Francis Daniel Pastorius and his immigrants might occupy three thousand acres close to Philadelphia, in what is now called Germantown, but the remainder of the grant was thirty miles away. The "navigable stream" was not to be the Wissahickon but Manatawney Creek.

Then, when the disappointed Germans went up to join with Daniel Falckner and his small group of mystics and wait patiently for the coming of the Lord in backwoods Pennsylvania, a sharp-witted swindler twisted the law to steal the land away. John Henry Sproegel swore that he was rightful grantee, and when Pastorius and Falckner produced their deeds, he charged that these were false. His lawyers rushed to court to cancel other claims. Pastorius, deserting his bees and his immense library of medical and scientific books, sought legal aid, too, but found, to his dismay, that Sproegel had already hired every lawyer in the province. No counselor was available to defend the proper owners. Pastorius was told that he would need to send to New York for attorneys, but that, even if he paid them their retainers and financed their passage to Pennsylvania, it was doubtful if the local courts would let them practice. His own superficial knowledge of the law, gleaned from the seven-language library where he delighted to stay, was wholly ineffective against the combined legal strategy of all the lawyers in the province. The farmers of the Falckner Swamp were thus obliged to buy their lands a second time.

Though the beginnings had been disappointing, Falckner Swamp had more than justified the hopes of those who came to settle. Here was a home of culture. Henry Antes, "the pious layman," had created a "Congregation of God in the Spirit" where all men might unite to worship in complete religious freedom. George Whitefield had preached in a near-by barn; Count Nicholas Ludwig von Zinzendorf had pleaded for a spiritual unity. It was from Henry Antes' home, where Washington now had headquarters, that Zinzendorf had gone into the wilderness to tame the savages. So gentle and so holy had he been, according to the tales that were passed down in Falckner Swamp, that the rattlesnakes would come to creep harmlessly across his body as he lay before the fire.

Henry Antes, too, had started here in Falckner Swamp the

93

first boarding school in the province. Thirty-four of the best lads of Pennsylvania and New York had come to work out their tuition. With them were, as an experiment in brotherhood, a Mohegan Indian and a Negro from the Virgin Islands. Antes planned to use these boys as missionaries to go to Greenland and Surinam, to the Indies and to Africa, and to all other backward places where there might be need for spiritual service.

The beautiful ideal was, however, wrecked by church dissensions. The cause, of course, was a trivial argument, as it almost invariably has been in such disputes. Antes took exception to the wearing of a white surplice. He left the church, though his missionary dream was carried out when his son John took the faith to Egypt.

Colonel Frederick, a younger son, was living now upon the ancestral farm, paying the annual quitrent of a shilling per acre to the heirs of land-grabber Sproegel. But Frederick had none of the quietist traditions of his father's time. He and his young son William enlisted at the very outbreak of the war.

Quite possibly the Antes patriotism had been fanned by reports which reached them from young Anna Maria Krause, who was a guest at Crooked Hill Tavern, near the entrance to the Swamp. Ruefully she confessed that she had been tricked by the gallantries of British officers. In December, 1776, she explained, a group of British prisoners en route from Reading to be exchanged had stopped at the Crooked Hill. Bad weather then set in; the Manatawney road had been impassable. Never had the staid Swamp folk heard such gay and sprightly conversation; never had they listened to such sweet flute music; never had young men been so debonair as these British captives. One in particular was especially delightful as a singer and a conversationalist. His name was Captain John André.

Anna had been smitten by the brilliant officer, and in spite of his devotion to the lovely Honora Sneyd there is small doubt that André exerted all his charm to captivate the pretty little fourteen-year-old Anna. They spent the better portion of the week together, but André made no love. His thoughts, even in the maiden's company, were of topography and military strategy. He asked incessant questions about roads and mills and forage, talked of farm land and of the number of livestock in the neighborhood, drew maps and diagrams all afternoon. Anna lingered close at hand, hoping that the little captain would grow tired of work; but when the roads dried out sufficiently the officers moved on. Then, to her regret, she learned from those who knew more about military intelligence requirements, that she had supplied to Britain's army a detailed account of the region's military strength.

Luckily, the British had made no use of André's complete information, though the debonair captain was awarded a promotion to be major; but Ensign Willie Antes felt that Falckner Swamp could win back self-respect only by exceptional devotion to the Continental cause. He rebuked his neighbors for protesting when the foragers fanned through the Swamp for food. He thoroughly approved the slaughter of so many cattle, though he did not enjoy the sight of little Speck Creek running blood-red, nor relish looking at the piles of refuse on the bank. These sights meant, however, that the army would again be fed abundantly.

Willie Antes was particularly worried when he heard the loud-voiced complaint of Christopher Ludwig, the baker-general, at the lack of bread. Even though the army came on

Monday, when the pantries should be bursting with fresh-baked loaves, the bread was wholly insufficient for ten thousand men. Ludwig fumed because the ovens were too few to bake sufficient rations; he complained because the commissaries had forgotten to supply him with sufficient bread-making facilities. His protests, couched in picturesque and forceful broken English, carried far in the frosty mountain air. No one in the camp was unaware that Ludwig thought that Falckner Swamp was most delinquent for the baker's purposes.

Ensign Willie Antes was happy to be at home, so happy that he could not bear to hear the baker's criticisms. If what the army needed, Willie thought, was better ovens, he would supply the need. The army should not go away from Falckner's Swamp with memories of hunger.

An ensign's pay was small, less than three dollars weekly in some regiments, and ovens were expensive. Bricks were plentiful near by, but hauling them might prove a costly matter. Antes, as it happened, had money of his own. Out of his resources he drew sixty dollars, more than a quarter's pay, to bring bricks from the kilns. Then, by the labor of his company, he built under a great sprawly oak, a magnificent bake house that won Ludwig's approval.

Ludwig kept the ovens roaring. The flour bins of Falckner's Swamp were emptied to the floor. All night by lanterns and by candlelight, the mills ground steadily. The wheat sheaves and the unthreshed rye were flailed for grain. Ludwig's baking went on without a respite until the entire harvests of the Falckner's Swamp were converted into army bread.

There was a famine when the army left, for all the food had been consumed for military use. No cows were left alive; no poultry clucked in near-by barnyards. The soldiers, after slaughtering the stock, had gone out through the valley and up the hillsides to scout for every living animal that might be used for food. The residents of Falckner's Swamp long remembered those September days when the Continental army ate up all the winter's stores. Until the spring brought fresh supplies of home-grown vegetables, the Swamp folk were obliged to go far north to Bethlehem and beyond Reading to get enough to eat.

The resting time at Falckner Swamp probably preserved the patriotic army. Beaten in battle, exhausted by long marches, ill nourished and worse clothed, the Continentals' morale was at low ebb when they came; they left refreshed and fed. Four days of fine, delightful weather restored the army's confidence, and though there was a heavy rain with hard winds all afternoon of Thursday September 25, the spirits of the soldiers remained high. When, early Friday, the order came to march again, the men stepped briskly through the clear, cool morning hours.

CHAPTER TEN

The British Fog

BRANDYWINE had shown how readily the American infantry could be taken by surprise; the ease with which Howe outgeneraled the rebels in the marches up and down the Schuylkill reemphasized the pressing need for an efficient detachment of light-horse scouts. The lessons were now heeded. During the stay at Falckner Swamp, Count Casimir Pulaski, thirty-year-old Polish adventurer, was given command of some four hundred cavalrymen. When the camp was broken, Pulaski's cavalry led the van.

The group lent color to the Continental force. Greencoated, red-vested riders in white buckskin breeches, their leader dignified by his great bearskin hat, they rode beneath a crimson standard. A bright gold eye, surrounded by thirteen gleaming golden stars, winked in the glare of the four hotburning sons which decorated the corners of the flag. Latin mottoes on the standard proclaimed that freedom must always rule and that honor was supreme; but few of the spectators took time to read the circular inscriptions. Their eyes were too dazzled by the gold and crimson banner of the Pulaski cavalry.

The renewed morale was not wholly due to Pulaski's bright trappings. Rested by the stay at Falckner Swamp, well fed by the Germans, confident again of ultimate victory, the infantry stepped forward briskly. Cutting capers to the quick-step tunes of fifes and drums, dancing ahead in the irregular fashion which so perturbed the professional French officers, the men skipped along the road, shouting jokes to one another, paying little heed to the entreaties that they march in more orderly array. Despite their losses at Brandywine and at Paoli, they were a happy, confident force.

Many of them, to be sure, were still ill clad; more than a thousand were shoeless. The impromptu moccasins made during the drenching rain had now been thrown aside as causing more severe pain than even the rough roads and the rocks; the stores of surplus clothing possessed by Pennsylvania Germans had been insufficient to outfit the needy troops. But Washington had issued orders for an impressment of footwear, blankets, and clothing for army use, and the troops were well convinced that new supplies would soon be brought to them. The march on Friday September 26 was not to be a lengthy journey; possibly the new supplies would come to the new camp at Pennypacker's Mills ten miles away almost as soon as the main body of the army should arrive. The men moved forward confidently.

Unluckily, the clothing did not come. Howe's raiders had done their work well; his golden guineas had proved too persuasive. Supplies which might have come to the Continentals from beyond the Schuylkill were either in British possession or destroyed. No other goods were available within almost fifty miles, and in the absence of sufficient army wagons and draft horses these distant goods could not be hauled to camp.

VALLEY FORGE

The Americans, nevertheless, were not despondent. The British, it was true, had now taken Philadelphia, the Tory-ridden capital, but this was no great blow to Washington's hopes. By some patriots, indeed, the fall of Philadelphia was almost accounted as a gain, for the commercially minded inhabitants had been insisting on a troop garrison which Washington could ill afford to spare. His refusal to detach part of his command to reassure the capital had led to murmurings against his leadership. In time, the whispered opposition would develop into a quiet conspiracy to replace him with a more amenable general.

Philadelphia in British hands might prove to be a trap in which Howe could be caught. Access to the city was impossible by sea, for the forts and warships still held command of the Delaware above Wilmington. Following the battle of Brandywine, Howe had shifted his base from the head of Elk to Wilmington and had thus given himself a shorter line of communication; but the upper river remained in rebel hands. After his withdrawal into the city, Howe's shortage of men had forced him to give up control over the interior of the state. Thus, he was penned between the Delaware and Schuylkill rivers, with no easy retreat. Conceivably, a quick successful thrust from the north might even result in Howe's surrender.

The American war council had thoroughly discussed the possibility of such success, but the time was not thought ripe for an attack in full force against Howe's veterans. By a ten-to-five vote, the generals had decided to wait until reinforcements could come to Washington's assistance. Harsh Colonel "Devil David" Forman was known to be approaching with a thousand Jerseymen; fiery General Alexander McDougall was yet to join his thousand Continental regulars to the main

100

body of the army. When these new troops should come, Washington's force would be increased to more than eleven thousand men, exclusive of two thousand poorly armed Virginia militiamen who were hurrying to the camp.

During four prematurely wintry days, while cold northeast winds blew over the oak-covered hills along the Perkiomen Creek, the army remained tented at Pennypacker's Mills. Within three hours after the arrival at the camp all the fence rails had been carried off for campfires; the hay and straw in stacks and barns had disappeared; the fowls, save one late-brooding hen, had been seized for food. By the next day, the whole community was stripped as bare of food and fuel as Falckner Swamp had been.

Pennypacker's Mills left a pleasant memory in soldiers' minds. News came on Sunday morning September 28 that General Horatio Gates had beaten the invading force of "Gentleman Johnny" Burgoyne at Stillwater, New York, and that the prospects for even greater victory were bright. Washington called the troops into parade formation to read them the good news and then, to celebrate the victory, he ordered the distribution of a gill of rum per man. Thirteen fieldpieces, of four-pound caliber, discharged a loud salute to Gates.

Next day, the men marched five miles closer to the city, moving down the curving old Skippack road. The day was exceptionally cold, and the winds were blowing strongly; but most of the route was in the shelter of the hills, and the brisk pace warmed the soldiers. Before noon, the army was encamped along the bank of little Skippack Creek, approximately twenty-five miles from Philadelphia.

Washington waited here until his spies brought word of Howe's activities. Reinforcements had now come, and though there were fewer Jerseymen than had been anticipated, the men were well equipped. For men with guns in poor repair or completely lacking weapons, Jacob Yost's near-by shop and tool factory, diverted from its usual task of making the best scythes and sickles of the colonies, worked constantly to manufacture rifles. His hand-hewn stone watering trough, used for tempering the steel, hissed day and night to cool the metal for gun making.

At last, on Thursday October 2, messengers brought the expected news, that Howe had sent some of his troops into New Jersey and others to Wilmington to aid in the reduction of the river forts. Knowing that the British force was divided, and that the Philadelphia garrison must now be smaller than his own army, Washington resolved upon attack. The hopes of Wayne and Smallwood, of frontiersman James Potter, of New York's rich and fluent but impolite James Scott, and of Pennsylvania's austere William Irvine were gratified. These were the generals who had pressed for action and who, at the war council, had been outvoted two to one. They were to have their wish. Battle was again to be attempted.

Washington's preparations were admirable. Cautiously he led his forces a few miles down the Skippack road to Methacton Hill, some eighteen miles from the British position. Taking his quarters at the quaint Dutch-style house of Peter Wentz, he called his generals into conference.

His spies had brought complete and accurate information. Washington knew that the bulk of the British army was encamped between Philadelphia and the pretty little settlement of Germantown. From the post of Knyphausen's Hessians, located to the west on Washington's old campground at Falls of Schuylkill, the British line ran two miles eastward across the main roads leading into Philadelphia. A few royalists under Cornwallis had gone five miles southward into the capital to prevent a possible American advance into Philadelphia by way of the Middle Ferry; other, smaller detachments were set at strategic road intersections; two regiments had been advanced beyond the main force of the British as outposts against a frontal attack from the Skippack country.

Howe's position was strong, and its advantages were numerous. Germantown, a small, one-street, tree-shaded hamlet, was an important distribution center for salt, sulphur, and saltpeter. Christopher Meng's vinegar house was an essential storehouse for hospital supplies, particularly for the vinegar used so extravagantly as an astringent to stop the flow of blood from wounds. John Bringhurst and William Ashmead made wagons for the Continental army; Henry Fraley's gun carriages were in constant demand; Germantown linens and stockings were famous throughout the thirteen states. Whoever owned Germantown would be well supplied.

Now that Howe's force had been divided, Washington believed the opportunity was ripe for recapturing the important little village. The American plans were carefully drawn. Singularly modern in conception, more complex than any former strategy devised by rebel leaders, the scheme depended for success on the two elements of synchronization and surprise.

For three successive days, Washington had arranged his great attack. Small scouting parties had been sent toward Germantown to snipe at the pickets in order that the final assault might seem nothing more than a similar slight action. On the night before the action the Americans were ordered to build huge campfires on Methacton Hill to deceive the British into thinking that no movement was in progress. Then, leaving their packs, blankets, tools, and all nonessentials in charge of a small guard of men judged unfit for a

103

long march, the main body of the army moved toward Germantown.

At seven o'clock in the evening of Friday October 3, four columns set off to their objectives. Old John Armstrong took the extreme right along the Schuylkill, with orders to engage Knyphausen's Hessians; Greene and Adam Stephens went to the left, with Smallwood and Devil David Forman's militiamen on the extreme left wing, while Washington, Sullivan, and Wayne struck straight for the British center. Each column was instructed to move with such speed that, by two o'clock of the dark, moonless night, all would be within two miles of the enemy. They were then to halt for two hours, advance the remaining two miles, and, precisely at five o'clock, to charge with fixed bayonets and without firing a shot upon the British outposts.

Three drawbacks only were anticipated. The plan was elaborate, and required exact management. Each general was provided, therefore, with explicit instructions as to which roads to take and which landmarks to use to gauge his progress. If the schedule were scrupulously observed, the attack would break out simultaneously upon a surprised enemy on four widely scattered fronts. To prevent advance report from leaking to the British, each column was ordered to take into custody any persons found upon the roads. Couriers, so essential for coordinating movements in this complex plan, were given special credentials to allow their passage. And then, because on mornings prior to the attack, the early hours had been foggy, each soldier was instructed to carry a large piece of paper in his dark hat, so that the troops might not fire on each other in the mist.

None of the precautions was effective. Twelve thousand marchers, dragging artillery, created too much clatter. By three o'clock in the morning, word came to Howe from witch-ridden Flourtown, four miles north of the British position, that the Americans were advancing. Fortunately for the rebels, Howe failed to realize the importance of the information and, save issuing a routine warning for his men to be alert, he took no precautions. Flourtown was known to be an unreliable source of news; since its credulity in witchcraft induced it to accept wild rumors from unsound sources. It had long since assumed the leadership in sorcery which once had belonged to the Swedes of the Great Valley.

The heavy fog, settling for the third successive morning, was more disastrous to Washington's carefully conceived plan. General Adam Stephens, mistaking the roads and, in his drunken state, confusing Meeting House Lane with Church Lane, turned too soon upon the wrong road. He met a force of soldiers, and, unable to distinguish their identity in the dense fog, he ordered his men to fire. The shots were sharply returned, and a brisk battle noisily continued, against all orders, until the drunken general, seeing white paper in his adversaries' hats, learned that he was firing upon his fellow Virginian, Colonel George Mathews of the Greene division. Mathews, shouting angrily that Stephens was too drunk to command, wheeled about and rushed his Tall Virginians back to rejoin General Greene.

Greene, too, had difficulty. Knowing that he was to start his assault when the more experienced General Armstrong attacked the Hessians, he slowed up his advance, in violation of Washington's express commands, until he should get word of Armstrong's position. But the latter failed in the fog to cover his allotted ground. Greene was without support. Mathews, hurrying to the place where Greene was supposed to be, ran headlong into the whole British army. The impetuous colonel, twice the victim of ill luck, surrendered the Tall Virginians.

The American center, led by Washington, Sullivan, and Wayne, was more efficient. Promptly at dawn, according to plan, Sullivan bayoneted the British pickets, beat back the awakened outposts, and marched steadily down the tree-bordered street. The American advance moved more than a mile into the heart of Germantown, Washington and Wayne following more cautiously.

By this time the British army was aroused. Kilted High-landers, in flowing tartans, ran at full speed; dragoons mounted and trotted into place; the grenadiers, heavy-armed and impressive in appearance, fell into line. Sullivan and the deliberate Greene faced a well prepared enemy.

The hope for a silent bayonet attack was now completely gone. British outposts, slowly falling back, fought from behind the fences, walls, and ditches. The American advance, slowed by the need for clearing out these snipers, lost its coherence. Instead of a simultaneous attack, with each of the four columns advancing from six or seven miles distant into one converging attack, each division accomplishing some action necessary to the success of all the others, the onslaught was mismanaged and uncoordinated. Armstrong came up too late; Smallwood and Forman were hopelessly behind time; Sullivan was too far ahead.

Germantown was wide awake. Women and small children, terrified by the constant fire, crowded into cellars. Many of them, huddling for safety, rushed to the centrally located house of Squire Joseph Ferree, where two dozen weeping women kept up a hysterical prayer for more than three hours. Most of the men were in the army, but half-grown boys, evading their anxious mothers, thronged the street or, climbing the tall trees surrounding the story-and-a-half houses, swung themselves upon the double-hipped roofs to see the fighting.

Little of the conflict was, however, visible from these coigns of vantage. After the first attack, the warfare took place chiefly in the open, fenceless fields on the outskirts of the settlement. Black-faced soldiers, their lips and cheeks grimed by the biting off of cartridges, fought almost hand to hand. Now that the rising sun had melted away the morning fog, it was no longer necessary to fire at the orange flames of enemy gunfire; the troops were in full view.

Had Washington's aides been better trained in military tactics, the battle of Germantown might even yet have resulted in an American victory. Sullivan was so successful that his British opponents were planning a swift retreat through the fields to Philadelphia. He had already gained the British camp and was in possession of a score of guns. But his rear seemed dangerous.

Shut within the great stone house of Tory Chief Justice Benjamin Chew were the British lieutenant colonel Thomas Musgrave and a force of a hundred and forty men. Most of the American underofficers favored putting a small guard around the Chew house, with perhaps one small fieldpiece to bombard its walls, while the rest of the army pressed on to assist Sullivan's victorious advance. The students of strategy, however, remembering the textbook warnings against leaving a garrisoned fort in the rear, insisted that the house must first be captured. General Henry Knox, bookish Boston artillery commander, won over a majority of his associates to this belief and arranged to throw the entire American center around the mansion.

Musgrave's defense was gallant. Guns cannonaded the

Chew house, splintering the woodwork, shattering the glass, and destroying the furnishings. A six-pound ball came through a front window, smashed four partitions, and passed out the rear wall. American volunteers, darting behind the row of cherry trees leading to the mansion, rushed up with flaming torches to fire the building. Musgrave's musketeers, fighting from behind barricades of broken furniture, coolly picked off the attackers. For more than an hour, while blood spattered every room of the Chew house, Musgrave's men held up the American advance. The unexpected delay ruined the carefully synchronized attack.

Sullivan, hearing the heavy continued firing, suspected that the British had flanked the Americans, and that they were now about to close in upon his own advanced guard. Word reached him, too, that Cornwallis was coming northward from Philadelphia at full speed to reinforce Howe's army. Fearing to hold his position longer, Sullivan wheeled rapidly and, abandoning the captured cannon, gave up the ground that he had won.

Again, Greene was unsupported. Despairing now of any help from the dilatory Armstrong, hearing nothing from Smallwood and Forman's wandering militiamen, unable to make contact with other American detachments, Greene, too, was forced to withdraw.

The news from the rear was not reassuring. General Francis Nash, handsomest and ablest of the North Carolinians, had been knocked from his horse by a cannon ball and was gravely wounded. Major James Witherspoon, son of the Reverend John Witherspoon, president of the College of New Jersey at Princeton, had been killed by the same shot that felled Nash. The British General James Agnew had also been killed, although not by an American soldier. A civilian sniper, firing from behind a tombstone, had shot him through the star on his uniform coat. Wayne had fallen heavily, when his horse was killed beneath him, and he was suffering sharp pain from a chipped breast-bone. He was never wholly to recover from the injury.

The battle was lost. The Americans, more disappointed than defeated, had dropped a victory when it was already in their grasp. Fog and confusion had wrecked a well planned and elaborate attack. Had the generals followed their explicit orders; had Armstrong performed his allotted task; had slow-moving Smallwood and Forman kept to schedule, instead of arriving at their designated posts when the battle was over; had Stephens not become confused, and had the bookish generals not clung closely to the standard rules of war, Washington's army would have won an overwhelming triumph. As it was, the Americans lost a hundred and fifty killed, and five hundred wounded. Four hundred rebels had been taken prisoners; the British lost seventy dead and four hundred and fifty wounded. The British prisoners taken by Greene managed to escape in the confusion.

The effect of Germantown was, however, not so disastrous to American morale as might have been anticipated. A well planned attack upon a supposedly fortified British position had been daringly attempted. American provincials, already defeated within three weeks in two serious engagements, had, in spite of their lack of equipment, been able to hold their own with a veteran victorious army. Washington's intelligence service, working smoothly from within the captured city, had proved its reliability. The rebels were far from discouraged.

They could not, however, hold their position. Howe and Cornwallis, bringing up the main body of the British troops, were now prepared to turn Germantown into a major engagement. Realizing that the whole effect of the surprise had been destroyed and that the superior artillery of the British would now be able to blast through the unfortified American line, Washington ordered a general withdrawal to the Pennypacker's Mills camp.

CHAPTER ELEVEN

Pastors in Politics

THE American retreat was far from pleasant. Five hours of exhausting battle, following an all-night march, had left the men completely fagged. Then came a hasty return march at midday in the humid heat, with cavalry pursuit upon their heels. The weary troops fought rear-guard engagements as far as Bluebell Tavern, six miles from the battleground. When the harassing cavalry turned back, the rebel force marched on. The withdrawal ended only at nine o'clock at night when the soldiers staggered back to Pennypacker's Mills. They had been on their feet, with but two hours' rest, for twenty-six crowded hours. Some had marched upwards of forty-five miles and had, in addition, fought a battle bloodier than Brandywine.

The rear guards left to protect the baggage were not astonished at the reappearance of the troops. For hours prior to the army's arrival, heavy wagons bearing wounded men had been rumbling to the Perkiomen bank. The cries of suffering soldiers, for whom there were no anesthetics, no opiates, and no dressings, shrieked above the noise of farm carts crashing over rugged roads. The beat of drums could scarcely be heard above the groans of dying men.

VALLEY FORGE

Little could be done to ease the anguish; the familiar camp site offered little real relief. Another campground, free from the refuse left when the camp was broken a week before, would have proved more sanitary and more comfortable. Pennypacker's Mills was safe against surprise attack, but the men who fled there hungry, tired, and thirsty after their prolonged ordeal found the region stripped clean of food and straw and firewood.

Luckily, there was no pressing need for fuel. The unpredictable Pennsylvania climate played, for once, into the Continentals' hands. The troops had marched out gayly a week before upon a day when all the men complained of cold; now, following the Germantown engagement, the soldiers gasped for breath during three full days of torrid heat. Water was cool and clean and plentiful; the men could bathe away the grime of battle; and though the food was limited, the troops could gain a respite for relief.

The men were hungry and exhausted, but they dared not relax their vigilance. Every Continental officer anticipated an attack in force. Over and over again the war conferences buzzed with astonishment that the British had failed to press onward beyond Bluebell. Had they advanced, the American leaders well knew, the enemy must inevitably have thrown the broken and dispirited rebel forces into headlong flight.

Washington was conscious of his danger. He could not understand why he was left in peace to reestablish the American morale. Then, to his amazement, his spies brought word that the invaders, far from moving north against the Perkiomen camp, were hurrying south from Germantown toward Chester. Tumult, disorder, and despair, it soon became apparent, existed in the British ranks. The same fog that had cost the Americans their victory at Germantown had prevented Howe from taking full advantage of the American retreat.

The men lay resting at Pennypacker's Mills for three full days. Then, when dawn broke on what promised to be a cool invigorating morning, Washington withdrew his troops from the exhausted camp. Word had reached him that not far away at Kulpsville, a tiny village of spick-and-span new houses set in a rich farm community, the thrifty Pennsylvania Mennonites had stored a heavy harvest of good grain. There was hope, too, that the Towamensing Meeting House, near Kulpsville, which had been used as a hospital for slightly wounded men, would yield enough recuperated soldiers to refill the regiments.

Washington set forth from Perkiomen at eight o'clock in the morning of October 8th, marching along the Skippack. The men were gay and hopeful, thinking that the worst was over, and that Kulpsville would provide sufficient food and shelter.

Ill luck pursued the Continental forces. The optimism was soon shattered. In his anxiety to leave the camp at Pennypacker's Mills, Washington had paid too slight attention to the weather signs. The seemingly fine dawn soon turned, as any experienced farm boy might have predicted, into a day of cold and violent rain. The roads were muddy and already rutted by the passage of the wagons carrying the wounded. Thin, summer uniforms, even the backwoodsmen's hunting shirts, were wet and clammy; boots were soggy; once again the ammunition pouches failed to keep the powder dry.

The scouts had not been good reporters. When the men arrived at Towamensing camp near Kulpsville, they found few good dwellings suitable for barracks. The soldiers were again obliged to camp in open country with but insufficient cover during two days of heavy downpour. The promised stores of freshly garnered grain, so eagerly anticipated by the Continentals, proved wholly mythical. The hay for army horses, while much more plentiful than at Pennypacker's Mills, was but a few days' supply.

There were other reasons, too, why Towamensing was a disappointment. The cold wet weather, followed quickly by the season's first killing frost, spread disease rapidly. Pneumonia cases mounted; colds were common; the men always remembered Towamensing as the place where thin-clad Continentals shivered as they starved. Death came to two of Washington's best officers, to Virginia's Lieutenant Matthew Smith and to gallant Francis Nash. Both had been wounded at Germantown, and both had been jolted in the rough wagon journey to Towamensing Meeting House, but the camp privations were the final cause of death. A homesick young Pennsylvania private, acutely aware that his family lived less than a dozen miles away, attempted to steal home to mother, but was caught while slipping through the lines and was condemned to die as a deserter.

The incident, while unimportant in itself, drew new attention to the deficiencies of Pennsylvania. Six regiments, one of them a crack body of well drilled State Guards, arrived from Virginia to join the army, but were astonished to discover that the Pennsylvania militia numbered a bare twelve hundred men, "whereas they should have as many thousand." The Virginians were amazed to see how lax was discipline, and how the hungry men, unpaid and poorly rationed, were selling off their military equipment to buy food and blankets. Some soldiers particularly welcomed sentry duty at the quarters of their officers because it gave an opportunity for stealing swords for sale to Tory sympathizers.

Civilian morale was also badly shaken. Fashionable Philadelphia was quite understandably Tory in its sympathy. The richer merchants and the more conventional among the Anglican clergy were always ultraroyalist. Whig sympathies were rare among the intellectuals.

The Reverend Jacob Duché, however, was an outstanding rebel. Poet, orator, and pamphleteer, he was widely known for daring and originality. He had been first in Philadelphia to dare to carry an umbrella, rather than the usual oiled linen cape called *roquelaure,* to keep off rain. In summer he had had the courage to use a parasol against the sun, and he had defied the ridicule of press and public who condemned him for effeminacy. From his pulpit at Christ Church he poured forth appeals to his parishioners to join the Continental Army, and he had announced that every cent of salary paid to him would be donated for the relief of families of men killed in battle. In flowery and well rounded phrases the sleek young cleric urged that Americans unite to resist encroachment on their rights. In recognition of his patriotic ardor, he was made the chaplain of the Continental Congress. Until the arrival of the British at Philadelphia, Duché was fervently rebellious; then, after one night's imprisonment by Howe, he turned his coat, denounced the independence movement, and invited Washington to abandon all resistance.

Duché's letter urging Washington to surrender came to the Continentals on the last day of the Towamensing encampment. It was a bitter disappointment, as indicating that the faint-hearted were giving up their hopes of victory, and as suggesting that the insurrection was a failure. General Washington dared not ignore the message, lest whispers magnify the importance of the Duché action, but he was in no position to punish the vacillating clergyman. He tried, therefore, to checkmate the peace proposal by referring the message to the Continental Congress. Duché was soon discredited and fled to England.

If the leading Anglicans were faint-hearted or even outright Tory, there were other clerics of stronger fiber. One of these was a neighbor of the Towamensing camp, and he, by preaching and example, stiffened the wavering morale.

South of Kulpsville on the Skippack road was the tiny Wentz Reformed Church, whose pastor, John H. Weikel, was an uncompromising rebel. From the very outbreak of the troubles, he was violently in opposition to the Crown. On one occasion, when his congregation included loyal constables and stamp-tax officers, Weikel broke away from his intended text to preach a violent extemporaneous sermon on the text: "Better is a poor and a wise child than an old and foolish king, who will no more be admonished." By every right of history and scholarship, by every consideration of personal safety, and, perhaps, by every right of polite etiquette, he should at such a time have centered his discourse on injustices in ancient Palestine; but the Reverend John Weikel used the text to talk about the colonies, the Crown, and George III's immediate advisors. Duché's gentlemanly moderation would never have produced so violent a tirade, even if the Anglican's "suicidal vanity" had allowed him to run such risks of royal retribution; but Weikel had neither fear nor restraint.

The dominie was not content with making fiery speeches. His was a faith that called for action rather than words. Thinking that the theme required dramatic illustration, Weikel closed the service, led his flock outside to where the horses had been tethered, held the bridle of his own mount firmly in one hand, and then began to fire his pistols close to the horse's ear.

"It's time," he pointed out, "that peaceful farm horses are made ready to be used in battle. I cannot waste time when war is here teaching this animal to stand still while I shoot. When we are called upon to fight I hope my horse will be a soldier, too."

The gesture was too pointed for the royal authorities to overlook. Promptly they ordered Weikel to be dismissed from the pastorate. It was pointed out that he was "given to intemperate habits and his behaviour was such that nothing good could be said of him." The fifty parishioners protested but were unable to resist the King's command. They did allow their fiery former pastor to remain upon the parsonage farm. Weikel continued to fire his pistols from the windows of the rectory over the head of the horse which he had tethered on the lawn.

Washington was witness to one of Weikel's demonstrations. As he passed the Weikel home, a gunshot fusillade burst from the little parsonage. Suspecting an ambush, the General ordered the place surrounded, and then dispatched an officer to demand surrender of the snipers. Happily the loyal parishioners of the deposed minister vouched for his complete loyalty to republican ideals.

The march from Towamensing to the new campgrounds at Worcester was not long, but the few miles intervening brought almost a complete reversal in the American fortunes. Towamensing had been the scene of misery and misfortune; almost all the news that drifted to the camp was pessimistic; Worcester—the name receives its full three syllables in Pennsylvania—gave good tidings. On two successive days, word came that raiding parties had ventured down to the Middle

Ferry, and that they had twice cut the ropes by which the flatboats were guided across the stream. After smart skirmishing the raiders had escaped unharmed. The accomplishment was not important except to indicate that the Americans on the west bank of the Schuylkill were still active and that the British were suffering a partial siege. After the succession of disappointments even these little victories were heartening. Then came the messages that threw the whole camp into ecstasies.

Excited couriers burst breathlessly into the Worcester camp to report that Gates had won the biggest battle of the war. The powerful army under General Burgoyne, moving south from Canada to occupy the Hudson River valley and thus to separate New England from the other colonies, had been trapped at Saratoga and had been twice beaten by the Continentals. "Gentleman Johnny" Burgoyne and all his troops were captives.

It was an amazing victory and one whose import was immediately recognized. The couriers had ridden night and day to bring the news. Faint hearts that were despairing at the hardships and at the disaffection of the weak civilians took new courage. The camp was jubilant; everyone was roistering.

Everyone, except perhaps Captain Charles Willson Peale, a thirty-year-old Marylander who combined warfare with the pursuit of art. Peale was painting Washington, after days of idleness. Peale was always, so it seemed, demanding that the General consent to pose. Wherever Washington might be, whenever light was favorable, young Captain Peale would call to ask an audience. His military duties, as officer of a regiment of foot, seem never to have worried Captain Peale when there was good north light for painting.

PASTORS IN POLITICS

That house of Peter Wentz, in which Washington again had headquarters, was made to order for a painter. The large square room on the second floor, built by a wild and wicked rover who resigned his privateering to settle down on his thousand-acre farm, was admirably fitted as a studio. Peale could not resist the opportunity. Poor Washington, anxious to reestablish discipline among his men, hoping to restore the shattered morale of his army, planning to hold war councils, was badgered into giving up some precious time to pose for yet another of the miniatures which Peale was indefatigably painting.

The General, barely out of bed, and scarcely risen from the breakfast which Black Hannah Till had made ready behind the locked doors of the tiny private kitchen, patiently returned to sit for Peale. The light was poor that morning, but it was the first reasonably fine day that Peale had been able to devote to painting since long before the Germantown engagement. Fogs and rains and wintry rawness had kept him from artistic work for three full weeks. Washington, if only to get rid of a persistent caller, sat well forward on the edge of the four-poster bed to put himself at Peale's disposal. The captain, Washington's subordinate, enthroned himself on the only chair in the room.

Rifle shots cracked out. Washington's temper flared at the open violation of a recent order. Only a day or two before, he had categorically commanded that "the Instant a gun is fir'd a Serjeant and file of men shall be sent to catch the Villain who is thus wasting ammunition and alarming the Camp." He leaped up to call an aide-de-camp. Peale, dismayed at interruption, angrily commanded his superior to come back to the bed; but, luckily for good discipline, Washington was already halfway down the stairs that led to his

119

first-floor office. The shots continued, shattering nearly all the tiny panes of ancient glass that Peter Wentz had built into his stylish mansion. When Washington learned that the firing was in jubilation at the capture of Burgoyne, he forgot to punish the offenders. He did not return to the bedroom-studio where Peale was fuming, but the loss of the model seems, in truth, to have made little difference. The miniature there begun is now reckoned among the masterpieces of the artist, and is preserved in the Metropolitan Museum of Art.

No more work was done that day. Washington issued a general order granting a holiday. "Let every face Brighten and every heart expand," he said, in asking the chaplains to prepare "short discourses suited to the Joyful occasion." Following the brief Saturday evening service, thirteen pieces of cannon were fired, after which a *feu-de-joie* was observed by every brigade and corps of the encampment. Beginning at the right of the front line, each soldier fired a blank cartridge until the last man at the left had fired; then the second rank took up the firing, starting at the left and running to the right. The salute was then to be complete, but the soldiers would not have it so. They insisted on a democratic participation by the entire army, not by merely the first two ranks of men. They were indignant because no order was issued for another distribution of rum such as had signalized other victories. American supplies were now too low to permit of such unnecessary luxuries.

Soldiers in the field are peculiarly susceptible to superstition, and Washington's mystic-minded Pennsylvania Germans were far from being an exception. They pointed to the date-stone set high in the wall by Peter Wentz and his wife Rosannah nineteen years before, as proof that Worcester was meant to be a place of peace. There in German were the words:

> *Jesu, kom in mein Haus,*
> *Weg nimmer mer heraus;*
> *Kom mid deiner Gnaden guet*
> *Und stelle meine sel zu friede.*

> (Jesus, come into my house,
> Never to leave again;
> Come with thy blessed grace
> And bring peace to my soul.)

It was a prayer particularly appropriate for a reformed privateer who had turned devotedly to church work—Weikel's Wentz Church was named for him—but the promise of peace seemed fraught with significance at this juncture.

CHAPTER TWELVE

The Morale Cracks

WASHINGTON'S new hope was to besiege the British in the capital. With the spiked barricades in the Delaware blocking the enemy fleet from advancing all the way to Philadelphia, with Potter's militiamen preventing Howe's troops from crossing the Schuylkill to draw forage from the Darby farms, and with the American army north of Philadelphia controlling escape from the city, the stage, at first glance, seemed well set for a successful siege.

Howe helped the plan. Two weeks after Germantown was fought, he concentrated his defenses. By building a pontoon bridge across the Schuylkill at the Middle Ferry and by throwing a temporary bridge over that river some distance farther south, he cleared the way for what he hoped would be a feasible passage from Philadelphia to his base at Wilmington. The road, lying between hills and marshes, was open to attack by rebel raiders; but it was out of range of the American gunboats, and it could not be shelled by the forts along the river. The British, too, were now in better position to protect their garrison. Howe no longer needed to guard the five miles of rutty, muddy road between his main army and the Germantown outpost. Knyphausen's Hessians were, accordingly, withdrawn to Philadelphia.

A siege was thus made easier for Washington. By Knyphausen's withdrawal, two hill ranges—one at Whitemarsh, close to the beginning of the Wissahickon gorge, the other at Chestnut Hill, the highest land near Philadelphia—were opened to American possession. Guns placed on these heights would protect Washington's position and would hinder Howe's escape.

Even more desirable was the narrowing of the territory to be guarded. Before Knyphausen's retreat, Washington patrolled more than forty miles of comparatively level ground lying between the Delaware and Schuylkill rivers. Now moving closer to the capital, Washington could take up a hill position where only nine miles of land lay between the converging rivers. Thus, his army could guard more effectively the highways leading north from Philadelphia.

To Wayne and his aggressive associates, the situation seemed remarkably favorable. Mad Anthony, happy because a court-martial was soon to be called at his request to investigate his responsibility for the Paoli affair, clamored for an immediate assault upon the British lines. If, Wayne warned, the attack were delayed, the British fleet might clear the Delaware of obstruction and so open an avenue of escape. Successful attack, however, might result in Howe's annihilation or surrender.

In answer to the impatient Wayne, Washington presented to his war council a detailed account of the man power of the controlling armies. Howe, he showed, had more than fifteen thousand veterans behind fortified barricades. Before an attacking army could reach the capital, it must cut its way through an abatis — a wide defense of trees felled length-

VALLEY FORGE

wise toward the rebels. The branches had been sharpened, too, to make marching still more difficult. The barrier stretched three miles, from river to river across the entire northern boundary of Philadelphia.

Against the British, Washington had eighty-three hundred Continentals and twenty-seven hundred militiamen. There were also, to be sure, fifteen hundred other militiamen guarding the Delaware River forts, or patrolling the west bank of the Schuylkill, but these could not participate in a direct attack upon the British breastworks.

Not all the eleven thousand men with Washington were available for duty. Some were sick; more were ill supplied; the thousand troops who had been shoeless had now increased by several hundred more. The awaited clothing had not yet come to camp but, because of the want of wagons and draft animals, remained in storehouses at Lancaster. Cold weather was approaching. The men, who were willing to endure the hardships of battle and had kept their confidence even after defeat, began now to murmur that they had been abandoned by the politicians of the Continental Congress.

Washington defended their interests. In writing to Congress to demand clothing, he pointed out that a special Congressional committee visiting the army at Falckner Swamp had seen for itself how seriously the men needed shoes and clothing. Evidently, he suggested, the report made then by Charles Carroll of Carrollton and Samuel Chase, "Maryland's born leader of insurrection," had been pigeonholed. Unless relief came soon, Washington warned, "two-thirds of the army will be incapable of acting." He hoped for immediate relief.

Under the circumstances, the generals in their war council defeated the Wayne plan for aggressive attack. They rec-

124

ommended instead that twenty more regiments be brought down to Pennsylvania from the north, and that, pending their arrival, the camp should be set closer to Philadelphia. At any rate, the British could thereby be harassed.

On Tuesday morning October 21, in the sharp, cold northwest wind, Washington cautiously crept closer to the city. Again, as on the night before Germantown, the main body of the army marched southeast toward Philadelphia along the old Skippack road. Soon Washington came to Center Square, recapturing the Swedesford road that led to New Jersey on the east and to inland Pennsylvania on the west. Once more his communications with New York and New England were good; once more he had good highways to the munition centers west of the Schuylkill. Each further step toward Philadelphia gave him additional control over fertile farming districts—though these, by the constant military occupation, had been well stripped of their supplies. Again he was coming into a small-scale industrial center where small furnaces and little forges could supply him with new guns, and where his broken weapons could be repaired. The advance was bringing him into more defensible positions.

The troops were on familiar ground. The old Skippack road had been their highway when they marched from Pennypacker's Mills to Germantown; after the disappointment of that battle, it had been their avenue of escape; now, rested and refreshed, they were marching back over it to exact vengeance.

To many of the men, there was an eerie quality to these broad, level lands of Whitpain township. Marching through the heavy fog that hung over the dense forests of virgin oak, they called to mind traditions of the spooks that ruled the Skippack. From Center Square the entire five-mile stretch of narrow road to little Sandy Run was known to be haunted.

Much of the spectral reputation was due to eccentric old George Bisbing, whose lonely bachelor's palace in the forest was a ghostly capitol. His paneled oaken double doors opened into the largest, most hospitable-appearing mansion in the Whitpain region; but his hearth, built of fifty flat tombstones taken from a near-by burial place, was awe-inspiring. The ghosts of all the dead whose graves had been despoiled gathered nightly by his fireside.

On clear days it was safe to travel between Center Square and little Sandy Run. Riders could speed safely past the white marble milestone where a careless cutter had made the distance to Philadelphia read "81" instead of the proper 18 miles. Abe Wentz's black brick tavern close to Center Square, together with the Bluebell and the Broad Axe inns, afforded comfort to wayfarers. The bright sun, shining cheerfully on the ancient road cut ruler-straight through the forest, inspired confidence and reassured the stranger.

The soldiers were, however, marching with no such reassurance. The shadowy trees that lined the road seemed in the mist to lean forward to enmesh them; the heavy frost crunched underfoot with a thin squeaking sound as though the spirits were complaining; white milestones assumed spectral, waving forms. The ghosts who had been Bisbing's familiars flitted through the trees. Some soldiers, peering into Bisbing's windows, saw the strange, old man himself, sitting in the corner of his fireplace, brooding over his cornstalk fire, with his ghostly comrades round about him.

There were further reasons for the Whitpain belief in spooks. Hard and grasping Christian Dull, keeper of the Spring House Inn, murdered lonely travelers, according to the common gossip, and buried the corpses in the Whitpain woods. The charge was certainly completely false, as were exactly similar accusations made against inn-keepers in many other parts of Pennsylvania, but the rumors could not be quieted. Dull even went eventually to the extreme of publishing newspaper advertisements to deny the reputation, but the denial only added to the firm conviction that he was guilty. The ghosts of Dull's victims were believed to haunt the Whitpain roads.

True it was that the popular Spring House Inn was none too immaculate in its appointments. Women travelers complained that sheets were seldom washed, but that German Mrs. Dull merely sprinkled soiled linen, ironed the sheets, and then, after a brief warming by the fire, replaced the sheets upon the tavern beds. The spirited Elizabeth Drinker, meeting such an experience, slept all night in her cloak and then, next morning, folded up her sheets, "nutmeg fashion, and left them covered up in ye Beds for the dirty, old Dutch woman to tag and scold at. May it be the means to mend her manners."

The inn's food was little better. A long poem by the ornithologist Alexander Wilson, though written after Washington's men had left, graphically described the table manners of the time:

> Here two long rows of market folk were seen,
> Ranged front to front, the table placed between,
> Where bags of meat, and bones, and crusts of bread,
> And hunks of bacon all around were spread;
> Pints of beer from lip to lip went round,
> And scarce a bone the hungry house-dog found;
> Torrents of Dutch from every quarter came,
> Pigs, calves, and sour-krout the important theme;
> While we, on future plans revolving deep,
> Discharged our bill, and straight retired to sleep.

127

Dull's reputation did not, however, cause the troops to shun his inn; indeed, to many of the soldiers who had heard of the Spring House but had lived too far away to frequent its taproom, the reputation was an additional allure. Throughout this Whitpain encampment, Dull's tavern was thronged by all the soldiers who could manage to get leave. The action of his rival John Porter, at "The Waggon," in asking Washington to station guards at the Waggon door with drawn swords to keep the stragglers from entering, gave Dull prestige as a steadfast believer in Independence. "Tory" Porter failed soon after.

Fearing ambush and suspecting traps, the Americans moved slowly on their advance. Washington stopped at James Morris' "Dawesfield" home, just off the Skippack road, a mile west of what is now the town of Ambler. Here in the old stone mansion, whose French windows, unlike the windows of almost all other country houses, opened directly upon the wide, stone terrace, he held his councils. The advance guard, under Wayne, pushed forward. By Thursday night, two days after their start, the van was back in Germantown.

Wayne's force came to Germantown almost at midnight. They were expecting to see the spectral horseman, dressed in British uniform, who, the natives swore, rode nightly on a gray horse about the foot of Spook Hill, rallying the redcoats to make another stand. Old Dr. Christopher Witt, an ancient Rosicrucian who in his lifetime had been known as "Hexen-meister," or chief of the witch-doctors, had been dead a dozen years, but the shade of the shriveled old mystic was still believed to toil up Spook Hill to join supernatural visitors who held nightly revel here until the bells of the old German church steeple tolled one o'clock. Then all the phantoms vanished, but spectral blue flames danced about their graves till dawn. Luckily for the Americans, however, the spirits did not hold their rites on the cold frosty night when Wayne returned to retake Germantown.

Good news came instead. A Hessian attack on the river forts had been repulsed with heavy losses. Two of the British warships, including the sixty-four-gun *Augusta,* had been blown up. The heavy sound of the explosion, which the Americans said was due to rebel fireships, and which the English said was caused by their own careless handling of powder, could be heard in Washington's quarters.

The Americans were in need of some such reassuring news. The weather had turned bitter cold. The Wissahickon Creek and Sandy Run were frozen over; even the broad Schuylkill had a film of ice. No answer had come from Congress concerning the imperative need for shoes and clothing. Washington himself was growing more disturbed over the unwillingness of Pennsylvania, "the most opulent and populous of all the states," to send more than twelve hundred militiamen to help dislodge the British from Philadelphia. "The disaffection of a greater part of the Inhabitants of this State— the languor of others, and internal distraction of the whole, have been among the great and insuperable difficulties I have met with, and have contributed not a little to my embarrassments this Campaign."

Rain increased the tribulations. For two weeks, the days were cold and wet. The soldiers huddled in barns or gathered round huge fires built from the trees that once were a special Whitpain pride, but the hardships were severe.

The Whitpain experience was a foretaste of the difficult times ahead. The army's morale was beginning to give way. Each state detachment muttered against the patriotism of other commonwealths; all talked angrily against a Continental Congress that fled across the Susquehanna to safety at York when the British took the capital, but that abandoned soldiers to privations. Talk of desertion began to be heard.

Wayne's court-martial, held during the worst of a long northeast storm, did little to relieve the situation. Mad Anthony was cleared of blame for the Paoli disaster, but the charges against the general ran through the camp. Most of the soldiers disbelieved the accusations, gladly accepting the court-martial's verdict that Wayne "did everything that could be expected from an active, brave, and vigilant officer," but a few gossipers insisted that there was truth behind the complaints and that Wayne had been whitewashed. The trial of two generals, Adam Stephens and Maxwell, for drunkenness, gave more material for whisperers. Stephens was cashiered for his Germantown behavior; "Scotch Willie" Maxwell, though acquitted, was rebuked because the evidence had shown that "the general's spirits were a little elivated by liquor."

In anticipation of an early arrival of reinforcements from the north, Washington moved still closer to the city. In the thick fog of Sunday November 2, the main body of the army left Whitpain for Whitemarsh, five miles nearer Philadelphia. The movement had not been unforeseen; for ten days past, scouting parties had closed in upon the town. John Nice's Rising Sun Tavern, eight miles south of Whitemarsh at the intersection of the roads from Philadelphia to New York and Germantown, was already an important picket post for American advance detachments.

The new Whitemarsh campsite was particularly strong. Situated on the hills in a thickly wooded country, protected on front and flanks by swiftly flowing, swollen creeks, the men were safe against surprise. By copying the newly in-

vented British abatis and by building a strong redoubt, Fort
Washington, the soldiers possessed a powerful defense. The
open plain, sloping for two miles before them, gave them
strategic advantage in case they desired to make a sudden
descent upon the enemy.

Washington's headquarters during the ensuing six weeks
were at George Emlen's many-windowed baronial hall which
stood at the foot of Camp Hill, a mile east of the little Whitemarsh hamlet. The long stay was not anticipated, for, from
the very day of arrival, hostilities were momentarily expected.
Leaves of absence were refused to both officers and men;
the army was instructed to be ready to go into action at a
moment's notice.

Washington spent busy days while waiting for the anticipated British moves against the Whitemarsh camp. Seated
at Emlen's desk, close to the enormous cedar mantel, he wrote
insistent letters demanding that Congress and the states forward an immediate supply of blankets, shoes, and stockings.
His men, he pointed out, were rapidly losing heart. Half-
clad soldiers, huddled drenched to the skin by icy November storms around green-wood campfires, were losing patience
with a seemingly indifferent Congress.

Safe in distant York, the Congress paid little heed. Benjamin Rush, the former surgeon general of the army who had
resigned in petulance when his medical advice was not accepted, was attacking the American generals as incompetent.
Greene, he said, was a bootlicker, Sullivan a braggart mad-
man, Lord Stirling a lazy, ignorant sot. Schoolmaster James
Lovell, son of a Tory, smirched Washington as a leader
whose only talent lay in flight. "You will be astonished,"
he said, "what numbers of troops have been collected near
Philadelphia to wear out stockings, shoes, and breeches."

John Adams, who had nominated Washington as commander-in-chief, swung to the side of Rush and Lovell. He protested now against what he called the growing tendency to idolize "Fabius Maximus Cunctator." Washington's dilatory tactics, Adams declared, warranted dismissal.

A movement developed to put Horatio Gates, victor over Burgoyne at Saratoga, in Washington's place. Braggart Thomas Conway, angry because Washington had just opposed his plea for promotion to a major generalcy, wrote a note to Gates in which he declared, "Heaven has been determined to save your country or a weak General and bad counsellors would have ruined it." Vain General Gates, flattered at the thought that he would soon be made commander-in-chief, showed the letter to an aide, the twenty-year-old marplot James Wilkinson, and Wilkinson, in a drunken burst of confidence, repeated the contents to his friends. Word reached Washington at Whitemarsh that a plot to displace him was in progress.

Other leaders, too, were known to be implicated in the so-called Conway Cabal. Pennsylvania's Thomas Mifflin, a handsome spendthrift whom John Adams had once called "the animating soul of the Revolution," was carrying on an extensive correspondence with both Conway and Gates. From the safe seclusion of his retirement at Reading, where he had gone to sulk because he did not like his duty as quartermaster general, Mifflin pulled wires to discredit his commander-in-chief. With the aid of eastern and southern Congressmen, he secured the appointment of a Board of War to take over the general supervision of military affairs. Gates was made the president, Conway was chosen inspector general of the army, Wilkinson was elected secretary.

The rain of criticism, abuse, and slander poured from all

directions upon Washington. Save Conway, the officers and men at camp were wholly loyal to their commander, but the evident dissension between Congress and the army helped to destroy their confidence. Soldiers who had cheerfully endured hardship and defeat were now certain that they were to be abandoned. The same men who had retreated, singing and joking, from Brandywine and Germantown, glumly talked of mutiny against the Board of War and planned desertion if their General were overthrown. Cold morning fogs, followed by afternoons and nights of driving rain, killed their enthusiasm. Louis Lebeque de Presle du Portail, newly arrived French engineer, wrote home in shocked surprise to predict that the rebel cause was hopeless. "Such are these people," he told the French war minister, "that they move without spring or energy, without a passion for the cause in which they are engaged, and which they follow only as the hand which puts them in motion directs. There is a hundred times more enthusiasm in any coffee house in Paris than in all the thirteen provinces united."

The letter was, to be sure, written on a day of gale and tempest, following a night "as cold as midwinter" when ice formed half an inch thick on the streams. During the previous five weeks, there had been, all told, but eleven pleasant days. All other days had been wet or frosty. If there had been no other cause for broken spirits, the bad climate alone might have explained the shattered morale. For the second successive month, the full moon had brought a storm.

Washington was, however, well aware of the other contributory factors. He knew, for instance, that lack of clothing was a vital cause. For more than two months, his own spare baggage had been missing. The men were coming on parade unkempt, unshaved, and ragged. The snows were beginning now, and Washington despairingly wrote to the Board of War: "We have no prospect of obtaining supplies of cloathing except by forcing them from the inhabitants. Such a procedure, I fear, would not relieve our wants and, at the same time, would greatly distress the people and imbitter their minds." Four thousand men lacked blankets. Some took advantage of the distress of their comrades by stealing the clothes of sick men in the rude emergency hospitals. Nor would the neighborhood help greatly for, as salty Major Samuel Hay wrote to his colonel, "The generality of the people would much rather take a blanket from a soldier at half-price than let him have one at double its value. The devil will get half of them yet."

The transportation agents were largely at fault. At the very moment when Washington's men were shivering in the Whitemarsh snows, six thousand blankets, more than enough to supply each soldier with a covering, were being carried westward toward Lancaster, directly opposite from the encampment where they were so urgently required. Three days later, when as Wayne pathetically reports, "Our poor naked soldiers begin to complain of the cold and look up to us for relief," a mere four hundred blankets came to the Whitemarsh camp. The rest of the great store stayed on the banks of the Susquehanna.

Food, too, was becoming scarce. Eleven thousand men camping in one region for more than two months had exhausted the grain and meat supplies. Congress seemed indifferent, however, for when the commissariat reported that not a single barrel of flour remained for distribution to the troops, the arm-chair bureaucrats returned a note expressing disbelief. "We cannot forebear our astonishment," the Congressional leaders replied, "that the army should be in dan-

ger of starving from want of flour when the very neighborhood of the camp is at this moment full of wheat."

The Whitemarsh position was, obviously, growing un-
tenable. In spite of bureaucratic optimism, food was not available; clothing was so scarce that Washington declared, "I think
the wonder will be how they keep the field at all." The Delaware River forts had fallen and, by November 23, all the ob-
stacles to British sea approach to Philadelphia had been
cleared away. Howe was now enabled to devote his entire
attention to crushing Washington's small, suffering army.

This risk of attack by a well fed, well supplied British
army kept the Americans in a state of nervous apprehension.
Six times within the month of November warnings had been
issued that the British were about to attack, and although
each time the warning was a false alarm the shaken Americans
could not recover their composure. Their morale was, at last,
broken.

The chief question now was whether to launch a desperate
attack upon the well protected British or to withdraw to
safety to some more secluded position. Now that wild and
boisterous Dan Morgan's Virginia riflemen had come into
camp, together with fifteen Massachusetts regiments and a
large detachment of New Hampshire troops, Wayne and his
fire-eating friends clamored for a fight. Three of the newly
arrived generals, all of whom, oddly, were naval men, urged
against immediate battle. Disappointed at the state of the
troops, Ebenezer Learned, pious Massachusetts innkeeper
whose military reputation had been enhanced by his whale-
boat squadron patrol about the British fleet in Boston harbor, Enoch Poor, the New Hampshire builder of fire rafts,
and John Glover, Marblehead fish merchant and naval
expert, joined the majority against Wayne's demand for

aggressive action. The war council decided that the hungry, ragged Americans were in no fit condition to storm the well entrenched British positions. By more than the usual two-to-one vote, the generals decided to withdraw to winter quarters.

CHAPTER THIRTEEN

The Bloody March

THE choosing of a site for winter quarters produced bitter argument. Throughout two stormy days, while cold northeast rain was beating down upon the camp, debate continued at the Emlen house. Anger was evident; animosities flared constantly; some of the leaders almost came to blows in the heat of their discussions.

Of the sixteen generals in the over-officered army, seven demanded that the troops retreat thirty miles inland to Reading, the great stores center on the Schuylkill. Housing, they said, could there be commandeered and, if necessary, additional quarters could be found in the villages that lined the roads into the iron districts.

Such a position, behind the first range of mountains, would have been proof against a possible attack, but there were serious drawbacks to the proposal. The rich Great Valley region, New Jersey, and the fertile acres north of Philadelphia would have to be abandoned to the British. The states would be fatally divided. All the easy highways from Philadelphia to the South would fall under Howe's control, leaving to the Americans only the mountainous wagon tracks to the north of Reading. Not only would it be difficult to rekindle the fires of revolution among those who would thus be abandoned to the enemy, but British light horse could intercept all rebel communications between New England and the rest of the rebellious colonies. In such condition, it was evident, the canny New Englanders would be cautious about continuing a war in which they alone would be obliged to bear the burden of supplying the money and the men.

Even more serious than loss of Southern support or fear of Northern withdrawal was the certainty that if the army fled so far into the hinterland the richest sources of munitions would be sacrificed. Warwick and Coventry would be secure, but other vital ironworks would be open to British raid. Nowhere in the thirteen states were sufficient substitutes available for the dozen furnaces that would be lost, nor for the score of gunneries that would be left in British hands. To camp along the Reading front would be, as nine generals argued, to invite national suicide.

Unhappily, the nine objectors could not agree upon a better site. Five generals, including Wayne and Du Portail, the French fortification expert, proposed a singularly dangerous plan of wintering at Wilmington. Not only would their scheme require a battle to dislodge the British from their river base, and not only would it abandon all the forges and furnaces to the enemy, but there were other grave probabilities. By one quick, successful thrust from near-by Philadelphia, the British could drive Washington's exhausted army into the flat peninsula between Delaware and Chesapeake bays. There could then be no possible retreat. Completely cut off from road connection with eleven of the thirteen states, penned in the level plains with not the slightest hope of natural defense, without money, munitions, or medicine, subjected to easy flank attack from Britain's blockading fleet, Washington could do nothing else than surrender. Not even the dilatory Howe with his peculiar genius for committing unexpected errors could muff the chance. He could sit down and win by waiting. So long as Britain remained mistress of the seas, a brief barricade across the twelve-mile plain from the Head of Elk to the Delaware would fence in the Continentals until they gave up in despair.

Twelve generals sensed the danger in the plan of Wayne and Du Portail, but the Pennsylvania Supreme Executive Council at Lancaster shouted the most effective warning. Flatly this governing group threatened that if Washington chose winter quarters outside the state, Pennsylvania would send no further troops, nor would it honor requisitions for supplies. If the Continental army wanted help from Pennsylvania, the Supreme Executive Council definitely warned, the soldiers must remain encamped close to Philadelphia.

Pennsylvania was completely selfish in issuing its ultimatum. The state was in political confusion. More, perhaps, than any other of the former colonies, the commonwealth was facing social as well as administrative revolution. Power was being stripped away from a privileged Tory class of rich farmers, prosperous merchants, and conservative intellectuals, and was being transferred to a comparatively radical group of unpropertied Whigs. The Supreme Executive Council, placed in power by the "redleg" poor white farmers of the hill country, by the debtor classes, and by the more turbulent city "mob," demanded that the army camp near Philadelphia in order to keep the Pennsylvania Tories under close control.

Rather than face the probable break-up of the united front against the British, Washington yielded to the Pennsylvania ultimatum. When it was evident that winter quarters must be found in Pennsylvania, and that Reading was unacceptable to a majority of generals, the best camp site was Valley Forge. A feeble voice mentioned Bethlehem, where the largest army hospital was located, but the suggestion found no favorable response. Valley Forge had greater possibilities and was better known. Wayne, who was familiar with the ground, accepted Valley Forge as his new choice; John Peter Gabriel Muhlenberg, son of the famous Trappe cleric, gave up insisting on Reading and also argued earnestly in behalf of Valley Forge.

Johann Kalb, the German waiter who had assumed the title "Baron de Kalb" in order to facilitate his entry into military life, was unconvinced. At Valley Forge, he told the war council, "the soil is thin, uncultivated, and almost uninhabited, without forage and without provisions." The statement was extraordinary, and was not based on personal knowledge of the terrain. Nor was Kalb's further statement true: "The idea of wintering in this desert can only have been put into the head of the commanding general by an interested speculator or a disaffected man." Wayne and Muhlenberg speedily proved that Kalb's comments were unfounded.

Pennsylvania's own General Jim Potter was even more positive in his objections. In spite of his open sympathies with the Supreme Executive Council, he was firmly set against establishing winter quarters in his native state. In a written communication to Washington, the semiliterate frontiersman forcibly argued for some choice other than Valley Forge.

"I assart winter Quarters is not to be found In the state of pennsylvania my Reasons for this Assartion is, the Capitale is in persession of the Enemy, and there is such large numbers fled from it, and the neghborhood adjasent, and the Towns

and Viledges along the River Dalawar, that all the Towns
and Viledges Back in the Country are full of Refugees all
Redey. What will be dun with those people Turn them
out of Dores to make Room for the Solders, god for Bid
it—that would be cruilty unexamplified by General How
himself."

Potter's protest came too late. The Valley Forge region
had been accepted. Its definite strategic value for guarding
mines and furnaces and for commanding highways into the
interior was evident. Its position on the hills commanding
fertile plains in almost all directions seemed to guarantee
as plentiful a supply of food as could be found at any camp
site within a range of many miles. Although its own forge
and flour mills had been destroyed by British raids, Valley
Forge was close to other mills and ironworks. Reading, the
great supply base, was not far distant and was available both
by land and by river. Yellow Springs, the favorite health
resort, lay but a few miles to the west, and could be made
available as a hospital for the sick and wounded.

Valley Forge, moreover, offered an exceptionally convenient base for operations against the British. Between the
camp's outpost at Matson's ford, the present site of Conshohocken, and the rear guard at what is now the town of
Phoenixville, no fewer than six convenient fords crossed to
the Philadelphia side of the Schuylkill. In sudden sorties,
Washington's raiding parties could thus swoop quickly upon
the northern approaches to the city. Similarly, upon the west
bank of the river, the Americans would hold an advantage,
for the newly created light horse could readily dash down to
harass any British forage parties who might venture across
the stream.

The army waited now for the heavy storm to cease and for

141

the roads to dry before marching to the newly chosen site. December came with clear, fine weather, and Washington, after sending off another message to the president of Congress reminding him, "The officers, or at least a large proportion of them, as well as the men, are in a most disagreeable condition as to Cloathing," drew up the marching orders.

He held them, however, until highborn Jedediah Huntingdon had brought his Connecticut brigade into camp. But even then they were not immediately announced. Before his men were ready to leave, word arrived that Howe was planning a surprise attack.

The news came to Washington's headquarters before most of the British army was itself aware that a sortie was contemplated. Howe's war council, meeting in Philadelphia at noon on December 2, arranged for several thousand men to march by a fourteen-mile circuitous route and fall upon Washington's unsuspecting camp. That evening, while the adjutant general was discussing the plans with fellow officers, Lydia Darragh, a Quaker midwife in whose home the adjutant had quarters, overheard the conversation.

Anxious to warn her son, Ensign Daniel Darragh, of the attack but not daring to tell her sternly conscientious teacher husband lest she be rebuked for eavesdropping, Mrs. Darragh conceived the plan of slipping through the British lines. She knew that it was possible, by special arrangement, for housewives to go northeast to Frankford to get flour from the mills. Although Frankford was six miles from Whitemarsh, she hoped that she might meet American scouts who would relay her news either to Washington or to her son.

The plan succeeded. Hiding her twenty-five-pound sack of flour in the woods, she walked from Frankford toward Whitemarsh. Soon she met Captain John Craig, light horseman of the Pulaski cavalry, to whom she told her story, insisting only that he should not reveal her name for fear the British might discover that she had disclosed their plan. Craig thanked her, promised to protect her identity, and then spurred back to Whitemarsh to tell his superior officers.

Mrs. Darragh was not wholly satisfied that she had fulfilled her purpose. She walked on to the Rising Sun tavern. Here she found tall and handsome Elias Boudinot, chief of Washington's intelligence service. Once again she told her story.

"A little, poor, insignificant old woman came in," wrote Boudinot. "She walked up to me and put into my hands a dirty old needlebook with various small pockets in it. Surprised at this, I told her she should return and she should have an answer. On opening the needlebook, I could not find anything until I got to the last pocket, where I found a piece of paper rolled into the form of a pipeshank. On unrolling it, I found information that General Howe was coming out the next morning with 5,000 men, thirteen pieces of cannon, baggage wagons, and eleven boats on wagon wheels. On comparing this with other information, I found it true, and immediately rode first to headquarters."

Another version of the story relates that Captain Allen McLane, also of Washington's scouting forces, first saw the enemy below the Rising Sun inn and hastened ahead of them to give Washington warning. It is, however, likely that McLane was carrying the Darragh message in advance of Elias Boudinot's arrival.

Mrs. Darragh herself later informed her close friends that the first news was sent to Washington through her own activities. After delivering her messages, Mrs. Darragh said, she had gone back to the Frankford woods, picked up her

143

twenty-five-pound sack of flour and, though she was small and weakly, had carried it back to Philadelphia in order to divert suspicion.

Washington, in any case, was forewarned. Boudinot believed that the eleven boats on wagon wheels showed that Howe planned to cross the Delaware under pretense of going to New York and then, at night, to recross the river above Bristol and fall suddenly upon the unguarded American rear. Washington thoughtfully considered the suggestion but then rejected it. "Mr. Boudinot," he said, "the enemy have no business in our rear. The boats are designed to deceive us. Tomorrow morning by daylight you will find them coming down a byroad on our left." He ordered cannon mounted to repel the anticipated attack.

At three o'clock on the cold Friday morning of December 5, American alarm guns announced that Howe's expected advance was in sight. All the American baggage was sent up to Trappe "except what a man might run or fight with," and the rebels prepared for action. General James Irvine with six hundred Pennsylvania militiamen went south to Chestnut Hill as an advance guard; but his troops, after a sharp skirmish in which Irvine lost three fingers and was taken prisoner, were forced to retreat.

No general engagement followed. Howe, finding the Americans strongly posted behind redoubts and barricades of fallen trees with fifty-two fieldpieces commanding the steep slopes of the hill, concluded that the rebel camp was too formidable to be stormed. Slowly he drew his attacking forces toward the American left, searching for a more vulnerable position; but when he learned that all the hill was similarly fortified, he ordered his men to withdraw to Philadelphia. By midnight on the cold, foggy December 8, the threatened attack was over.

THE BLOODY MARCH

The retreat was more disastrous to the Americans than the advance had been. As Howe's men returned to their Philadelphia camp, they plundered farmers of grain, forage, and livestock. Houses were set afire at Beggarstown, now called Mt. Airy, north of Germantown, and at the other little settlements along the road. The Rising Sun inn, the American picket post, was burned. Seven hundred head of cattle were driven down to the capital.

No obstacle now remained for Washington's withdrawal toward Valley Forge. Orders were again drawn up for the departure. At four o'clock in the morning of December 11, the troops were to leave, by way of Matson's ford and Swedes' ford for the Valley Forge camp site.

By direct road over smooth country, Whitemarsh is only thirteen miles due east from Valley Forge, but in the cold, snowy December days Washington's thinly clad, half-starved soldiers required more than a week to complete the journey. Ill luck, bad weather, poor management, and fright combined to make the march the most painful and the most difficult ever undertaken by the Continental forces.

Jim Potter's Pennsylvania militiamen caused the first confusion. When Sullivan's van arrived at Matson's ford to cross to the western bank of Schuylkill, the troops methodically set army wagons in the shallow river bed and then laid planks upon the wagons for the army to cross dry-shod and in good order. No sooner, however, was the work complete than a terror-stricken crowd of Potter's men came rushing down to tell that all the British army was upon their heels. "Old Corncob" Cornwallis, they said, had crossed the Middle ferry, had met Potter's outposts at Black Horse tavern, and was rushing to Matson's ford to attack the rebel army. The Potter men, frightened into headlong flight, had thrown away their guns and run for safety.

Only a few of the British, as it happened, had been in the action, and these had come without a thought of starting full-fledged battle. Cornwallis was seeking forage, but when Potter's men took flight the raiding party followed after. Now, lined upon the steep hills on the western shore, controlling the winding roads that led inland along the swiftly flowing creeks, they looked on in amusement as the Potter militiamen gasped out their tale of danger.

Sullivan retreated, destroying his wagon-bridge behind him. The Americans, prevented, as they thought, from crossing at Matson's ford, plodded northward to Swedes' ford where passage was less easy. A full day was thus lost, for again the cautious Americans, fearing to advance into what might well be a British trap, delayed until dusk before trying to pass over the river. More wagons were sunk in the stream, replacing the thirty-six carts lost at Matson's ford; fence rails were laid across the wagon tops; and, in single file, the army moved across. The passage took all night.

Snow had now begun. Ragged troops, with legs naked and feet completely bare, with shirts hanging in strings above torn breeches, tramped down the west bank of the river in the dark to meet the British at Matson's ford. The wind, sweeping unchecked from the plains across the river, blinded them with heavy snow; the remnants of their uniforms were soggy; they were unfed; not even rum was available to give them temporary solace.

By sunrise the larger portion of the army had worked its way to where the British army was supposedly awaiting, but the enemy was nowhere visible. The small force which Cornwallis had brought up to watch the crossing had long since returned to warmth and comfort at Philadelphia. The Americans struggled on through the deep-cut creek paths to Gulph

146

Mills, where with high pine-clad hills at their backs they strove to build campfires from the dripping wood. There were no tents nor baggage; these were far distant at Trappe, for the Signal Service had guessed that the weather would be clear and warm, and that the men would have no need for shelter. During four days of snow and driving sleet, in bitter cold, the troops huddled close to their fires.

In such emergencies the Continental troops rose to their best heights. Though in good weather they might grouse and grumble at the stupidity of a Congress which subjected them to such privations, yet, when the times were hardest, the rebel soldiers showed comparatively good humor. Their eyes smarting from the thick, acrid smoke that rose from green pine logs, their scanty bowls of thin soup filled with burned leaves and dirt, "sickish enough to make a Hector spue," their clothes steaming from the heat, they laughed and joked and sang. Some ventured in the snow down to the overhanging rock which jutted over the narrow trail, and hammered saplings under it to give the impression that the rock was unsafe and about to fall. Then they warned their comrades that the road was dangerous and that all passers-by must scramble over the huge ram's-head boulder to regain safe footing.

Four days after the arrival at Gulph Mills, the tents caught up with the army. They were not immediately pitched, however, for again the Signal Service erred in its predictions. "The weather being likely to be fair," the orders read, "the men are to be in readiness to march at four o'clock tomorrow morning."

During the night, the snow turned to cold rain so that by daybreak, the ground was thick with slush. Barefoot soldiers who might march with reasonable comfort along dirt roads

147

in warm midsummer would risk freezing when they trod to Valley Forge. The mercury fell lower; the slush froze into hard and icy ridges. Not for three days more did the weather clear sufficiently for the march to be resumed.

In midmorning of December 19, the day after one which a thoughtless Congress had ironically ordered to be observed as a fast day for thanksgiving, the troops began the final section of the journey. Around the spur of the South Valley hill, through the small streams close to the Gulph, climbing the twisting rocky slopes of the Old Gulph Road toward King of Prussia, the exhausted, hungry army plodded doggedly forward. It was a slow and painful progress. So few horses were available to pull the artillery that the men had to be harnessed to the gun carriages. The snail's pace of artillery progress compelled the infantry to inch along. Frequently the column halted to enable the guns to be pulled out of some deep ditch, and each time as the soldiers rested "two or three men in each platoon would be seen standing, supported by their guns, fast asleep." Then came the order to move on; and as the sleepers roused themselves, pushed by the platoons from behind, they stumbled and fell. The sharp ice ridges slashed the feet of barefoot men. The men left trails of blood.

Six hours of marching barely a mile an hour, brought the worn-out army to the old white oak at King of Prussia. Here the men, crouching around quickly built campfires, heated up their scant rations of frozen thin stew, made mostly of frostbitten potatoes with but small bits of meat. Some had not even this but swallowed crumbs of stone-cold army bread.

The officers were only slightly better off, but they were warmer. The King of Prussia inn, standing at the crossroads, offered hospitality. Washington and his immediate family of officers dined sparsely in the great second-story chamber. Colonels and majors tarried below in the huge taproom, warmed by the great fireplace, where many an ox had roasted, but where now the eight-foot logs flamed under lesser provender. Outside the thick stone walls, horses were tethered in the dense oak woods, temporarily safe from the biting wind that howled from off the icy hills.

High on the outer wall, the inn sign creaked in the gale. Presumably painted by Gilbert Stuart, it bore the image of Frederick the Great, King of Prussia, sitting erect in his blue coat and his buff knee breeches upon the back of a high-headed chestnut charger, his cocked hat slightly tilted in a rakish style. The artistic signboard was a relic of the days when Frederick had helped both Britain and the colonies in the Seven Years' War against the French. The fifty French officers were not pleased to see the portrait of their former enemy, although some hoped that Frederick might yet join the war to help the states throw off the English yoke.

At four o'clock the drums beat for the men to move along their last three miles. They now were climbing once again, but they were going uphill for the last time. The rising hills of Valley Forge were in plain sight against the brown woods ahead; the terrible march was almost over.

North Carolinian Tarheels, leading the van, tried hard to push forward, followed closely by ex-privateersman Aleck McDougall's men, and by the forces under young Lafayette. But the march was even slower than it had been during the morning. Many of the soldiers, staggering from fatigue, had to be supported by their sturdier comrades. Tired and exhausted, they blundered into one another; they slipped more frequently upon the frozen road; they fell heavily, cutting themselves upon the icy ridges. Too weary even to complain, the desperate group pushed on. Some, trying to find rest by sinking into snowy fields, had to be forced to their feet to save them from freezing where they lay.

Dusk was closing down when the army came at last to Valley Forge. The heavily timbered hills, thick with ice and almost bare of cultivation, were inhospitable. Food had not arrived. The men, completely worn-out, could not yet take rest. Wood for the campfires had to be cut; rude shelters for the ill had yet to be erected; a few tents must be pitched.

Little effort was made that night to set a watch. The soldiers were too tired, too hungry, and too ill to mount guard in a snow-swept camp against an enemy which had not stirred from comfortable Philadelphia. For this one night, at least, the army was too completely fagged to follow military rules.

Never in the entire Revolution had the men felt so despondent, so weary, or so hopeless. Defeat at Brandywine had left them disappointed but still confident of ultimate success; failure at Germantown had seemed an accident of weather. Had the fog not intervened to save the British, they were convinced, the well planned attack on the British van would have proved completely successful. But now, at Valley Forge, the men were losing hope. Their seeming desertion by a cowardly Congress deprived them of all heart.

Washington, knowing the spirit of his broken men, enforced no rigid discipline. He and his officers, huddling round their fires on the unprotected plains, suffered with their men. The Commander was bitter cold, but he resolved that he would seek no better shelter for himself until his freezing soldiers were more adequately housed.

CHAPTER FOURTEEN

Shelter in the Snow

MORNING brought more intense cold weather. Soldiers, ringed close to the fires, who had tried to sleep upon the icy ground, woke to find the snow still falling, the Schuylkill frozen fast. Hungry, numb, ill from exposure, they set to work to build shelters.

As soon as these were built, the highest officers would be adequately cared for. Billeting agents had already gone out in advance of the army's arrival to mark with chalk the houses set aside for the Commander and the other generals. For Washington, the billeters had chosen the great two-and-a-half-story stone mansion built twenty years before for John Potts, master of the Mount Joy Forge.

The Potts estate was not now intact. Eleven children had shared the property when old John Potts had died. The forge had gone to William Dewees, a son-in-law; Isaac Potts had moved next door with his religious young bride; the big house had passed to Deborah Hewes, a daughter-in-law, who had remarried since her first husband's death. The large Potts family was scattered over the long stretch of country between Philadelphia and their ironworks upstate.

Patriotic Mrs. Hewes was willing to release her home for Washington's occupancy, though she had but recently returned from her town house in Philadelphia. The rental of a hundred pounds which Washington insisted on paying, was of less interest than the chance to be of service to the General. She asked only for time to move her personal belongings into her neighbors' houses. Colonel Dewees, who owned the house with the great bake ovens at the crossroad, found room to care for Mrs. Hewes and her possessions.

The delay pleased Washington, who was reluctant to take up comfortable warm quarters while his men were exposed to cold and snow. He ordered his big marquee pitched upon a hillock underneath a gum tree, proposing to remain in this thin shelter until his troops had built log huts.

Exact and definite instructions were issued in the General Orders of this first day in winter quarters, specifying precisely how the huts were to be constructed. The work was to be accomplished in as cooperative a manner as was practicable, though Washington made it clear that each regiment was to "reap the benefit of its own labor." A prize of twelve dollars was offered to that group of twelve men in each regiment "which finished its hut in the quickest and most workmanlike manner."

Meanwhile, he promised that while the men were building huts, foraging parties would survey the countryside to see what food might be obtained. Most of the grain had been used up, but he knew that it was customary to store wheat, unthreshed, in the barns until there should be time to flail it during the winter. Washington ordered, therefore, that farmers turn in their unthreshed wheat at once under penalty of having it confiscated at the price of straw. In return for the immediate threshing, he promised, he would order that the troops should spare the fences and should not ruthlessly rob farmers of their stock.

THE WASHINGTON MARQUEE

(*Courtesy Mrs. W. Herbert Burk and Valley Forge Museum of American History*)

THE SOLDIERS' HUT

Reproduction, by Valley Forge Park Commission, of the huts used at the time of the encampment. (Courtesy Dan J. Voorhees and the Albertype Company, Brooklyn, N.Y.)

SHELTER IN THE SNOW

The work of hut building commenced, therefore, in hopes of putting all the army under roofs before Christmas. Washington, shivering in his canvas marquee, wrote letter after letter to Congress complaining that the troops were without food, and that "unless some great and capital change takes place" in the commissary department, "this army must inevitably be reduced to one or another of these three things: starve, dissolve, or disperse in order to obtain subsistence in the best manner they can." He grew bitter in his remonstrance against those who "seem to have little feeling for the naked and distressed soldiers."

Experienced frontiersmen, meanwhile, applied the arts that they had learned in western mountain clearings. Axmen hurried to the woods to cut down oaks and to hew the trunks into sixteen-foot lengths. Others searched for cedars, preferably straight-grained and of good diameter, to make roof shingling; some, armed with broadaxes, hacked out rough slabs from the smaller trees. Such slabs, rough-barked on one side, splintery on the other, would provide material for doors and, with cedar shingling hard to find, would also serve for roofing. Some officers thought that the men could floor cabins with these slabs, but most of the huts had no flooring but the frozen earth.

Horses hauled the larger logs to sites selected for the company streets; men, harnessed by ropes about their chests and shoulders, pulled the smaller pieces through the snow. The work was heavy, and the ropes tore through the thin hunting shirts the soldiers wore, but, with a dozen men working on the materials for each hut, the task was soon accomplished.

Once the logs were dragged to the assigned positions, the actual building progressed rapidly. Skilled workmen notched the logs and fitted them to their places. Warmed by the roaring fires of small, discarded branches and chunks of chopped logs, the men speedily raised the cabin walls to the six-and-a-half-foot height prescribed by Washington. The chinks between the logs were plugged by stones or clay or bits of slab; the roofs were similarly tightened; doors were fitted into place. Meanwhile, inside the huts, wooden fireplaces, clay-lined to prevent their catching fire, were speedily constructed.

Cabin building on the frontier customarily required three days, ending in an all-night dance, but the troops at Valley Forge were working much more speedily. Even before the second day was done, many of the cabins had been crudely finished. The finer touches were not yet complete; the huts lacked the built-in bunks, the crude tables, and the usual pegs about the walls on which the clothing could be hung. No buckhorns had been fixed above the fireplaces as supports for rifles; the cranes were not yet ready. These were niceties to be finished later when rations might be generous enough for men to give "housewarming" parties.

Meanwhile the huts were proof against the icy winds, save for the draughts that blew beneath the bottom logs to chill the men as they lay sleeping on the hard dirt floor. They banked earth about the huts to keep these draughts from blowing, and they sought straw and cedar boughs to make their sleeping softer. The huts were badly ventilated, too; the ill built chimneys were too short. Great gusts of choking green-wood smoke made breathing difficult and caused the troopers' eyes to run with blinding tears. These were, however, evils that could readily be borne. The chief purpose of the huts had been accomplished. Most of the men were safe against the heavy snows that fell on Christmas Day, and against the biting northeast winds. Within the huts, during this week of "amazing cold," the majority were comfortably warm.

Not all the troops were, however, under cover. The city soldiers, unaccustomed to hut building, lagged in their tasks. These were helped by the frontiersmen now that they had finished all the building for themselves and for their officers. Not until a full week of January had passed were the eleven thousand men under sufficient shelter.

The officers, meanwhile, had been distributed to quarters in the neighborhood. Old houses built by the Welsh and English Quakers were still usable, but the British raid had left few houses standing. Within a four-mile radius of Headquarters, fewer than twenty stout, stone houses were in fit condition for immediate occupancy. Few of these were within the actual encampment grounds. Powerful James Varnum, the quick-thinking lawyer whom Washington called "the Light of the Camp," was the Commander-in-chief's nearest neighbor on the south; but Varnum's quarters, at David Stephens' house, were almost a mile away.

Varnum was, however, in the center of a group of lively officers. Fiery Aleck McDougall, who enjoyed writing controversial pamphlets which just skirted the libel laws, lived in a new-built hut across the road. Close by was the log house of Thomas Conway, the newly appointed inspector general who was plotting to displace Washington by Gates. Devil David Forman, petulant because of his constant disagreements with his New Jersey legislature, also had a hut in Varnum's neighborhood, though he was seldom at Valley Forge. Jedediah Huntingdon was quartered in a stone house just down the road.

The cluster of officers in the Varnum neighborhood made his quarters, close to the present site of the Washington Memorial Chapel, a convenient gathering place for war councils. Washington frequently rode up to the old Welsh farmhouse to discuss camp affairs. More often, the brother generals whiled away the tedium of the winter by coming here to talk with the scholarly Varnum and to discuss, as Greene so frequently did, such unmilitary matters as the Latin poets and the latest news from their Rhode Island home.

The Varnum neighborhood possessed a strong New England flavor. Connecticut and Rhode Island infantry, manning the river defenses at the Star Redoubt, fraternized with John Sullivan's New Hampshiremen who guarded the Fatland ford. Scorning the Pennsylvanians and the Delawarean "Blue Hen's Chickens" who stood between them and the Headquarters, these New Englanders looked upon their portion of the camp as the heart of the encampment. Their central location and the frequency of Washington's visits to their chief led them to believe that all other Continental troops took second place in the Commander's regard.

A much larger group of soldiers encamped along the outer line, guarding the high ground where the Memorial Arch now stands. Muhlenberg, whom the Hessians called "Teufel Piet," posted Virginia regiments on the extreme left; with the fellow Virginians from George Weedon's brigade close by. Big John Paterson's Massachusetts men, still chattering about their leader's narrow escape from being killed when his horse was shot from under him, guarded the center, together with Glover's Bay Staters and the lonely Rhode Islanders whom Learned led. Poor's New Hampshire troops, separated by the entire width of the camp from their friends in Sullivan's brigade, held the right in company with Wayne's Pennsylvanians. Vigorous Charles Scott, plain-spoken and distrustful of the social graces, watched the right wing of the outer line.

The defense was powerful. Before the entrenchments of the eight brigades which protected the front, a wide, flat plain sloped for almost two miles toward the King of Prussia. No enemy attack could catch the watchers unawares. Any British advance must march straight forward, without cover, under American fire.

In such event, the engineers assured Washington, the British losses would be heavy. Fieldpieces posted in the outer line redoubts could decimate the enemy long before the British infantry could fire successfully upon the rebels. Round shot aimed at an advancing column was effective within a thousand yards, but rifles such as were used by the British carried less than a fifth that distance. Rifles, moreover, were slow in loading. Before a second rifle volley could be fired, the guns, reloaded with grape, could devastate the British ranks. American muskets, effective at a hundred yards, could then complete the task of stopping an advance.

If, the engineers went on to reassure the Commander-in-chief, the British should succeed in breaking through the field-gun barrage to come within bayoneting distance of the trenches, the "redan" formation of the outer-line breastworks would provide additional security. By building the intrenchments in angular fashion, so that salients projected toward the enemy, the Americans could subject the British to a deadly crossfire. During the interval that the enemy would be occupied in reducing this redan defense, the artillery could be drawn off to new positions on an inner line of breastworks, behind a well built abatis.

So secure were the defenses that several of the generals felt safe in choosing quarters well beyond the outer line of breastworks. Little Trout Run, more than half a mile south of the entrenchments, was bordered by good stone houses. In these, Wayne, Poor, Weedon, Pulaski, Kalb, Sullivan, Potter, Muhlenberg, and Morgan found accommodations.

157

The most picturesque shelter was that selected by Dubuyson, a French artillery officer. Finding no houses available, and preferring to live in quarters of his own, Dubuyson chose to winter in a cave.

A cavern in the yard of Abijah Stephens' home, near Trout Run, served the Frenchman as a home. Stephens had long used the cave as a springhouse. A natural pit, three feet below the surface, had been lined with interlaced saplings and with straw to make an underground chamber almost twelve feet square. Here Dubuyson lived, coughing from the smoke that could not easily be ventilated from his cave, until spring brought weather warm enough for tents to be pitched outdoors.

Greene at "Rehobeth," Scott and Virginia's William Woodford at New Centerville, three miles from Headquarters, and brisk Colonel Thomas Bradford, deputy commissary general of prisoners, whose quarters were near Howellville, were even more remote from camp. Their daily horseback journeys to inspect their men or to consult with Washington, during the worst weather of the winter, sometimes exacted a great toll of strength, though Scott and Bradford, in particular, relished the opportunity for working off excess energy. Lame Nathanael Greene stayed often overnight with Washington rather than endure the strain of long riding on the snowy nights. He feared that exposure might aggravate his asthma.

Almost a mile north of the outer line of breastworks, a second, shorter inner line of trenches was dug. The left, resting on the Star Redoubt, was held by Huntingdon's Connecticut brigade, with Conway's Pennsylvanians in the center, and "Scotch Willie" Maxwell's Jerseymen upon the right. The inner line was equipped with field guns which could, in case of necessity, command the outer trenches. Between the

158

two entrenchments was Henry Knox's reserve artillery, ready to be hauled by sturdy soldiers to whichever breastworks seemed in most need of defense. At either end of the inner line, square gun emplacements, Fort Huntingdon and Fort Washington, stood to receive the heavy guns that would command the approaches to the camp.

There seemed but little need for defense upon the rear. The road that now winds along Valley Creek had not then been cut. Hostile troops seeking to take Valley Forge from the north would be obliged to ford the creek, climb a precipitous wooded hill, and then attack the Americans in their trenches. The danger of such assault was slight, particularly as the trenches were designed to be defended almost equally well on either side.

The one practicable approach upon the rear was by the road that led from Valley Forge into the iron regions. This was guarded by Lord Stirling's men, and by the close proximity of the North Carolinians and the Delaware regiments on the south bank of the creek. General McIntosh was quartered on the north shore of the stream, living in a small cabin owned by a free Negro. Later in the winter, Baron Steuben, the Prussian drillmaster, was to take quarters at the little inn which, because of its stone doorstep, was called Slab Tavern.

All the major generals thus lived outside the campground. Charles Lee, who was billeted with Bradford, and Thomas Mifflin, the quartermaster general, did not spend all the winter at the camp; Greene and Kalb lived south of the outer line; Steuben, another late arrival, was well to the north of the encampment limits. Stirling, Lafayette, and Knox were stationed west of the campground.

Farthest of these from the Headquarters was the home of

"Lord" Stirling, eccentric New York claimant to an extinct Scotch earldom. Farmer, manufacturer, and miner, this adventurer, whose rightful name was William Alexander, had won fame by capturing, with forty men in a pilot boat, the British transport *Blue Mountain Valley*. Tireless, resourceful, and energetic, he was invaluable as the army's master mechanic. Realizing that Dewees' Mount Joy Forge was wrecked beyond repair, he persuaded Washington to let the skilled ironworkers of Valley Forge specialize on making small tools, repairing broken guns, and blacksmithing. Forges in the hills, closer to the mines and furnaces, he thought better fitted to carry on the heavy industries.

The work did not absorb all of Stirling's tremendous energy. On the lawn of his quarters, sheltered on one side by the Reverend William Currie's stone mansion, and on another by the springhouse and the bake oven, he set up a small telescope. Here, on the clear winter nights, while Dr. Currie shivered at his side, the fifty-year-old general, one of Washington's oldest aides, took observations.

His host, Dr. Currie, was himself a colorful eccentric. For thirty years, the crusty octogenarian had been rector of three churches, with parishes that stretched from Yellow Springs through Radnor, past Valley Forge into the strongly Lutheran regions of the Perkiomen.

Currie was a Whig in politics, but he was royalist in his religion. Because the formal Church of England prayers required that every congregation pray for the health of King George and the royal family, the rector confined his rebel sentiments to unofficial weekday talks; on Sundays he prayed earnestly for British victory. No one could convince the argumentative Scot that Independence had modified the wording of the formal prayers. He would not listen to discussion.

Eventually, he gave way, but he did it in a typical Currie fashion. When, one Sunday, his congregation filed into the tiny vestibule of charming old St. David's Church, where the Waynes had been vestrymen for sixty years, they found a letter pinned to the vestry book. Signed by "your loving pastor," the note ran:

"You are not to expect me at Church any more till Circumstances are altered when it shall please God to restore me to a better State and I can with safety return to ye Exercise of my function."

Parson Currie retired into the Great Valley to live there until the Revolution should be over. He was delighted when the accidents of war brought him as a guest a fellow Scot with many of his own tastes. Mentally Stirling and Currie were kin.

Lafayette and Knox lived in stone houses on the east bank of Valley Creek. Each was outside the limits of the encampment, but neither was in an exposed position. Pickets gave ample protection against surprise attack.

Comte du Portail, the French engineer who was Washington's master of defense, was quartered near Lafayette and Knox. Unpopular among his fellows because of his cold, distant mannerisms, he had dared to rebuke Washington on the very day of his arrival in the army. "Learn then this lesson," he had lectured the astonished General. "See that you have an army of regulars before you attack. Remember, too, retreat is not defeat. The British can never conquer America so long as her army is intact." The perfection of the Valley Forge defenses was almost wholly due to Du Portail's sage counsel.

Now that his men were hutted and the officers assigned to quarters, Washington moved into his Headquarters. Mrs. Deborah Hewes had used the week to good advantage. Aided by a squad of soldiers assigned to assist her, she had transferred the major portions of her personal belongings to the near-by home of her Potts relatives. The mansion was available for Washington's use. Early in January, 1778, he entered into occupancy.

CHAPTER FIFTEEN

The Starving Time

THE Revolution was at its lowest ebb. The starving, freezing men who came to Valley Forge, seemingly deserted both by the Continental Congress and by their home states, were suffering privations. For a hundred days they had endured unspeakable conditions. Less than a third of all that time had been pleasant weather; the remainder of the long period had been marred by snow and rain and cold, by fog and by excessive heat. Their clothing was torn and water-soaked; their shoes, worn out; their health, seriously undermined. Their spirits were at last depressed.

The huts afforded some relief, for there was, at least, protection from the swirling snows. In the first hours of the camp, the residents of Valley Forge could offer comfort. By boiling up their small stock of coffee and by making flapjacks from their supplies of flour, the housewives cared for the immediate needs of a small portion of the army. Little ten-year-old Rachel Peck brought a pan of dried-up gingerbread, planning to wet it with water and feed it to sick soldiers, so that she, too, might show her patriotic ardor.

These were, however, only palliatives. The men, worn out

by their long marches in the storms, needed medicine and rest. They needed thousands of pounds of flour, and of rich, red meat. None of these were to be found at Valley Forge. For six long months the men were to suffer before they could emerge from camp a drilled, confident, and well fed army.

In every such emergency, the good humor of the soldiers was unquenchable. Although the men had scant patience for the selfish machinations of the politicians, and although they were quick to talk of mutiny and of desertion when Congressional stupidities or self-seeking ambition caused unnecessary hardship, they endured privation in good spirits. When, for example, rations were at their lowest quantity, soldiers opened their hut doors by a narrow crack to call after their captains, "No bread, no soldier," shutting the doors quickly when the officers wheeled about to see from whence the call had come.

Sullivan's brigade, hearing that Wayne's Pennsylvanians were ordered to dress up for a cleanliness parade, put on a special show to spoof Mad Anthony. Though they were in tatters, "with the remaining parts of their garments hanging in streamers behind them," they stuck sprigs of evergreen in their hats, and powdered their heads snow-white with flour that they had spared from their too scanty rations. The spectacle moved even the chaplain "to forget his gravity."

Albigence Waldo, the alert Connecticut surgeon whose diary is so packed with sparkling observations, reports that during the worst time, when the troops were drenched with icy rain, he heard two soldiers greeting each other with an exquisite politeness:

"Good morning, brother soldier, how are you this morning?"

"All wet, I thank 'e; hope you are so."

Waldo also mentions that during the bitter Christmas snowstorms at Valley Forge, while the freezing men were still shelterless and half starved, a soldier entertained his fellows in the evening by playing on the violin "in that soft kind of Musick which is so finely adapted to stirr up the tender Passions."

The most moving instance of all the camp, however, was that provided by Richard Wheeler of New York, who, during the privation period in January, 1778, wrote home reassuringly to tell his mother, "We are very comfortable and are living on the fat of the land."

The food supply was exhausted. Men complaining because they had eaten no meat during two full days of blinding snow, and because there was no bread, learned that there was not a single food animal in camp, and that the entire army of eleven thousand men must live on cakes of flour and water baked on flat stones set by the fires. The scanty rations were tasteless and repellent, resembling nothing quite so much as dried pasteboard, but the cakes were hot and stilled hunger temporarily. Not even this could long be offered for there were only twenty-five barrels of flour left in the cantonment.

Foraging was strictly forbidden but, under the circumstances, soldiers braved the threatened hundred lashes to secure mouthfuls of food. Friendly neighbors shared their little stores of food, and when better fare was not available the men snatched small handfuls of grain to chew the dry wheat fine and then wash it down with water. Chickens were fair game; a milch cow was regarded as a prize.

To protest against illegal raiding was not only unpatriotic but even inhuman; yet some of the near-by residents, realizing that their tiny food supplies would soon be gone unless they made complaint, plodded through the snow to Valley Forge. The generals listened sympathetically and promised to endeavor to restrain the men, knowing that little effective action could be taken. Five times within the first week of the arrival at Valley Forge, Washington issued peremptory commands forbidding his troops to leave camp for foraging, or for any other purpose, but the orders were invariably ignored. Even the officers connived at violation of the injunctions, preferring to regard their little shares of stolen food as did Albigence Waldo when, at midnight, "Providence sent us a little mutton."

After two weeks of indescribable privation, in January a slight spell of warmer weather thawed out the roads sufficiently for wagons to bring provisions into camp. The provender was not first-class, for it consisted largely of casks of salted herring so badly spoiled that the fish could not be drawn out singly but "had to be shovelled up en masse." The wagons brought a little flour and some rum, casks of vinegar which the men might use in place of fresh vegetables to ward off scurvy, and a trifle of fresh beef, so lean that, as the irrepressible jokers of the camp declared, "you could see the butcher's breeches through the meat." There was food enough on hand to grant each man four days' supply of fresh provisions.

The relief was only temporary. The January thaw was short-lived; new storms blew drifts of snow across the narrow roads. Great quantities of pork and beef, sent from New Jersey, could not be brought to camp for want of sufficient animals to haul the carts through heavy snows. Hundreds of barrels of flour lying on the banks of the Susquehanna perished for want of proper protection from the wet weather;

some, indeed, stayed on the river banks until spring freshets washed them downstream. The troops were again on the verge of starvation.

Much of the difficulty was traceable, no doubt, to the complete collapse of the commissariat. Sulking General Mifflin, presumably in charge of furnishing the army with sufficient food, was idling at Reading, carrying on his secret machinations in behalf of Gates and Conway. No one at Valley Forge was responsible for the carriage of supplies, nor for the securing of sufficient horses and wagons. Congress, now reduced to a dozen active members and these chiefly unimportant people not needed in the local governments, cared little for the army's needs.

The lack of horses and wagons worked extraordinary hardship on the men. Camp transportation of food and fuel and munitions had to be performed by soldiers yoked to sledges or to long poles dragged Indian-fashion upon the snow. Patiently, they carried wood upon their backs, or buckets on their heads. A wagonload of straw would undoubtedly have saved the lives of many sick men forced otherwise to die upon hard boards or even on the cold, wet earth, but close to camp the straw was not obtainable. Three thousand shovels, needed for entrenching tools, a large amount of tent cloth, and fifty wagonloads of clothing were ready for army use, but had to be stored in distant barns because there was no transportation.

Congress, however, took little heed of these conditions until the military aspect of the matter was brought home to it by Francis Dana, the inspecting officer. "Should the enemy, encouraged by the growing weakness of your troops, be led to make a successful impression upon your camp," he told Congress, "your artillery would now undoubtedly fall into their hands for want of horses to remove it." Dana added that the loss of the artillery would be a smaller and more tolerable evil than the imminence of famine; but the money loss involved in replacing the cannon weighed more heavily with Congress than the sacrifice of men. Congress felt that it had done its duty when it ordered eight thousand barrels of flour to be sent to the army storage house.

Finding the flour was more difficult than Congress had assumed. The rich Great Valley, once the most fertile section of the state, had been exhausted of supplies. During four months, foragers from both the British and the American armies had drawn their food supplies from the immediate vicinity of Valley Forge. Twenty-four thousand men, relying for almost their entire support upon the farms of this locality, had drained the granaries. The British could rely for further food on southern New Jersey and, indeed, on provender brought up the Delaware in ships, but the Americans had no such recourse. Their food could only come from distant in-land farms.

The narrow roads were blocked by snow. Great drifts filled up the passes through the hills. Heavy four-horse wagons, caught by the storms, stood frozen in the ruts. The riverside road from Reading to the camp was lined with stalled carts, abandoned until warmer weather should release them from the ice and snow.

Further difficulties stemmed from the plan of organization of the service of supply. The wagonmasters were a virtually independent group. Using their own horses and their own covered wagons, hiring their neighbors as assistants, they were often free from army discipline. Officers could ask for definite supplies, but if the wagonmasters thought that need for other goods was greater, or that search for different commodities would take them over better roads, the wagoners might disregard the orders. Because they paid in cash for flour, meat, straw, and fodder, trusting to be reimbursed from military funds, certain of the wagonmen preferred to speculate. Under the chaotic methods of administration, with no strict, central control, the transport system acted almost as it pleased.

Even when the food did arrive, it often came in bad condition. Wagoners hauling heavy loads through snowy passes soon learned to lighten their wagons by pouring off the brine in which the meat was kept, or by dumping the flour from the barrels into the body of the wagon. Often the food was spoiled by such exposure to the weather.

Even spoiled meat was often impossible to secure when snows swept the camp. In theory, the men drew regular daily rations. Congress had laid down a rule that each man should receive a pound of bread and a pound of meat per day, together with a pint of milk, a gill of peas or beans, a small amount of butter, and a quart of beer. After the arrival at Valley Forge, the ration was cut down, omitting the milk and beer and vegetables and reducing the meat allowance to three-quarters of a pound, but raising the issue of bread or flour to a pound and a half. But even so the camp did not possess sufficient food to grant each man his regular allowance.

So hungry were the soldiers that when supplies trickled into camp the men pounced upon the food without waiting to cook it. "I found a barrel of shad," wrote one hungry militiaman, "and voraciously fell to eating them raw and I thought them the best I had ever eaten."

Hundreds of the officers, considering that the cause was lost, resigned their commissions; some of the army's fourteen chaplains, realizing that men in such straits "would not listen to sermons," went home; even the hard-pressed surgeons sought leaves of absence. Wayne himself talked darkly of desertion unless he was granted leave of absence.

Yet, while the generals were despairing, and while Varnum was telling Greene that "in all human probability the army must soon dissolve," the men were steadfast. Only after some brigades had gone a week without a taste of meat, and when word leaked out that the quartermasters were considering a still further reduction in the already tiny rations, did they begin arriving at Headquarters, hat in hand, to ask Washington for help.

At such a juncture, while a howling snowstorm blanketed the hills with icy torture, Washington wrote to Governor George Clinton of New York his famous tribute to the common soldier: "Naked and starving as they are, we cannot enough admire the incomparable patience and fidelity of the soldiery."

Lafayette, too, was expressing wonder at the devotion of the troops. "The unfortunate soldiers were in want of everything; they had neither coats, hats, shirts, nor shoes; their feet and legs froze till they had become almost black, and it was often necessary to amputate them. . . . The patient endurance of both soldiers and officers was a miracle which each moment served to renew."

Reluctantly, Washington was compelled to issue orders to requisition food, animals, and clothing. Using authority conferred upon him by Congress prior to his arrival at the camp, he wrote instructions to Anthony Wayne and other generals.

"I authorize and empower and command you forthwith to take, carry off, and secure all such horses as are suitable for cavalry or for draft, and all cattle and sheep fit for slaughter, together with every kind of forage for the use of the army, that may be found in the possession of any of the inhabitants, causing certificates to be given to each person for the number, value, and quantity of the horses, sheep, cattle, and provisions so taken."

Under such commissions, foragers were sent into the already well scoured regions of Pennsylvania and New Jersey, and even into Maryland, Delaware and Virginia. Seven thousand cattle and eighteen thousand barrels of flour would, it was estimated, be required for a three months' stay at Valley Forge. No such vast quantities were available, but Wayne found sufficient livestock to gain himself the nickname "Wayne, the Drover."

The resort to commandeering did not imply that communities should be completely stripped of their possessions. Devault Beaver, living on the farm next to Wayne's quarters, complained to Mad Anthony that a soldier came each morning to rob him of milk. When Wayne, preoccupied, seemed not to listen, Beaver impatiently asked what action he should take.

"Shoot him," snapped Wayne.

When the marauder called at dawn to milk the Beaver cow, young Devault followed the suggestion. He shot the soldier. Then, fearing court-martial for murder, the boy secretly buried the body at a fence corner on the farm. Years later, when a post-hole digger accidentally uncovered the bones, the soldier was reburied near Fort Huntingdon in Valley Forge Park.

Because some farmers preferred to sell their wares directly rather than receive commandeering certificates, Washington ordered markets to be opened. Twice a week, at each of three different places in the camp, goods could be sold at definite prices fixed after consultation between the farmers and the commissary officers. Horses and wagons hauling food to camp were safe against impressment, and officers were stationed at the market places to guard farmers against thieves.

In comparison with the prices paid by the British during the partial siege of Philadelphia, the schedules set at Valley Forge were low. For butter, the British had given seven shillings a pound, but the Valley Forge market set three shillings sixpence as a proper price; potatoes had fetched sixteen shillings a bushel at Philadelphia, but only ten shillings at the encampment; fat chickens like those for which redcoats had paid ten shillings were sold to Continentals for two shillings and a half; veal had brought four shillings per pound at Philadelphia but only tenpence at Valley Forge.

The prices asked at Philadelphia had been inflated. They had dropped considerably by the time that Washington's market opened at Valley Forge, but there was still sufficient difference between the scales to induce some loyalist sympathizers to smuggle food into the city. Most of the near-by supplies were sold, however, at the encampment markets.

Soldiers competed eagerly for the privilege of buying at the market. Few had hard cash, and even the less valued Continental currency was rare; but by chipping together their pence, hutmates could buy a fat goose or a dozen eggs for a shilling; or, for four shillings, they could buy a barrel of hard cider. Some sold their clothing or equipment in exchange for liquor.

Army officers, fearing the effects of too abundant cheap liquor, then established a special sutler system for alcoholic drinks. To discourage the use of whiskey, rum, and brandy,

172

prices were raised to four shillings a quart; cider was increased to a shilling a quart; but beer was reduced in cost. Soldiers could buy "small beer" at the sutlery for a shilling a quart instead of the old market price of a shilling tenpence. No other liquor selling was permitted within seven miles of the camp.

As an additional encouragement for near-by farm products to be brought to market, access to the camp was made easier from the eastern bank of the Schuylkill. During the first part of the winter, arrivals from the Fatlands were obliged to cross the river on the ice or to ford the stream. Later, when the coldest period was believed to have passed, Sullivan was ordered to build a bridge over the stream, close to the Fatland ford.

Sullivan and his New Hampshire men, tired of camp routine, welcomed the opportunity for employment. Log piers were driven deep into the stony bottom of the shallow ford and were protected against ice floes and freshets by stone-filled log boxes. Timbers were laid from pier to pier across the stream and split logs were put down for flooring.

The bridge was rough and narrow. The split tree-trunks, laid flat side down against the sleepers, offered only a rounded, rugged surface for the traveler, and cart wheels caught in the grooves between the logs; but dry passage was now possible. The twelve-foot width was enough for most of the anticipated traffic, and although the floor was not much above the level of the water, the height was believed ample even for the spring freshets.

The men, proud of their quickly built bridge, decorated it with carvings. Each span between the piers was carved with the name of a major general, the central honor being reserved for Washington. Then, because Sullivan expected that the

173

bridge would remain "until the wood decays," the date 1778 was cut deeply into the timber as a memorial of his work.

Sullivan's Bridge allowed the camp limits to be widened. A large detachment of the troops was no longer needed to guard the western Schuylkill shore, and men could be transferred into the Fatland regions. More mills and farm lands were thus drawn into the constant service of the camp. Pickets were thrown farther into the countryside; more good houses were available for quarters. Sullivan's Bridge, guarded by a small picket party on each shore of the stream, afforded opportunity for wagons to haul more abundant food supplies into the encampment proper.

The worst starving times were drawing to a close. Wayne the Drover was forwarding supplies to camp; Nathanael Greene, newly appointed quartermaster general, was increasing the supply of wagons and was making the commissariat into a more efficient agency; new food areas were being opened for camp use; the confidence of farmers in the Continental cause was being steadily revived. The army's morale was strengthening.

Then, dramatically, the famine completely ended. Countless thousands of fat shad, swimming up the Schuylkill to spawn, filled the river. Sullivan's men, accustomed to treading out fresh-water mussels in the stream, were astonished to see the water almost boiling with the struggling fish.

Soldiers thronged the river bank. Then, at the advice of Pennsylvanians accustomed to the yearly fishing, the cavalry was ordered into the river bed. Carrying huge bushes, broken tree boughs, and long sticks, the horsemen rode upstream, noisily shouting and beating the water, driving the shad before them into nets spread across the Schuylkill at Pawling's ford, where the Perkiomen flows into the river.

So thick were the shad that, when the fish were cornered in the nets, a pole could not be thrust into the water without striking fish. Thousands of the tasty, rich shad were netted at each haul. The netting was continued day after day, with more than a hundred horsemen continually beating the water, until the army was thoroughly stuffed with fish and in addition hundreds of barrels of shad were salted down for future use. The lavish fish feast was a dramatic close to a long period of privation.

CHAPTER SIXTEEN

Fighting the Fever

COLD could be attacked by blazing campfires, hunger might be stayed by thorough foraging, even insufficient clothing could be eked out by the men's borrowing garments from one another; but the suffering Continentals faced an even graver enemy than these. The men were sick, and, in their weakened condition at Valley Forge, the illnesses were spreading.

Washington had no adequate medical service; his hospitals were small, scattered, and inefficient; his drug supply was unreliable. Ships from the West Indies and from France brought needed medicines, but not at stated times. The drugs came unexpectedly and with no regard for army requisitions. The few physicians with the troops relied on makeshift medicines, experimented with substitutes, or tried to cure the cases without drugs. Wherever possible, they sent their sick men home. Even the wounded were often thrown upon their own resources.

Not all of this neglect was due to mismanagement or to carelessness; more was caused by the general medical ignorance of Revolutionary times. In most respects, the better cared-for British army was in the same plight as the American soldiers. The Britishers, however, had the great advantage of comforts and resources the rebels wholly lacked.

When Washington hurried out of Philadelphia to fight at Brandywine, his men were ailing. Fully a quarter of the army should have been on sick leave, but instead the men marched on during weeks of heat and almost endless rain, sleeping in the soggy fields and eating insufficient, badly prepared food. The invalids did not falter.

Even the wounded carried on. Six hundred men hurt at Brandywine and four hundred more shot in the Germantown engagement were quickly sorted into groups. Those with minor injuries struggled on foot to medical attention; graver cases were hauled in open, springless wagons fifty miles or more to the base hospitals; only the most serious casualties were cared for on the spot. In many cases, especially after Brandywine, hours elapsed before the hard-worked surgeons could attend to all.

Such was the vigor of the farm-bred boys that, even under conditions of neglect, ill feeding, and exposure, the rugged lads survived. Many of the ill even regained their strength and returned to active duty. Malnutrition, hardship, and lack of sanitation were endured. In spite of their fatiguing marches, the men long remained in a surprisingly healthy state.

Not even the strongest constitutions could, however, endure the long continued strain on their vitality. Wet weather, hunger, and privations sapped the army's strength. Three thousand men were reported as unfit for duty in the first sick roll at Valley Forge. Within a month, eleven hundred more were added to the list. On one day alone, more than a third of all the soldiers were ordered sent to hospitals.

No hospital facilities were available for such an enormous

total as the four thousand men certified as sick. Bare log huts, equipped with crude bunks and a rough board operating table, had been hastily run up for emergency hospital use at Valley Forge; but these slab-floored hovels cared for only a small proportion of the seriously ill. Less than 5 per cent of the invalids could be treated in the eleven so-called hospitals.

Private homes, churches, meetinghouses and the few existing schools were commandeered for medical quarters. The beautiful church at Trappe, where Muhlenberg was pastor, was among the first to be filled with sick and wounded. Its well proportioned pews were torn away; the curious gallery from which restless boys had peered down upon their elders during the long German sermons, lost its rows of benches; the tall white pulpit became a storage place for the scanty medical supplies. Valley Meetinghouse, on a rolling knoll close to Rehobeth, was filled with ailing soldiers; its near-by burying ground, donated by pioneering Lewis Walker, became crowded with the dead.

Sympathetic folk of the Great Valley willingly granted the use of their barns and other buildings for hospitals, but a few Tory partisans resented the taking of their property for even humanitarian purposes. Forcible entry was sometimes necessary in such cases, and inevitably injustices were perpetrated on the innocent. Quakers, who conscientiously objected to all forms of force, complained that they had been bound and beaten. In one instance, a man had been dragged along the roads by ropes tied to horses, because he would not yield his barn for army use. Such abuse was, however, rare, and was almost always due to soldier tactlessness in failing to make clear that the commandeering was for noncombatant and medical purposes.

HEADQUARTERS IN MIDWINTER

(Courtesy Valley Forge Park Commission)

ARMY HOSPITAL

THE SURGERY

*Reproduction, by Valley Forge Park Commission, of huts
used at the time of the encampment. (Courtesy Valley
Forge Park Commission and Mrs. W. Herbert Burk)*

The shortage of special hospitals prevented the isolation of the sick. Men suffering from minor ailments stayed in their huts where they infected their healthier comrades. Thus the bothersome itchy scabies passed through the camp until the army was intolerably affected by the disease.

Soap and water could have cured most cases of this burning itch between the fingers and the toes; but soap was scarce. Three ounces of soft soap per week, or a single ounce of hard cake-soap, was all that could be spared for a man to cleanse himself, his cooking kit, and his clothing.

Water was too scarce to be used except in the rarest emergencies. After an autumn of incessant rain, when the men had been constantly drenched to the skin, the soldiers were undergoing a veritable drought. Their diaries indicate the straits to which the encampment was reduced.

"We had no tents nor anithing to Cook our Provisions in, and that was Prity Poor," wrote Elijah Fisher, "for beef was very lean and no salt, nor any way to Cook it but to throw it on the Coles and brile it; and the warter we had to Drink and to mix our flower with was out of a brook that run along by the Camps, and so many a dippin and washin it which maid it very Dirty and muddy."

The water supply was always a serious Valley Forge problem. Save the New Englanders posted along the Schuylkill, few of the troops had easy access to a stream. Trout Run, half a mile south of the encampment beyond the outer line of entrenchments, was the most convenient, for the only other running water was at Valley Creek, at the foot of a steep, thickly forested hill. Only two wells, at extreme ends of the campgrounds, were available.

Experiments made by the Pennsylvania Germans were failures. Taught by their *Hexenmeisters* that water could be discovered by magic rites, the trusting boys called in witch doctors to find hidden springs. Carefully, the diviners cut forked witch-hazel sticks, pronouncing proper incantations. Then, holding a branch in each hand between their thumbs and forefingers, palms held toward their faces, the twig ends pointing down, the hexers slowly walked through the encampment. When a spring was passed, they knew, the magic rod would suddenly bend downward.

Although the experiment was tried with witch-hazel and with peach-tree twigs, no sudden twisting of the rods betrayed the presence of a spring. The twigs were cut, the *Hexenmeisters* explained, at the wrong season of the year. Nor would rods cut in other regions prove successful, they declared; each district answered only to wands found in its own locality.

While the snowstorms were heaviest, the troops got a little water by melting fallen snow; but the supply was small. Snow was soiled too quickly, nor were even the heavy falls sufficient to give water for eleven thousand men. During the six months' stay at Valley Forge, most of the water was laboriously carried uphill from the creeks and river. Soldiers detailed on water duty carried splashing buckets in both hands for the comrades in their huts.

So long as the army had been moving, some of the more serious diseases had been avoided. By quick removal of the men from one encampment to another, much of the danger of infection had been averted. Filth-bred sickness and the carriage of germs by flies and mosquitoes had been thus cut to a minimum.

There was, however, no escape at Valley Forge. None knew during the Revolutionary War that germs were spread by parasites and that the primitive sanitation methods condemned a stationary army to typhus and smallpox epidemics. The latter might be partially controlled, physicians believed, by inoculating soldiers with mild cases of the disease, and orders were accordingly issued compelling soldiers to receive inoculation; but no means were known for stopping the dreaded typhus, or camp fever.

Both ailments began with very similar symptoms. High fever, rigor, headache, and sleeplessness were the first indications; the sufferers turned dusky red. Soon the smallpox patients could be detected, by characteristic vomiting and by the appearance of the telltale blisters; but typhus was more subtle and more deadly. A stage followed in the development of camp fever when the patient seemed to mend; the headaches passed; the condition seemed much easier. Over and over again, the Revolutionary doctors were deceived into the belief that the disease had been averted.

The errors were costly. The apparent relief was disastrous. Soon the typhus patients lay in wide-eyed stupor on the straw pallets of the badly ventilated huts.

Even when the disease was properly diagnosed, the treatment was often ineffective. Typhus patients need nothing quite so much as milk, cleanliness, good nursing, sedatives, and delicate attention. These were difficult to guarantee at Valley Forge. The parasites which carry the disease were not regarded then as dangerous, and thus infection was renewed; opium was scarce; the instruments which doctors so urgently required were almost wholly absent. Mutton broth and wine were inadequate substitutes for the milk which the patients needed.

Medical supplies were difficult to secure. Drugs were unobtainable, especially in pure condition; bandages were insufficient; molasses, then the chief sugar substitute, and wine, a necessary stimulant, were completely exhausted long before the epidemics were stopped. Coffee, tea, chocolate could not be procured; salt was lacking; even vinegar, essential as a preventive against scurvy, was high-priced and scarce.

Dr. Bodo Otto, friend of Muhlenberg and chief surgeon of the middle states, tried to guarantee a constant supply of necessary goods by encouraging the establishment of monopolies for the manufacture of vinegar and whisky. Otto pointed out that whisky could be produced at a dollar a gallon, instead of the prevalent price of two dollars and a half, that vinegar could be made for ten dollars a barrel, about half the current cost, and that pigs, fed on the waste products of the distilleries, could yield pork at seven dollars a hundredweight instead of the thirteen dollars then paid for pork. The Government, Otto pointed out, would save about sixty thousand dollars yearly if the plan were accepted; but the influence of speculators was too strong in Congress. The scheme was disapproved.

At Washington's suggestion, Dr. Otto was commissioned to build a big base hospital at Yellow Springs, eight miles west at the forks of Pickering Creek, where Wayne's men had enjoyed their beef feast after the abortive Battle of the Clouds. Yellow Springs had long been famous as a health resort. Its chalybeate waters, deeply tinted with iron, were regarded as particularly healing for palsy, nervousness, rheumatism and "all complaints showing debility and languour." Fashionable Philadelphians, often to the number of four hundred daily, had frequented Yellow Springs as a summer resort. Old Adam Ramsower, later host at the Spread Eagle, had made the resort a place of gayety and comparable to England's Bath.

So merry, indeed, had Yellow Springs become under the

Ramsower regime, that near-by Uwchlan monthly meeting had expressed a deep concern that the frivolities of Yellow Springs might prove corrupting to Quaker youth. The Uwchlan influence had been sufficiently strong to cause Ramsower to abandon Yellow Springs for the more centrally located Spread Eagle.

Yellow Springs became, then, the site of the chief Revolutionary hospital. Aided by Dr. Samuel Kennedy, patriotic owner of the springs, Otto erected the only hospital specially designed for soldier use. The three-story Washington Hall, begun in January, 1778, was a hundred feet in length and thirty-six feet wide, surrounded on three sides by wide porches on which, in warm weather, convalescents might rest. During the Valley Forge encampment period, more than thirteen hundred patients, chiefly typhus cases, were cared for by Kennedy, Otto, and their few assistants. So skillful were these men, in days when medicine was crude, that fewer than one-sixth of the patients died. One of these, unhappily, was Dr. Kennedy himself, a victim of the typhus which he fought so earnestly.

Other hospitals, more remote from Valley Forge, received their share of patients. Forty miles west, the Spiritual Virgins of the Adventist community at Ephrata turned over their tall, steep-roofed cloister buildings for hospital purposes. The veiled and hooded Sisters, trailing their long woolen gowns up the narrow, ladderlike stairs, nursed the men incessantly. Their few leisure moments were devoted to smoothing linen with the heavy blocks of wood which Ephrata preferred to "sinful" iron tools, and to chanting, in the well trained voices which Ephrata cherished, hymns for the recovery of the wounded. Meanwhile, the long-bearded Solitary Brethren, cowled and gowned, labored in the fields and mills, or helped with the emergency operations in the gloomy cloisters.

Northeast of Valley Forge, at Bethlehem, fifty miles away, the song-loving Moravians turned their entire town into a hospital. Their medieval buildings, centered round the old Sun Inn, housed hundreds of the Continental sick. Lafayette was brought here after Brandywine; the Germantown wounded found solace among the peaceful Druid-looking brethren. These nonresistant pacifists worked hard, for after their nursing hours they served in prayer bands to keep up "hourly intercessions"; they sang chorals in their *Stunden;* they held all-night vigils in their chapel and in the big Bell House that had been built across the main street of the settlement.

Gradually, as the Yellow Springs base hospital grew larger, the auxiliary hospitals closed their doors. The institution at Lititz, in the Pennsylvania German country, closed; Bethlehem transferred its patients to Otto's care at Yellow Springs; the smaller, temporary hospitals at Princeton, Burlington, and Trenton, at Reading, Allentown, and Trappe, at Easton and at Manheim, where the lordly glassmaker "Baron" Henry William Stiegel lived, were no longer necessary. The emergency quarters for the wounded in the Quaker meeting-houses and in wayside churches were restored to their congregations.

At no time, however, during the period of the Valley Forge encampment were sufficient medical men available. The few surgeons, working by rush-light candles well into the night, worked incessantly with their heavy saws and long unsterilized shears to care for wounded men. Gangrene was a common ailment, for the surgeons, wholly unaware of the ill effects of their treatment, allowed wounds to fester; pus

184

formation, it was thought, was cleansing for the body. Cartridge burns were disregarded; often, the physicians deliberately dropped burning powder into a wound to cauterize the hurt.

Trained assistants were impossible to secure. Nursing was not yet a skilled profession. The "surgeons' mates" who aided in operations, and who gave the small amount of after care then provided for a patient, were too frequently either convalescent soldiers or volunteers conscientiously opposed to bearing arms. Seldom did the surgeons' mates possess much knowledge of medical matters. Chosen haphazardly, their work was often inefficient, if not indeed actually harmful.

Physicians, too, were chosen with too slight regard for their attainments. Formal medical training had not yet been established. Young apprentices, observing the methods of their masters, gained a sketchy knowledge of scientific practice. Frequently they began to care for patients with no real knowledge of the art of healing. The army accepted almost anyone who cared to offer his services as a physician.

The annals of the Pennsylvania Line reveal an unusual case in a surgeon of the Seventh Pennsylvania. During the period when medical men were most needed, a prepossessing foreigner, apparently well versed in military matters, arrived to seek a Continental commission. Giving his name as John Rose, he said that he had been a medical student, and that he had served in the Russian army. On the strength of his supposed experience, the suave Russian was appointed surgeon, but after Brandywine and Paoli he was found so incompetent that he was reduced in rank and was transferred to hospital duty as a surgeon's mate.

Rose almost immediately disappeared, to turn up later during the Valley Forge winter, under the new name of

Gustavus Henderson. He had deserted, he declared, in order to study surgery. The pressing need for medical men caused his desertion to be overlooked, and Henderson, or Rose, was reinstated. The hostility of his mates, however, caused the Russian to resign his army career and to join the navy as surgeon of the *Revenge*. Captured almost immediately by the British, he was exchanged and, under his old name of John Rose, he rejoined the army as lieutenant and aide-de-camp to Pennsylvania's General William Irvine. When the war had finished, he had so regained his popularity as to be chosen as an army lobbyist to secure bounty lands from the State of Pennsylvania. He returned to Europe in 1784 and died in 1830.

Years later, in October 1893, the true story of John Rose was discovered. Born Gustavus H. de Rosenthal, baron of Livonia, he had killed another nobleman in a duel within the precincts of Catherine the Great's palace at St. Petersburg. Fearing the Tsarina's anger, he had fled to England and later to Baltimore, where he took a brief course in surgery. After his failures at Brandywine and Paoli, he had gone back to Baltimore for further medical instruction. After the Revolution, winning Catherine's forgiveness, he returned to Russia and become Grand Marshal of Livonia. At the express wish of the democratic Alexander, tsar after 1801, Baron de Rosenthal invariably wore the emblem of the Order of the Cincinnati.

The ease with which the quickly trained John Rose twice gained appointment as a surgeon indicates the low standards in existence. Such men, however, cared for only the more extreme cases of suffering; in most instances the men were thrown upon their own resources.

For the prevention of minor ailments, Washington ordered

that the huts be purified. Each day, during the long winter, a cartridge was burned to dispel the noxious air. When spring brought warmer weather, the clay which chinked the logs against cold drafts was knocked away. To the distress of many of the men who thought the night air dangerous, fresh winds blew through the huts.

The spring brought new relief. Almost all the soldiers, particularly those versed in wilderness lore gleaned from the Indians, were firm in the belief that certain common herbs were sovereign remedies. As soon as weeds began to grow, the soldiers scattered fan-wise through the open fields to search for these specifics.

They sought, especially, the sour sorrel dock, for this was good to cure the burning itch between the toes. Sores that still remained unhealed, after the hard winter of neglect, could now be salved by the inner bark of elderberries, or by young magnolia bark if burned to charcoal and mixed with fat. Burdock cured the fever, as did fern; the mustard-yellow sassafras blossom purified and thinned the blood; bark of wild cherry and of cedar trees was good as tonic; even torn, frostbitten feet might be restored, the soldiers thought, by bathing them in beech-leaf tea. So confident were the soldiers that the worst privations were now over that they gave more thought to their appearance. They gathered up the big white dogwood leaves, stripped the trees of bark, and made a brew to make their hair grow thicker. Unquestionably it was a happy sign of a restored morale when Continental soldiers spruced up, of their own accord, in the bright warm sunshine of Valley Forge.

CHAPTER SEVENTEEN

"We Fear the Yankees"

DISPIRITED and hungry men are never reasonable. Cold and hardship, disappointment and defeat, tried the temper of the troops. Each separate state contingent, proud of its own record, accused all the rest of being lukewarm to the Revolution.

Pennsylvanians, for example, hated and distrusted Yankees. Mild-mannered Major Persifor Frazer burned with indignation at the "low, dirty, griping, cowardly, lying rascals" who came from New England. It was strong language for a patriot to employ, especially for one who had entered the war with such high regard for Massachusetts' brave stand against oppression, but Frazer was disillusioned. He thought the Yankees undependable; he believed them soft; he questioned their cleanliness; he did not like their looks.

"The miserable appearance, and what is worse, the miserable behavior of the Yankees is enough," he told his wife, "to make me sick of the service." He was a pioneer abolitionist, and he was a thorough believer in human equality, but he could not endure the New England mixed battalions. "Among them is the strangest mixture of Negroes and Indians and whites, with old men and young children which, together

188

with a nasty, lousy appearance, makes a most shocking spectacle." Frazer wished that the New Englanders would stay at home.

Frazer was, to be sure, but one individual, and his hot prejudice was not the general opinion of all the middle states, but he was, next to Anthony Wayne, the most influential citizen of his locality. His fears that New England planned to substitute a Yankee tyranny for that of England gripped the farmers in the neighborhood of Valley Forge. Undoubtedly his strictures against Northerners were potent in rousing public sentiment against the Massachusetts men.

There were, however, more evident causes for anti-Yankee feeling. Chaplains and surgeons, fleeing the rigors of the camp, gave New England a bad reputation. "The Boston surgeons" were notorious for seeking furloughs during the worst days of the suffering. Physicians from other New England states joined with the doctors in charge of the medical department in criticizing their Boston colleagues. When one of the worst offenders was cashiered "for lying and deceit" in applying for a furlough, forthright Albigence Waldo of Connecticut approved the sentence. "I wish," he said, "that his cursed tongue was pulled out for thus giving an example of scandal."

Mary Taylor Frazer, Persie Frazer's wife, made it her business to acquaint the neighborhood with her husband's idea of New England character. She and her indefatigable companion, Jane Sheward Gibbons, were no quiet, self-effacing housewives content to stay at home wringing their hands while history was in the making. They had already descended upon Howe, demanding their cattle and insisting that British jailers give the prisoners enough to eat. Their energy, intelligence, and force of character were familiar to the farmers.

Through their tireless efforts, the neighborhood, already "middling well reconciled to independency," began to think that Pennsylvania ought to set up a nation of its own. "We very much fear," she said, "the heavy taxes which are to come upon us, but above all we fear the New Englanders." George III was preferred over the "Eastern people."

If the white facings of the Yankee uniforms were not well liked in Pennsylvania, however, neither the New Englanders nor the blue-uniformed Southerners approved the Pennsylvanians. There was, to Massachusetts minds, something sinister about the red trimmings of the Pennsylvania costumes. The known Tory sympathies of prosperous Philadelphians, the pacifism of the Quaker farmers, seemed to smack of redcoat sympathy. Pennsylvania was accused of being niggardly in offering supplies, of being slow to enlist her militiamen, of arrogance in her demands.

The intercolonial quarrels were love feasts in comparison to the intense feeling against the French. From the very highest quarters in the army down to the lowest recruit there was resentment over the preference granted to the foreigners. Washington complained of the "swarms" of French adventurers who were applying for commissions as field officers in the Continental army. He feared "the driving of our own officers out of the service and throwing not only our army, but our military councils, entirely into the hands of Foreigners." He protested against the appointment to the army of field officers who had "no attachment nor ties to the country further than interest binds them," and he appealed to Colonel Alexander Spottswood, in creating a headquarters guard, to "send me none but Natives and Men of some property, if you have them." But, with characteristic caution, Washington added, in his Spottswood letter, the request that the colonel "give no intimation of my preference of Natives, as I do not want to create any invidious Distinction between them and the Foreigners."

Kalb and Lafayette were conscious of the antiforeign feeling, but they were more acutely aware that certain of the foreigners well merited the opposition. While Lafayette was recuperating from his Brandywine wounds he wrote to his wife: "All the other foreigners now employed here are discontented and complaining; they are filled with hatred toward others, and they are hated themselves." Kalb, writing to his wife from Valley Forge, was more specific. He mentioned "the mutual jealousy of almost all the French officers, particularly against those of higher rank than the rest. These people think of nothing but their incessant intrigues and backbitings. They hate each other like the bitterest enemies and endeavor to injure each other wherever an opportunity offers."

Among the upper officers, the international conflict could be conducted by political intrigue and poison propaganda; the lower rankers had no such delicate recourse. When the common soldiers clashed, the customary arguments were with knives and guns. The soldiers went so far as to demand that Burgoyne's British troops be given arms to help the Continentals fight the French allies!

As though the conflicts between the natives and foreigners and between the soldiers from different sections were not sufficient to wreck good-fellowship, the morale was further weakened by jealousies among the officers. The claims of Continental privates to outrank the state militia officers were soon dismissed, but the regulars continued to demand superiority over militiamen of equal rank. Quarrels over precedence created much disturbance, despite the ruling by the high command that length of service should be regarded as the final test. An army that supposedly was democratic set great store on social status.

All the officers, whether national or local, were agreed, however, on their right to special privilege. Whenever the troops were on the march an unconscionable proportion of the wagon train lugged huge trunks of spare uniforms and many chests of household wares. Even when battle loomed, as in the week before Brandywine, certain dandies refused to part with their finery. The army did not dress for dinner, to be sure, but the practice would surely have been welcomed by the more fastidious set. In a period of charming weather, when the mornings were cool but the middle of the day was sultry, the daintier leaders insisted that both winter greatcoats and summer uniforms be carried as essential baggage. Washington was induced to yield the point although he hoped to limit each man's baggage to blankets, greatcoats and three shifts of underwear. The dandies were quite ready to sacrifice the army's elasticity of movement for the vanity of a well groomed appearance.

The élite refused to yield one other perquisite. High rank implied the right to ride; to walk seemed a confession of inferiority. Washington complained that the number of horses had so increased that the animals were a nuisance. He hoped that none but the higher leaders would keep mounts, but he reckoned without full knowledge of the pride of position. Prestige required that every officer be furnished with a batman, but Arnold demanded a personal guard of twelve men; and one happy clique of two generals and two colonels believed that twenty-four soldiers should be assigned them for their private service. Even these assistants thought it was beneath their dignity to walk with common rankers. Indeed, as the march progressed, the lower officers, who were not entitled to the ease of horseback travel, commandeered farm horses for their private use. Legally, no requisition should be honored unless the officer produced an order from the quartermaster general or a special permit from the Commander-in-chief, but farmers dared not protest against the seizure. To enter an objection was too sure a proof of Tory sympathy.

By January, it was evident that the presence of a herd of unauthorized horses was a decided drain upon the limited supply of forage. Supposedly, each saddle horse was allowed fourteen pounds of hay and six quarts of oats per day; draft animals received a larger ration. But there was insufficient fodder to provide for all the horses, and, when the quartermasters refused to feed the privately owned animals, the owners rode out from camp to plunder the neighbors.

Washington tried in vain to limit these illegal raids. On Christmas Day he ordered strict punishment to any person "caught riding in or out of camp." Two weeks later, finding that his orders were evaded, he asked officially that no one keep a horse unless expressly authorized to do so by act of Congress. "Even to them it is recommended to part with their horses if they can."

The recommendation was unheeded. The desire to maintain prestige was paramount. As a result, fifteen hundred horses starved to death. Meanwhile, for want of good draft animals, scores of army wagons, full of needed stores, lay helpless along country roads. So many horses perished that the hungry soldiers had insufficient strength to bury the carcasses. Dead horses accumulated faster than they could be hauled away. The camp became intolerable. Washington, riding through the lines, was aghast at the uncleanliness. The health of Continental troops was undermined by the appalling lack of sanitation in the camp.

Undoubtedly, the soldiers had but slight respect for official orders, particularly when strife was evident within the high command itself. The lack of confidence by troops was a direct reflection of the disturbed conditions among the higher officers themselves. For weeks after the arrival of the men at Valley Forge, the camp was torn by jealousies, recriminations, and suspicions.

Even the generals did not trust one another. When Congress planned to push Du Coudray over the heads of native-born American generals, Nathanael Greene, John Sullivan, and Henry Knox threatened to hand in their resignations. Congress was prepared to let them go rather than allow the army chiefs to dictate to the civilian government, but the crisis passed when Du Coudray was drowned in fording the Schuylkill.

Washington pathetically pleaded with his officers to cease their bickerings and to look upon themselves as "a band of Brothers cemented by the Justice of the Common Cause." He asked for perfect harmony and urged that they resolve their personal disputes in amicable fashion, but the generals were not so easily persuaded. Feuds continued; jealousies were common. Hotheaded General Jim Potter, for example, trained on the frontier to distrust the sleek and polished city dweller, distrusted his lawyer-comrade General Sullivan. In private counsel and in military message Potter cast disparagement upon his fellow Irishman, nor did he voice a syllable of sorrow when Sullivan, attacked for inefficiency, stormed later out of army service.

John Lacey had neglected a minor order from Wayne and had received a mild rebuke. This reprimand struck deep. "This was a Thunder Bolt I had not foreseen nor expected, therefore, taken by Surprise, an Electricity that Vibrated through every nerve." He considered himself humbled by a tyrannical and haughty autocrat. Wayne, evidently startled by the underofficer's reception of the hasty reprimand, tried to mend matters by inviting Lacey to dine with him "off a roasted pig." Lacey obeyed the order, though he considered it another proof of Wayne's capricious temper; but he certainly did not enjoy the meal. "It was well Cooked and very nice, but I felt such a load of Degradation, of injured innocence, of the purest motives of Patriotism, such a deadly blow to all my future hopes of comfort or preferment under such an absolute, such a Tyrent and Partial, commander, I had not appetite."

Lacey tried to resign, but Wayne refused to let him go. Instead of realizing that the sensitive subordinate was cut to the quick, Wayne requested him to appear upon Parade as though nothing had happened. Lacey was afraid not to obey, lest Wayne "gratify his spleen in punishing me for my reluctance in yielding to his arbitrary and unjust mandate." The introspective captain went back from parade to sulk in his tent, drowning his sorrows with rum. When called to mess he found himself in further trouble. He had drunk too much on an empty stomach and was "louder in conversation than I ought to have been." He was again rebuked by Wayne, although, as Lacey reports it, "my friends all agreed I was the soberest person in the Company." Wayne pressed no charge, and this, too, seemed suspicious. To Lacey the forbearance proved that Wayne was "Waiting only like a beast of Prey to make a sure and safe stroke on his victim." He thought that Wayne's sycophantic clique was sneering.

Fortunately for Lacey's peace of mind, the badgered patriot was transferred. He was promoted to become a brigadier general, which seems sufficient indication that Wayne's vindictiveness was purely a matter of the Lacey imagination; but even this recognition failed to make the poor officer happy. He meditated resignation, declaring that all his friends "advised him to abandon the American cause." One uncle assured him that the British would only be too happy to recognize his merits. Lacey decided not to leave, but he never ceased to suspect that Wayne was plotting to degrade him. The detail as general in charge of Pennsylvania militia to guard the nine chief highways leading north from Philadelphia soothed his vanity and made him feel that proper talents were really recognized in Continental ranks; but later, when his force was taken by surprise, Lacey was again convinced that he had been betrayed by crafty traitors. General John Lacey was ready to believe that there were malevolent demons hovering round him for the sole purpose of bringing him renewed dismay.

Calmer, cooler judgment of a later year would free the individual states of sinister designs against the freedom of their fellows, but men in wartime do not weigh the merits of a controversy. Especially when luck is breaking badly, there is a human willingness to seek a marplot on whom to pin the blame.

More probably, the whole militia system was at fault. Irregulars, carelessly enlisted, serving for too brief a period, untrained, undisciplined, and too often unarmed, whose only military experience had been skirmishing with Indians, could scarcely be expected to maintain their morale against the veterans of Clive's campaigns. Over and over again, the generals complained that the militia would not fight, that they were cowardly and inefficient, that they would flee a battle if their period of enlistment was drawing toward its close. Many an officer discovered, in a time of grave emergency, that the militiamen would not obey orders but would fight the battle in their own unmilitary fashion.

"I suppose," wrote one colonel to his general, "there is a new cargo of militia coming out. They might as well stay at home, for not one-fourth of them is of any use about three-fourths of them Run off after the first fire and their officers foremost and it will ever be the case while the People have the choosing of the officers. There is no more regulation among what I have seen of them than there is among a flock of Bullocks."

In such a situation, the gravest need was discipline, but there were comparatively few leaders in whom the common soldier would place implicit trust. The upper rank of generals found grave difficulty in securing complete obedience to all commands; officers of lower ranks, unable to enforce their orders, were compelled to try cajolery, pleas, or persuasion. The camp sorely needed an iron hand; luckily there was soon to come a foreigner whose past experience in war was sufficient to command respect. That drillmaster was General Frederick William Steuben, veteran of the Prussian army.

CHAPTER EIGHTEEN

A Camp in Chaos

Sɪᴄᴋ, hungry, tattered soldiers, torn by dissension and racked by jealousies, crowded the cantonment. Disappointments and nervous tensions fanned suspicion and distrust. Small spites grew into vendettas; oversights, once forgivable, became proof of cunning treachery; unintended slights were magnified into unpardonable offenses. A plague of courts-martial cursed the camp. The dapper foreigners, accustomed to the unquestioning obedience of European troops, were horrified. Trained in professional armies which set great store by precedence and social status, they were shocked at the democratic Americans, who had small sense of discipline and slight regard for rank.

Steuben, a martinet for precision, was amazed at seeing soldiers use their bayonets as spits on which to broil their beef. He shuddered at the sight of officers mounting guard "in a sort of dressing gown made of an old bed cover." He fumed and swore in conference with his chief officers when he learned that not one of them had the faintest inkling of how many men he had at his command. He thought it unpardonable that the army kept no records, and that the men were hopelessly disorganized.

A CAMP IN CHAOS

The truth is that the officers were terrified. Chosen for personal popularity rather than for military genius, they dared not risk a mutiny. Men who held commissions because of their success in raising companies could not compel obedience from tired and ill paid privates. They might, to keep the records clear, issue orders for the guidance of their troops; but neither officers nor men expected that real attention would be given to the solemn statements.

Too often, therefore, the leaders were content with empty threats. Genial "Joe Gourd" Weedon, for example, listened to the Commander-in-chief's strictures against burning fence rails and then went back to his regiment to ask the men to humor Washington's strange whims. That day, the army was on the march, and there was little time to gather fuel; so the order was not heeded. Three days later Weedon again asked cooperation in the matter; but rain that night made green wood difficult to burn, while the fence rails were well weathered. Faced by a double violation of his order, "Joe Gourd" made a vague threat that the theft of fence rails would subject "the Mess to which the fire belongs" to some unspecified penalty. He wished that his troops would please stop thieving.

When Washington exerted further pressure, poor Weedon whimpered that continued disobedience was causing him concern. Angrily he ordered that ten lashes be visited upon offenders; but both he and his men were well aware that nothing would be done. Instead, he followed up his threat with a most plaintive reminder that "no fences are to be burned on any pretext whatever" but that, "if unavoidable necessity compels us to do it, license must first be obtained from the Commander-in-chief." Imagination boggles at the thought of a Virginia private going cap in hand to Washington to ask if he might fling a fence rail on the fire. Finally in mid-January when the cold was most intense, he shook his finger at his freezing men and said, "The General positively forbids the burning of the farmers' fences." But by that time there were no fences to be burned.

Steuben could not understand the leniency of Continental officers. In the matter of the fence rails, where there was at least a slight excuse for laxness lest the soldiers freeze to death, rigid discipline might not necessarily be enforced; but Steuben thought the officers should not allow the man to violate the orders with impunity. This, to the classic military mind, was suicidal.

Evidently no strict control could be enforced over the commissariat. The quartermasters, usually without sufficient food for the troops, shrank from the violence of disappointed soldiers. They no longer waited until proper requisitions were presented to distribute stores; instead, they gave out their supplies haphazardly to the first applicants. Later comers were convinced, and probably with justice, that the commissariat commanders gave their special friends advance inklings when fresh supplies became available. Undoubtedly, a large amount of missing clothing and accouterments passed into the quartermasters' hands as bribes for favors.

Washington's orders bristle with stern commands against such practices. Again and again he warns that soldiers "who shall loose, sell or otherwise dispose" of army equipment "shall be punished in the most Exemplary manner without the smallest mitigation"; but again the orders seemed impossible to enforce. Colonels were supposed to inspect their troops daily to check up on the presence of arms, clothing, and munitions; but the officers soon learned that it was advisable to do that duty in a most perfunctory manner.

A CAMP IN CHAOS

In such circumstance even the well disciplined troops began to lose respect for their superiors, especially when officers were quarreling among themselves. Many of the younger firebrands flung hasty accusations of cowardice against their brother officers; charges of drunkenness were rife; the Virginians, in particular, questioned the gentlemanliness of their associates' behavior. Washington was compelled to rid his army of several fiery young subalterns whom he found guilty of thus undermining the military morale.

To Steuben the laxness was intolerable. Generals must never yield to the opposition of their men. But the violation, though a dangerous breach of military regulations, injured civilians rather than the army; and civilians, to a graduate of Frederick the Great's crack Guards, were comparatively unimportant. There were more serious offenses against discipline which would surely undermine the welfare of the army. Steuben undertook to stiffen the discipline.

Within two weeks after the arrival at the camp the problem of disposing of wastes and refuse had become acute. So long as winter reigned the sanitation squads could clear the camp; but with the steady breakdown of morale, and with the lessened energy of half-starved men, carelessness grew common. Steuben had not been two days in the camp before he made it clear that no army could continue to survive the unsanitary conditions.

The men were quite as willing to ignore the orders of a German general—for, after all, they said, he is no better than a Hessian—as they had been to disregard their own commander; but Steuben was adamant. He did not waste his time in writing his "requests" and "hopes." When a second order, ten days later, effected no improvement, Steuben introduced a Prussian sternness. The generals were told to mount a brigade guard, with a major in command, ordered to shoot any man who violated regulations.

He gained obedience when even Washington was forced to compromise. The commander's pet detestation was gambling. He may himself have relished good horse racing, and evidently he spent, at times, a moderate amount at cards, but he was utterly opposed to gaming in the ranks. "Games of hazard" were absolutely forbidden during the stay at Valley Forge, even to the point of punishing "two lads of the Third Virginia Regiment" for the offense; but the soldiers were uncooperative. To avoid a subtle discrimination between "play" and "gambling," he forbade both cards and dice, classing them in his headquarters orders, with "the Itch," as matters that unfitted troops for duty. The soldiers listened with grave faces to his strictures, nodded attentively, and proceeded to ignore the warning.

Even the generals were grumbling at the democratic administration. When orders came down from headquarters, each underling assumed the right to nullify such rules as he personally disapproved.

Certainly the officers were setting a poor example for their men. To prevent straggling from the army, Washington required his colonels to muster their forces at regular intervals. Absences could thus be marked, and nonattendance could be promptly punished. Scouting parties were sent out to catch stragglers who wandered more than half a mile from camp. The methods thus provided against unlawful wanderings were excellent on paper, but, like so many of the Continental regulations, were honored in the breach. On six occasions during the Valley Forge encampment Washington put forth reminders of his roll-call rules, but each time the colonels paid little heed. Food was too scarce and pillaging too easy;

personal popularity was too precious to be risked by holding roll-calls thrice a day as Washington had asked. The threats of court-martial for officers who failed to do their duty were regarded as empty warnings. In the presence of such leniency from both the generals and the lesser leaders it is not astonishing that more than eleven hundred men deserted from the rebel ranks. To get the stragglers back, the colonels actually tried advertising in the local newspapers.

But if deliberate breach of regulations was not always punished there were some offenses judged worthy of cruel retribution. Washington's mercy did not extend to civilians who sought to smuggle food to Philadelphia. Two hundred and fifty lashes was a common sentence. Fifty lashes were administered daily, after which the stripes were washed with salt and water. The victim was whipped daily until all installments were complete.

Officers were less cruelly punished. A Virginia lieutenant who bought a soldier's shoes and thereby rendered the man unfit for service was discharged from the army. A Connecticut lieutenant who stole a comrade's whisky and, after drinking it, refused to pay was likewise dismissed. A Pennsylvanian who accused a brother officer of cowardice, and who not only ran away in time of danger, losing a wagonload of wheat, but aggravated his offense by lying about it, was cashiered. In comparison with the brutal physical penalties exacted from the private soldiers the errant officers seem to have escaped with extremely light sentences. After all, the psychic injury occasioned by dismissal from an army in which the culprit had but slight desire to serve would not be unbearable.

Possibly, however, the cashiering was not always as painless as the bare entries on the orderly books might indicate. One unhappy lieutenant was fetched from the guardhouse, mounted backward on a horse, bareback, with his coat turned inside out and his hands tied behind him. All the fifes and drums of his division drummed him from one end of the parade ground to the other. Three times he rode this gantlet. Hoots and jeers and, when the officers turned their heads, blows and missiles rained upon the disgraced officer. Then he was drummed and beaten out of camp with orders never to return.

Common soldiers were more roughly treated. They were marched from the guardhouse, with halters round their necks, and were forced to run the gantlet, naked, through the whole brigade. Brother soldiers, formed in double line line to make a narrow lane sometimes half a mile in length, lashed them with switches as they passed. If it was suspected that the prisoner might run too fast and thus escape an undue proportion of the switching, a man would be detailed to point a bayonet at his breast and force him back down the gantlet line.

Evidently the punishments were not restricted to the male civilians and soldiers. By General Greene's command a woman was condemned to receive a hundred lashes and was drummed out of camp for attempting to carry messages through the Continental lines to the British at Philadelphia.

Steuben's methods ran the gamut from gay infectious laughter to the sternest violence. Appalled by the slimness of supplies, he made a joke of the short rations. To greet his officers and to set up a sort of camaraderie among his military family, he gave a dinner but invited only those whose breeches were patched. His dapper cook, imported in his train from France, was asked to fix a feast of tough beefsteak and frozen potatoes, with hickory nuts for the dessert. The beverage was water, with a liqueur of "salamanders"—rum set afire

STEUBEN DRILLS THE TROOPS

From the Copley Print of a painting by Edwin M. Abbey

(Courtesy Curtis & Cameron, Inc.)

THE COMMANDER REVIEWS HIS ARMY

From a Trego painting. (Courtesy Mrs. W. Herbert Burk and Valley Forge Historical Society)

and brought blazing to the table. The chef quit in disgust at Steuben's plebeian tastes and at the meager food provided for the culinary artist.

He was by turns indulgent to his men and unrelentingly exacting. "In Europe," said he, "I drill a man three weeks and then I have a recruit; here in America I must make him a finished soldier." But he did not shirk the task. "I drafted 120 men from the line as a Guard for the commander-in-chief. I made that Guard my military school. I drilled them myself twice a day and to remove that English prejudice which some officers entertained, that to drill a recruit was a sergeant's task and beneath the status of an officer, I often took the musket myself to show the men the manual of arms."

In telling the story, however, Steuben softened the facts. He did not confess that it was his daily practice to rise at three o'clock in the morning, and after a frugal meal of coffee and a pipeful of tobacco, to start the drill before the sun was up. He did not tell about his fits of passion when, after his awkward squad had failed to carry out some simple maneuver, he swore at them in a vocabulary of foreign oaths, French, German and his own private Franco-German dialect which none but he could understand. No one of the soldiers, however, failed to grasp the import of his oaths; nor did they laugh when the intense and harassed leader threw up both his hands and shrieked to Benjamin Walker, his assistant:

"Viens, Walker, mon ami, viens, mon bon ami. Sacré dam de gaucheries of dese badauts, je ne puis plus. I can curse them no more."

The methods were successful. Steuben drilled his company. He made them perfect in the manual of arms, until they could march in unison and execute simple military movements with precision. Then he sent them off, each man to drill a company of his own. Woe betide thereafter any underofficer who dared to deviate in any manner, however trivial, from the methods laid down by the Steuben school. All must be "pointedly exact in carrying out instructions— the strictest uniformity must be observed."

The uniformity could not extend to uniforms of troops. French officers, fresh from the newly regimented troops which had been arrayed in beautiful new uniforms by Etienne François Choiseul, were aghast at the sight of Washington's parti-colored army. We are accustomed, at this long distance from the Revolutionary War, to think of Continentals smartly dressed in buff and blue; but even at the most prosperous period of the war the rebel army was never wholly so. More usually the troops were in brown or green, in gray or tan. Some, indeed, wore uniforms quite like the red coats of the British.

Lafayette's description of the men at Brandywine is probably the best account of the men's appearance. "About eleven thousand men, ill-armed and still worse clothed, presented a strange spectacle to the eye; their clothes were parti-colored, and many of them were almost naked; the best clad wore hunting shirts, large, grey linen coats." Under these long loose hunting shirts were long breeches to which were attached gaiters made of tow cloth steeped in a tan vat until they were the color of dry leaves. These were held down by straps under the shoes. Ruffles of the same material ringed the neck, the wrists, the bottom of the shirt, and ornamented the shoulders and the elbows. A black stock was wrapped about the neck, a white belt slung from the shoulders held a cartridge box, and over all was a dark, broad-brimmed hat turned up at three places. One of the flaps usually was decorated by a colored cockade or by a sprig of green.

It was a workable costume for a backwoodsman, but scarcely for an army on the march; and certainly it was not trig enough to captivate a Frenchman. It could not stand up against the rigors of the rain, nor was it proof against the Pennsylvania mud. Even by December, 1777, the clothing was in tatters, the shoes were worn out, and blankets were imperatively needed. Two months earlier Washington had ordered William Henry of Lancaster to seize all the blankets, shoes, stockings, and clothing "that could be spared by the inhabitants"; but lack of draft animals prevented the arrival of the needed supplies. There was, with odd irony, a "Clothiers' Store" at Valley Forge, but the shelves were so bare that the room was used for the commissary-general of prisoners.

It would be pleasant to record that these deficiencies were merely special instances, albeit grievous ones, and that at all other times the rebel troops were amply cared for; but the facts are adverse. Almost exactly a year before, Washington had referred to the deficiencies of his commissariat. Many of the soldiers were then described as "entirely naked and more so thinly clad as to be unfit for service." Colonel Israel Angell of Rhode Island, writing to his governor, said that the condition of his regiment was such that the members of other corps and the people in the villages called his men "The Ragged, Lousey, Naked Regiment." Washington was constantly complaining that thousands of uniforms lay for months in distant parts because "our public agents cannot agree on whose business it is to transport them."

But the Valley Forge ordeals were by far the worst of all the hardships. Part of the trouble rose because the endless rains wore out the fabrics and because when trampled mud froze into ruts, the rough edges cut like knives. The men tore strips from their blankets to bind about their feet, or cut the tents to make some sort of cover for their wounds. Under such conditions it is small wonder that the men, obliged to huddle round the fires all night for want of blankets, stole forbidden fence rails for fuel.

CHAPTER NINETEEN

The Capital Is Lost

Meanwhile the British were living in comparative comfort at Philadelphia. A craven Congress, hearing at one o'clock in the morning of September 19 a false report that the British were on the eastern side of the Schuylkill less than twenty miles away, had "decamped with the utmost precipitation." The statesmen had fled to Lancaster and then, after only a brief delay, had pushed on across the Susquehanna twenty-five miles more to York.

Orders had been left to strip the city of materials useful for war. Copper, brass, lead, and other metals had been hastily packed for hauling to safe refuge at Easton, Allentown, and other distant points; six tons of church bells, and the famous Liberty Bell which had rung out the news of Independence from the State House, had been moved away; public records and army stores had been taken out of the city. Even wounded soldiers in the hospitals were hurriedly hauled in oxcarts to Bethlehem, Easton, and Allentown.

Philadelphia had feared that it would be burned to the ground. Two suspicious characters, arrested by the night watch, had confessed their intention of firing the city. Messages from Cornwallis, however, from his resting point at

Germantown, quieted these fears by promising that no one would be molested in life or property so long as the populace remained peaceful. For a week after the first announcement of the impending capture, Philadelphia had been expecting his arrival, but not until the early morning of September 26 did word come that the British were within the city limits.

Led by the thickset, grayish Cornwallis, resplendent in his scarlet and gold-lace coat, white buckskin breeches and well polished top boots, the confident grenadiers came with the British van into the capital. Three thousand strong, they marched down Second Street to Society Hill in the heart of the city. The Tory sympathizers cheered loudly as the royalists advanced; the rebels, fearful that silence might seem proof of traitorous intent, joined weakly in the applause.

In spite of the appearance of loyalty, however, several dozen American sympathizers, including Parson Jacob Duché, were at once arrested. Known Tory leaders were given administrative positions: Joseph Galloway became acting mayor and superintendent of police; Jonathan Roberts, well known miller of Merion, was assigned to persuade his fellow Quakers to join the British cause; Abraham Carlisle, a carpenter, was put in charge of the gates leading through the redoubts into the city.

Galloway's orders made the Philadelphians seem as though they too were prisoners. No one was allowed to appear upon the streets after half past eight at night without a pass; neither river might be crossed except by special British permission; no wood was to be cut, no provisions marketed, no blankets or other clothing sold without a British license. The rules went further, Philadelphians believed, than mere military necessities required. They particularly resented Galloway's command that they sweep the streets in front of their houses every Saturday morning, and that they clean their chimneys at regular intervals.

At their first arrival, the British were courteous about commandeering quarters. Officers called politely at the houses to ask if they might have accommodations. When they were refused, they raised their hats and left quietly. Mrs. Henry Drinker, whose husband, a nonresistant Quaker, had been deported by the Americans to Virginia, gained a respite of two months by pointing out that, "as my husband is away, I should be pleased if they could obtain some other place."

In spite of promises that, if the inhabitants remained quiet, they would not be molested in their persons or their property, looting was continuous. Punishment of four hundred lashes proved insufficient deterrent; the hanging of a man for stealing six dozen bottles of wine and the bed-clothing from four of Mary Pemberton's beds, did not prevent other thefts. Philadelphians protested that foragers took hay and gave receipts for only one-tenth the amount, and that Hessians and British alike stole food necessary for the people. The effect was to destroy the hope that nonresistant Quakers would be won over to the British cause.

After the hope of enlisting Quaker support had faded, the invaders were less tolerant of the wishes of householders. Major John Crammond, of the King's Own Fourth, moved into the Drinker home on the promise that he would be a quiet guest, keeping early hours and entertaining rarely. Two days later he filled the Drinker barn with three horses, two cows, two sheep, and several fowl, added three British servants and three Hessian orderlies, and had eleven officers as dinner guests. When the rooms proved inadequate, he requisitioned two front parlors, a bedroom, a baggage room, the kitchen, and the entire stable. Night after night, when he was not entertaining large parties, he woke the neighborhood by returning home singing and shouting in the small hours of the morning.

"The ravages and wanton destruction of the soldiery will, I think," wrote diarist Robert Morton, "soon become irksome to the inhabitants, as many who depended upon their vegetables for the maintenance of their families are now entirely and effectually ruined. . . . I mean not to dictate to men of whose superior abilities I have a just appreciation, but had the necessities of the army justified the measures, and had they paid a sufficient price for what they had taken, then they would have had the good wishes of the people and perhaps all the assistance they could afford, but contrary conduct has produced contrary effects."

The change of policy was dictated by the failure of the conciliation methods to win over any appreciable number of the Americans. On his arrival at Head of Elk, Howe had hoped that the pacifists would flock to his standards; he had believed that the well born landed gentry would prefer British rule to an independent commonwealth dominated by the redlegs of the infertile hills; he had overestimated the loyalty even of the merchants and of the conservative city folk. Disillusion at the failure of his plans and realization that his lavish spending of golden guineas had not won the province caused him, after his first futile efforts to enforce his non-looting laws by lashes and by hanging, to overlook subsequent violations.

Captain William Cunningham, bullying keeper of the "British Provost," or Walnut Street jail, Philadelphia, was particularly hated. "Former pimp to a gin-shop drab in a blind alley" of London, he had been a "scaw-banker," or kidnaper of child labor, until he had come to America as a horse breaker. He had joined the British army and had been made provost marshal. Executioner of Nathan Hale and torturer of Ethan Allen, the brutal sadist took delight in starving and abusing the nine hundred rebel prisoners whom he had in charge at the jail in Philadelphia.

By British army regulations, Cunningham was paid a definite amount each day for proper feeding of the prisoners. Cunningham kept the money and, instead of giving the regular rations authorized by General Howe, fed the prisoners on moldy bread and a few ounces of spoiled meat. Even of this, there was, however, no regular allotment; often the prisoners were starved for days. Although relatives of prisoners were supposed to be allowed to send special food into the jail, Cunningham delighted in beating the captives away from the food with the butt end of his heavy whip. On numerous occasions, he kicked over kettles of soup, to see the starved prisoners lap up the spilled food from the stones. As a special treat, Cunningham had a diseased cow shot dead in the prison yard for the rebels to eat raw. Scraps of leather, chips, even pieces of the prison pump, were chewed by the starving prisoners under Cunningham's control.

The prisoners in the Walnut Street jail suffered as severely from the cold as did Washington's men at Valley Forge. Cunningham pocketed the money provided for the purchase of blankets. The rebels, shivering in ragged uniforms without extra coverings and usually without fires, had no relief. Snow drifted through the broken window panes. The death lists rose rapidly.

Cunningham continued, however, to draw money for the feeding of his prisoners. He grew rich, as the Americans declared, on the bodies of the dead and on the starvation of the living. It was impossible to register complaints against him, for these passed through Cunningham's own hands or through those of Joshua Loring, his immediate superior. Loring, commissary of prisoners, was himself accused of having murdered two thousand American prisoners and of embezzling funds entrusted to his care. He was safe from punishment because Howe was infatuated with his wife, Elizabeth Lloyd Loring.

News of the abuses reached Washington through the cleverness of Mary Taylor Frazer and Jane Sheward Gibbons, the tall, imperious "Queen of the County," who had called on Howe to demand the return of her cow. Persifor Frazer had been taken prisoner after the battle of Brandywine. The two aggressive women insisted on receiving permission to visit Frazer in the jail, and Howe, anxious to win favor among the Quaker farmers, unsuspectingly allowed them to pass Cunningham's guard. They saw the mistreatment of the prisoners and, noticing the marks of starvation and abuse, suggested that Frazer and his fellow prisoners write a formal letter of protest to Washington.

Cunningham and Loring had been careful to prevent leakage of such information. When the women were about to leave the jail, sentries demanded that they submit to search. Mrs. Gibbons stubbornly protested and acted as though she were trying to escape; Mrs. Frazer, who had concealed the note in her petticoat under a strip of braid, seemed acquiescent. Tory women called in to make the search, finding nothing on the angrily struggling Mrs. Gibbons, gave only a cursory glance at Mrs. Frazer. She carried off not only the statement of protest but also a small sample of the bad bread served to the prisoners.

Once past the sentries, the women rode to the Middle ferry, passed the guards as though on their way to the Brandywine, but then wheeled their horses northward toward the American camp. Under the escort of an American colonel found with a roistering group at Swedes' Ford tavern, the women spurred onward to Washington's headquarters. Their information was immediately used as the basis for an official protest sent to General Howe. Conditions thereafter were improved for prisoners.

Stories of ill treatment continued to be current. Wayne warned his men that Americans who deserted to the British were bound and gagged and were then transported into lifetime slavery on West Indian sugar plantations. The fear of British abuse was a powerful factor in limiting the amount of American desertion.

Albigence Waldo's fears were typical. "Our brethren who are unfortunately Prisoners in Philadelphia meet with the most savage and inhumane treatments that Barbarians are Capable of inflicting. Our Enemies do not knock them in the head, or burn them with torches to death, or flee them alive, or gradually dismember them till they die, which is customary among Savages & Barbarians. No, they are worse by far. They suffer them to starve, to linger out their lives in extreme hunger. One of these poor unhappy men, drove to the last extreem by the rage of hunger, eat his own fingers up to the first joint from the hand, before he died. Others eat the Clay, the Lime, the Stones of the Prison Walls. Several who died in the Yard had pieces of Bark, Wood, Clay, and Stones in their mouths, which the ravings of hunger had caused them to take in for food in the last Agonies of Life. These are thy *mercies*, O Britain."

"For five months," said Charles Wallace, a Pennsylvania volunteer, "we fed on peameal biskit broke up into small pieces full of worms and we thought often horse beef with now and then small bit of pork about a good double handfull of the biskit for four days. In the crown of our hats when boiled the soup would be covered with worms." In more picturesque phrase, he wrote in his diary, "We fed on trouble with hungry bellys."

Quite as fearsome as the actual treatment of the captives were the threats held over them. Wallace relates how the prison keepers "kept us in a little house with a stone floor without fire or heat, threatening to hang us or to transport us to Botany bay."

Poor Herman Zedwitz' story, written in a wild note of protest to Washington, was still more startling. He feared electrocution! Three "high germans," he said, had "privit Instructions to thacke thrugh their Electric Instruments entirely a way my senses." This threat, he said, "they Confirmed with the haviesd Oath I ever hard of." The frightened Zedwitz somehow smuggled letters to both Washington and Howe pleading for his life and warning against the "dangerous villains" with their electric machines. Whether because of the letters or because the threats were merely empty words, Zedwitz escaped with no other punishment for his rebel service than a short jail sentence.

Tory raiders were as dangerous as many of the British prison camps. Inspired by cold Joseph Galloway, American-born lawyer who supported Howe rather than see the former colonists turn radical, roving bands of desperadoes ravaged the countryside.

Night after night, in the rich farm lands across the Schuylkill from Valley Forge, residents were awakened by the noise of horsemen in the barnyards. Farmers were faced by masked men armed with swords and muskets, while other bandits drove off the few horses and cattle left by the foragers. No one knew the identity of the marauders, though it was suspected that the robbers were Tory agents.

Vigilante groups were organized to track down the raiders. Foremost among those who demanded vengeance was Joseph Doane, a Quaker teacher. His father Moses Doane and two schoolboy brothers joined with the schoolmaster to punish the outlaws. No family was more noisily patriotic. The Doanes were determined to avenge the sufferings inflicted upon two other brothers held prisoners at the Walnut Street jail.

A band of riders came one night to the farm of John Shaw, a fellow vigilante. Shaw was dragged from bed and was badly beaten. His favorite riding horse was stolen. On the same night two other vigilantes were seized, bound to trees and whipped. None could identify the masked desperadoes, but one vigilante, hiding in a wood, took a quick shot at a rider, and toppled him from his horse. The other outlaws escaped.

The wounded man was immediately captured by the rebels. To the astonishment of the law-enforcing band, the prisoner was Joseph Doane, the pro-rebel teacher. The other robbers, he confessed, were his father, the two schoolboys, and the two other brothers supposedly prisoners at Philadelphia. The Doanes were in the pay of Galloway and the British. Teacher Joseph escaped from jail and disappeared for a year, but later he was discovered and hanged. The other Doanes were similarly punished upon their capture, months later.

The disorder was typical of conditions faced by many sections of America during the encampment period. Fear of Tory raids and fear of treachery were common. Rumors grew into extravagant form. People of the Great Valley heard that England was about to import an army of a hundred thousand

Hessians, and that mercenaries were being enlisted against the United States from every quarter of the globe. Moors, Eskimos, Laplanders, even Persian archers, Fiji islanders, and Japanese were, it was said, about to embark in a tremendous fleet of British transports to attack the American farmers. No rumor was too absurd to find acceptance.

War hysteria developed into a spy mania. Nonresistant Quakers who would not aid the rebels because they sincerely believed all wars wasteful, sinful, and barbaric, were looked upon as traitors. To enthusiastic rebels the Quaker reluctance to fight or to pay taxes for the continuance of the war became clear evidence of guilt. Even Washington went so far as to declare that the neighborhood of Valley Forge was "to a man disaffected." The Congressional Board of War officially accused the Great Valley people of betraying the American cause.

Six wagonloads of prominent Philadelphia Quakers had been deported to Virginia immediately after the battle of Brandywine; other deportations followed. Most of them were treated well, though a few of those judged strongly pro-British were kept in close confinement. None of the Philadelphia Quakers was as badly treated as were the Loyalists condemned to the terrible Simsbury mine of Connecticut seventy feet underground. The Pennsylvania deportations were designed to take the Quakers away from a center likely to be captured by the enemy.

Howe's men, always nervously anticipating an attack, suffered severe fright soon after New Year's. Sudden thaws broke the river ice and permitted a slight degree of navigation. Rumors spread that Americans were about to float down the Delaware from Burlington and thus make a water attack on Philadelphia. Howe, fearing that his fleet might be separated from the city by rebel rafts coming between the vessels and the docks, ordered his ships warped close to the river bank. The movement would also safeguard his squadron from being frozen in midstream in the event of a return of freezing weather.

The precaution was well taken. Early in the morning of January 5, British sentries spied a curiously shaped keg floating down the river. Remembering their previous experience in August, 1776, when Sergeant Ezra Lee had almost blown up a British frigate by paddling David Bushnell's clam-shaped "submarine" against the British fleet, the sentries were terrified. The Delaware River keg looked different from the Bushnell device, but the British were suspicious. The egg-shaped cask seemed dangerous. When a boat's crew attempted to hoist the keg out of the water, it exploded, killing four sailors and injuring several others.

Bushnell had tried a second time to blow up the British fleet. This second keg was not manned by an "engineer" but was so arranged as to explode its hundred and thirty pounds of gunpowder by contact with the copper-bound hulls of the fleet. The sailors who had tried to lift the keg into their boat had inadvertently set off the percussion cap inside.

Other kegs followed the first arrival. The British fired upon them, exploding a dozen or more. Troops on shore, hearing the bombardment, rushed to the wharves and began firing at every floating object in the river. Citizens became panic-stricken. Wild rumors ran through the town that the kegs were filled with armed rebels, and that bayonets had been seen sticking from the bungholes. Some frightened Tories feared that the kegs were infernal machines so built as to roll up the wharves and then to roll flaming through the city streets. Firing continued from dawn until dark before this so-called "Battle of the Kegs" was finished. Francis Hopkinson, chairman of the Continental Naval Board, wrote a satirical poem on the British terror.

Howe's own officers were turning against their leader. His action, soon after issuing orders against looting, in appropriating Mary Pemberton's coach and horses as his own, his evident preference of the company of dissipated younger officers to that of the more mature men with whom once he had associated, his reluctance to leave the comforts of Philadelphia when, it was believed, Washington's army lay at the British mercy, and his capriciousness in making appointments destroyed their confidence in Howe's good faith. His arrogance led one of his men to write:

"This Trait plainly shews the wide Difference of a Desspotical and Monarchial Government. Lord have mercy on the Poor People that are always subject to the peevish spleenitical whims of an unreasonably headstrong Despot."

Once Philadelphia had been fortified against American attack, with breastworks running across the two-mile northern front that lay between the rivers, and with a well built fence shutting off the waterfront from the center of the town, the British officers had little to do beyond guard duty. The British camp gave itself up to gayety and amusement; gambling increased; drunkenness became common. Balls and parties were everyday occurrences.

In some respects the round of parties gave a gala season to Philadelphia society. The same girls who had gallantly marched out, in triple columns, to visit Washington's men at Falls of Schuylkill a month before Brandywine, and who had there drunk double bowls of claret lemonade with the Pennsylvania troops, now were entertained at British parties. The high-coiffured, hoop-skirted belles, decked out with quantities of gayly colored feathers, were merry at plays, concerts, teas and balls. "No loss for partners," wrote one girl to an out-of-town friend, urging her to rush into Philadelphia for the excitement; "even I am engaged to seven different gentlemen for you must know 'tis a fix'd rule never to dance but two dances at a time with the same person."

The social season reached its peak at the famous *Meschianza,* an elaborate regatta, tournament, banquet, and ball presented by Howe's chief officers at the time of his departure for England in May, 1778. The spectacle, arranged by André, Captain John Montresor of the Engineers, and others of the younger macaronis, was an overpowering demonstration of the artistic resources of the British camp.

From a mile north of High Street to more than a mile south of that central thoroughfare, a procession of gayly decorated barges, bearing the Howe brothers, fat General Sir Henry Clinton, Sir Billy Howe's successor, polite, sharp-faced Knyphausen, dark, heavy Banastre Tarleton, and other British leaders, moved along the waterfront. The shores, inside the protecting fences, were lined with troops on dress parade. As the barges, each with its band of music, were rowed "regular to harmony," a fleet of lighter skiffs moved along on either side to keep off the swarms of private boats that filled the broad Delaware.

On arrival at the Wharton estate in Southwark, the British generals walked along a double line of saluting grenadiers to a lawn laid out as a tournament field. On opposite sides of the field two pavilions had been erected for the ladies. Before each pavilion sat seven "of the principal young ladies of the country," each dressed in Turkish costume and each wearing in her turban the favors with which she was to reward her chosen knight. Toward them dashed seven Knights of the Blended Rose, in white and crimson on gray chargers to defend their ladies' wit, beauty, and accomplishments against the black and orange Knights of the Burning Mountain.

The contest was then carried on, with lances shivered against each other's shields, with pistols fired into the air, and with swords in mock duel, until, after a single combat between the leaders of the opposing Knights, the ladies on each side signified that they were satisfied with the proofs shown of their Knights' devotion. The party continued, with dancing, fireworks, and a magnificently elaborate dinner of twelve hundred dishes, in a mirrored banquet hall, until an hour after sunrise. It was, said André, "the most splendid entertainment ever given by an army to its general."

The *Meschianza* was, however, costly and magnificent beyond all due proportion to the successes it was intended to celebrate. Howe was going home to answer charges of inefficiency. After eight months in Philadelphia, he had not added an inch of territory to the British possessions. He had kept one British soldier in the capital for every ten inhabitants, but had not been able to win over the city to its old allegiance. The populace was more pro-rebel at his departure than it had been when he arrived.

Almost immediately after Howe's departure, Sir Henry Clinton gave orders for the British to prepare to evacuate the city. Clinton was planning to reunite the British army by returning to New York and then to start a more intensive campaign for the reconquest of America. He announced that he would cross the Delaware into New Jersey and march straight for New York.

The British officers packed their belongings. André, quartered in Benjamin Franklin's house, carried off with him a parcel of rare books; other British officers took keepsakes from the houses of their unwilling hosts. In sharp contrast was the scrupulously honest action of Wilhelm, Baron Innhausen und Knyphausen, who called in the agent of General John Cadwallader, head of Philadelphia's crack "Silk Stocking" City Troop, to certify that none of the Cadwallader possessions had been disturbed. Alone among the British and Hessian leaders, the quiet taciturn Knyphausen, ridiculed for his strange habit of spreading butter with his thumb, insisted on paying rent for his occupation of the quarters.

The departure of the British, in the last week of June, was a signal for general rejoicing. Old Crazy Johnny Brinton, jailed for months because every time he was forced to shout "Hurrah for King George" he added an even louder "Washington," shouldered a musket, waded into the river and fired two shots at the retreating frigate *Roebuck*. Then, considering his duty done, he marched back to his farm at the Brandywine battle field. For thirty years thereafter, as long as he lived, he continued to wear the Revolutionary uniform.

CHAPTER TWENTY

Camp at Play

Mid-March with its un-seasonable heat revived the spirits of the troops. The men were full of energy; they felt that spring had come to stay. The worst privations of the camp were over. There was time to frolic and to play.

Traditionally, St. Patrick's Day was set aside for Irish jubilation. Even the Scotch-Irish from the hills laid aside their hatred for the shamrock to join their Irish rivals in the celebrations. From time immemorial, the Irishmen enjoyed the holiday.

The Britishers at Philadelphia carried on the custom. The Irish sentries at the gloomy jail drank heavily all day. They left their posts to make merry in the taverns and, unmindful of their duties, were robbed of the prison keys by rebel spies. Many Continental captives, including Colonel Persifor Frazer, who had been taken prisoner soon after Brandywine, gained their freedom. They took advantage of their oppor-tunity to slip through the British lines to Valley Forge.

At Valley Forge, however, St. Patrick's Day almost brought dissension. The Pennsylvania Germans, who never had had much love for Irish neighbors, hung up by night a grotesque figure which they plainly labeled "Paddy." When St. Patrick's Day dawned, the effigy was in full view, swinging on a tree limb in full view of Morgan's Irish frontiersmen.

The hot-tempered riflemen were furious. They threatened to avenge the honor of their saint by murdering the culprits. No one, however, had seen the image hung. The Pennsylvania Germans, gleeful at the success of their prank, then tried to stir up trouble. They told the angry Irishmen that New Englanders had hung the effigy. Morgan's men, muttering their indignation, prepared to fire on their Massachusetts neighbors.

Washington, summoned to restore order, quelled the trouble by diplomacy. "This day," he said, "is the second anniversary of the evacuation of Boston. It is also St. Patrick's Day and I, too, am a lover of St. Patrick. I must settle this affair by requiring all the army to take a holiday."

All day the men played. Stacked at the camp were heaps of eight-pound cannon balls brought down from Warwick by the wagonmasters. The new sport of "Long Bullet" was contrived, the men competing to see who could roll the cannon balls farthest. The winner won a swig from the canteens of his opponents; the weakest rival was obliged to gather up the balls of each of the contestants. The game, a variant of classic Gaelic weight casting, long continued in the neighborhood as a favored athletic event.

Captain Allan McLane's small band of Oneidas carried off the honors. Fixing a copper coin to a thin stick, they stood fifty yards away and aimed arrows at the coins. They showed uncanny accuracy, hitting the little target at almost every shot.

The frontiersmen, already famous for their musketry, were frankly envious. They themselves were skillful with the bow, but they lacked the deadly Indian precision. Believing that the Indian perfection was due to better balanced arrows, they begged the Oneidas to tell them the secrets of properly feathering the shafts. The Oneidas answered by borrowing the arrows of their white competitors and splitting the bull's-eyes with the same skill.

These St. Patrick's Day games of 1778 may mark an important innovation. For the first time in history, entry is made of what may well have been the ancestor of modern baseball. "We played at base this evening," reports George Ewing. Possibly he refers to the newly invented game of "Rounders," just then coming into fashion in Great Britain. This game of ball and bat, with posts for bases, seems to have been introduced into America at Valley Forge. "Rounders," two generations later, in 1838, developed into the nation-wide game of baseball. It is, however, possible that the Ewing entry may refer to the children's game of "prisoner's base," already known for more than three full centuries.

More dances might have been held at the encampment, with farmer belles and army wives as partners, had not the ladies known of Lafayette's aversion to dancing during wartime. Such dancing parties were held at York and Reading, so frequently indeed as to call forth warm protests from staider patriots, and Washington himself, it is well known, was fond of the diversion.

Whispers spread, however, that Lafayette, stopping off at Baltimore on his way to join the Continental army, had rebuked the maidens of that little town when they asked him to a party. "Ladies," he is reported to have told the girls, "you are indeed very handsome; you dance very prettily; your ball is very fine; but the soldiers have no shirts."

The ball ceased; the ladies ran home to sew. By the next

day a large number of shirts were on their way to clothe the soldiers.

Among the ladies, Lafayette's lightest wish was law. His courtly manners, his handsome face, his light and graceful figure, were irresistible. They hastened to anticipate his wishes. Largely through their anxiety to follow his supposed unwillingness to dance in wartime, Valley Forge society was willing to forgo its pleasure. Only in the more remote quarters, at Coventry in the iron regions, at King of Prussia and at Greene's house, were dances held.

The story of the Frenchman's gallantry to little Betty Stephens, daughter of the Valley Forge physician who lived at what is now the Varnum House, was well known in the camp. Coming to the Stephens home for a treatment of the wound received at Brandywine, Lafayette saw a subaltern forcing a kiss upon the unwilling girl. He kicked his aide downstairs. Then, bowing politely to the frightened girl, he assured her, in the name of France, that such an outrage would not recur.

Benedict Arnold, in comparison, made a poor appearance. After his success at Saratoga, Arnold had come down to Pennsylvania to nurse his wounds. When he had recovered, and when warm weather had returned, Arnold commanded the commissary to provide him with a banquet for twenty-one guests.

A long table was laid under a cherry tree by the creekside near Valley Forge. The ranking officers were invited to attend. Few of the major leaders accepted the invitation. Washington sent a cutting note refusing to take part in an expensive entertainment, and though Lafayette and Wayne stopped to drink a glass of wine each made his excuses on the ground of urgent business. Arnold was furious. He never forgave the Commander-in-chief for what he rightfully considered a rebuke, nor did he forget the casualness with which Wayne and the Marquis had treated their invitations. Allan McLane believed that this incident first disclosed Arnold's willingness to sacrifice the interests of the soldiers for his personal enjoyment.

Wayne, however, expressed the bitterest criticisms of Arnold's selfishness. Already convinced of Arnold's unreliability "both as a Gentleman and a Soldier," Wayne now let loose unbridled comments. "Honor and Virtue," said Wayne, "are Strangers to his Soul." Wayne believed that Arnold was a coward, that he never ventured upon any enterprise except when he was drunk, that he "retailed the publick Liquors for his private Emolument and furnished his Quarters with beds and other furniture by paying for them with Pork, Salt, Flour, etc. drawn from the Magazines," and that he even stooped to steal the savings of private soldiers. "The dirty, dirty, acts which he has been capable of committing," said Wayne, "beggar all description and are of such a Nature as would cause the Infernals to blush." Mad Anthony's comments were, of course, extravagant, and most of them were untrue; but they are indicative of the distrust felt by certain of the leaders for the brilliant Arnold's honesty.

Washington's own parties were of very different nature. He made a special point of asking that the officers of the day dine with him at Headquarters. The meal, especially during the first days at the camp, was extremely frugal. The only courses might consist of a scanty bit of meat, a few frozen potatoes, and some army bread, and a dessert of nothing more than a plate of hickory nuts, cracked open with a tomahawk upon the stones. The toast, invariably drunk to the health of the nation, might be no more than simple rum-and-water toddy. But the spirit was invariably kindly and cheerful.

Washington's three o'clock dinners to his officers were most important social events.

The conversation, to be sure, was neither sparkling nor sprightly. The Continental officers, drawn from a somewhat different social stratum than their British rivals, lacked the swift riposte, the malicious repartee, the keen incisiveness that marked the table talk at British army messes. At Valley Forge, official conversation dwelt rather on material affairs. The diners talked of foragers and hospitals, of prospects for a French alliance, of the resolutions passed by Congress. Occasionally the officers spoke guardedly of the achievements of absent generals, but such comments were frowned upon. Washington was not fond of gossip.

In the more retired quarters of the officers, however, the talk was unrestrained. Especially when things were moving less favorably than usual, hot tempers flared into dispute. Red-faced William Smallwood, almost perpetually angry, shouted hasty denunciations at all those who would not grant the superiority of Maryland, at those who questioned the valor of militiamen, at every foreigner, especially at Steuben who enjoyed the drillmastership which Smallwood coveted for himself, and, above all, at the stupid Congress which would not promote him faster. Smallwood's temper was a constant trial to his associates.

When tongues were loosed at these informal gatherings in quarters, the air was often electric with accusation. Sunburned Lord Stirling, whom Washington was said to love because, next to the Commander-in-chief, he had the most military mien of all the officers, flared into anger when a critic described his round red face as brandy-colored. He would not forgive a heavy jibe about his claim to noble rank. Kalb and Steuben, though born on the same side of the Rhine, were

229

constantly at odds. For years they had been fighting in opposing armies. Genial but irascible Steuben, his glittering star of the "Order of Fidelity" sparkling in the firelight, accused Lafayette, too, of plotting against him. The Frenchman, bowing his deep-red head toward the powdered Steuben, passed off the charges with a Gallic wit. He bore with patience Steuben's complaints against his supposed presumptuousness and vanity. A quicker-tempered soldier might have challenged Steuben to a duel, but the amiable Lafayette disarmed the heavy German by charming him with compliments.

As food supplies grew more abundant, the regimental officers adopted the fashion of entertaining their associates at dinner. The colonels asked the staffs to dine; then the underofficers returned the courtesy in order of seniority. These were gayer dinners than the more formal affairs at Headquarters, with more jokes and pleasantries. At one such party, the squad passed a stone jug purporting to be filled with excellent rare brandy. Each man, in turn, drank from the jug. He found the contents only water, but kept the secret to himself, smacking his lips and praising the quality of liquor, until every man had been deceived and disillusioned. The pleasures of the camp were simple joys demanding no great strain upon the intellect, but they were innocent diversions to beguile the weary days of waiting.

The ladies added greatly to the comforts of the camp. Pretty little Catherine Littlefield Greene, young bride of General Nathanael Greene, came down from Rhode Island with her boarding-school store of French conversation to make her quarters a salon for young French officers. They could not always understand the academic phrases which she pronounced so quaintly, but they understood her eagerness to be a gracious hostess. They appreciated her, too, her thoughtfulness in bringing in the neighbor girls, Sarah Walker and Margaret Beaver, Elizabeth and Priscilla Stephens, Jane and Elizabeth Moore, to teach them how to be as brightly vivacious and as capital at story-telling as she herself. And they admired little George Washington Greene, baby of the camp, whom Catherine brought down to Valley Forge after the food supplies had grown more plentiful and comforts were more easily obtained.

Round little Lucy Knox, wife of the fat and florid Boston bookseller general, became the veritable life of the encampment after her arrival in the last days of the stay at Valley Forge. Lively and perhaps meddlesome, bluntly forthright and free from social pretension, her tactlessness and unbounding energy put her in the forefront of all activities. She and her voluble, excitable, and unbridled spouse, whose apparent pompousness belied his true character, were extravagantly fond of each other; and though the general sometimes publicly rebuked his wife for interference in army politics they were, as Greene told Catherine, a perfect married couple.

Older women from outlying farms rode into the camp once or twice a week, bringing saddlebags filled with bread and pies. Mrs. Mary Bowen, in particular, who lived in the Great Valley somewhat to the west of Valley Forge, won Martha Washington's particular friendship by teaching Martha how to darn the General's stockings in a more becoming fashion. She came so often, according to the legend handed down to her descendants, that by the time the army left the camp the Bowen horse was too worn out for further use. When Washington broke camp, he ordered that an army horse be given Mrs. Bowen to replace her mount.

Martha Washington was, of course, the dominant lady of the camp. Each day at Headquarters, her second-story sitting room overlooking Valley Creek was filled with wives of officers, who spent their time in sewing garments, patching torn uniforms, darning old stockings and knitting new ones, and in preparing baskets of food and medicines to be taken to the huts of ailing soldiers.

Many of the baskets were distributed by little Mary Mc-Donald, a seven-year-old colored girl who pilfered potatoes, nuts, and apples from her master to give to the men. She trudged through the snow with her small hoard hidden in her apron underneath her coat, knocked on the Headquarters door, while the sentry looked on amusedly, and announced that she had come to join the army. Martha Washington took her to the General. He patted her on the head and smiled. "He was so grave and dignified," said Mary McDonald, years later on her hundredth birthday, "that I felt afraid at first; but after he smiled and spoke to me, I did not feel at all afraid. Even the highest officers would raise their three-cornered hats and bow with much courtesy whenever they met me on my rounds."

The wives of many of the soldiers, especially in the Pennsylvania regiments, resided also at the camp, and, with their children, took part in military duties. Eleven-year-old John Geyer, for example, a drummer boy, stayed on, after his discharge on New Year's Day, to help his mother with the regimental washing. Though, like his father, he was twice wounded in action, he refused to leave the army. The patriotic devotion shown by the wives and children of the soldiers was extraordinary.

In spite of mid-March balminess, the spring was backward. The end of April usually finds the cherries white with blossom, the apples gayly pink, the forests filmed with green. A clear and brilliant sunlight drenches the valley with fresh brightness. The atmosphere in April often seems crystal-clear at Valley Forge. None of these delights appeared in April, 1778. The warm March sun which had brought the birds and called the lilacs into bud gave way to raw and rainy weather. The cold returned; late April was as frigid as February. The early blooms of pear and plum, the long drooping yellow willow branches, the first sweet cherry blossoms were cased in ice. The river froze from shore to shore.

Men knew, however, that the summer was at hand. The signs of spring, still evident in the frozen blossoms, revived the spirits of the army. Washington made plans to sow the near-by fields in wheat; the soldiers hoped to plant little patches in early vegetables. Confidence grew strong that food would soon be plentiful again.

A company of Virginia cavalrymen brought romance into camp. Following the arrival of three girls from the Old Dominion to marry their soldier sweethearts and to set up housekeeping in crude log huts at the camp, other comrades married girls from near-by Chester County farms. Then, on the coldest day of this belated winter, Captain Berryman Green, commander of the company, climaxed the series of six weddings by his own marriage to a girl in whose house he had been billeted.

Then the days grew warmer; trees burst suddenly into leaf; the fields grew green again. Spring was belated, but its joys were welcome. The ultrarevolutionist Sons of St. Tammany, named for the friendly Lenni-Lenape chief, who was buried but a few miles east of Valley Forge, planned for their annual May Day celebration in his honor. The Pennsylvanians were particularly active, for the Indian saint was closely identified with William Penn. They were accustomed to parading, wearing bucktails tied with black ribbons in their hats, to defy the aristocratic Tories. This year, the Pennsylvania patriots resolved, the holiday should be extraordinarily observed. Their desire was made more possible because, on the eve of May Day, news came that France and Holland had signed a treaty of alliance with the new United States.

May Day this year was thus a triple celebration, honoring the May Pole, King Tammany, and the news of the alliance. Cheers began at reveille. Then the soldiers, decked out with cherry blossoms, passed in review before the regimental headquarters, waving their hats in salute and cheering lustily.

The ceremony was distinctively an affair arranged by the common soldiers. A sergeant, dressed in Indian costume to represent King Tammany, stood at each regiment's May Pole, in company with thirteen other sergeants, dressed in white, each holding a bow in the left hand and thirteen arrows in the right hand. Thirteen fifes and the same number of drums provided the music for the march. Past them marched the private soldiers, drawn up in groups of thirteen platoons of thirteen men each. The officers of the regiments were conveniently absent.

Having saluted the May Poles the men moved off to the Headquarters to do honor to their Commander. The noise was extreme; discipline was lax; the men, entirely good-humored, roared in excited laughter. They halted at the top of the hill leading to the Headquarters to re-form their lines and to march in better order.

Washington took refuge in a convenient indisposition. He heard the men's approach and, preferring not to face so hilarious an audience, asked an aide to halt the march. John Marshall met the troops, informed them that the General was unwell, and asked them to retire. They did so "with the greatest decency and regularity."

The party was, however, much too pleasant to be ended. The men went back to the top of the hill and then marched back and forth before the quarters of the generals, hurrahing at every May Pole that they passed, until the officers gave each man a generous drink to toast the day. The songs and dances lasted until midnight. All was done, the diarists report, "with the greatest regularity and without any accident happening throughout the whole day."

Lafayette and his brother French officers set aside the next day, while the men were still recovering from their jubilation, to hold a dinner in celebration of the Alliance. They now were no longer soldiers of fortune, offering their swords as volunteers; they had become the advance guard of a mighty army of French troops fighting in the common cause of freedom.

A more formal acknowledgment of the French and Spanish alliance was yet to come. Washington issued an order forbidding sentries to remain on duty more than forty-eight hours at a stretch, a rule which the men believed was due to the imminent arrival of many French reinforcements. Then Washington ordered a thanksgiving celebration. The chaplains made speeches of appreciation at the head of every brigade; a review was held by Steuben and his chief assistants. Then a grand *feu de joie* occurred.

Washington and Greene, flanked by Lafayette and the leading French officers, took place upon the high ground overlooking the Grand Parade. The army, drilled for the first time as a unit, moved toward the General. Thirteen cannon shots were fired. A blank cartridge fusillade broke out, running along the front line from right to left, back again from left to right along the second line, and so continuously until ten thousand men participated in the firing.

The festivities of the day closed with a collation. The officers marched, linked-armed, thirteen abreast to open marquees. Frugal bread and beef and pork and beans formed the main dishes of the grand spread. Bountiful supplies of rum and cider had been provided.

Tradition, for which there seems but slight verifiable authority, reports that a captured British spy, held prisoner at the camp, was set free on this occasion on the express condition that he return to Philadelphia to inform the British of the American happiness. There is much more basis for the parallel tradition that American soldiers, confined to the guardhouse for slight violations of the regulations, were freed to take part in the celebrations.

A later generation, accustomed to reverencing John Marshall as the scholarly Chief Justice of the United States Supreme Court, finds a peculiar pleasure in reading, too, how the youthful captain, barely come of age, ran races in his stocking feet. The white heels of the hose just sent him by his mother won him the nickname of "Silver Heels" on this occasion.

To climax the celebration, the officer-actors performed Joseph Addison's *Cato*. The choice was not, perhaps, the happiest possible, for the sixty-five-year-old tragedy showed Marcus Porcius Cato, the friend of freedom, besieged by Caesar and betrayed by both associates and allies. Washington could not have relished the implication that the only alternative to surrender was death by suicide, but he did admire the skill with which the soldier actor "made an excellent die." The throngs who crowded the parade ground to see the tragedy performed in the open air were loud in their approval of the cast.

The *al fresco* theatricals were, in one important aspect, a distinct improvement over the indoor dramas which had been given at intervals during the winter. For the first time in the series of events, the common soldiers were enabled to catch at least a distant glimpse of the festivities. The hills bordering the parade grounds were dotted with observers who, if they could not hear the spoken words, could at least enjoy the spectacle. By moving the festivities out of doors, moreover, the entire officer corps could be invited to attend. At previous events, too slight attention had been given to the capacity of the improvised theaters. More tickets had been issued than the hall could hold. Officers holding tickets for the entertainments would arrive to find the theater already overcrowded, and be obliged to find some other diversion.

Occasionally the alternative, according to rueful accounts in various diaries, was a drinking bout from which the participants emerged with aching heads and woeful recollections. Not every such party was as disastrous as the famous "Barrel Fever Epidemic" which resulted in a plague of black eyes and bloody noses. More often the disappointed ticket holders repaired to the hut of one of their number to play at cards or to prepare an elaborate joke upon those who had been luckier than themselves.

Pennsylvania's Major Thomas Forrest, for example, heard at such a party that a newly arrived regiment of Jerseymen were fearful of smallpox. He and his fellow artillery officers spent the time while the play was in progress in making huge placards reading "Smallpox Here." After dusk, the plotters posted the signs on the huts directly opposite the Jersey quarters. At dawn, the Jerseymen awoke, saw the warning placards, and fled in terror. Not a man remained. Forrest was reprimanded for the prank and was obliged to bring the soldiers back to Valley Forge.

CHAPTER TWENTY-ONE

Scouting the Enemy

VALLEY FORGE was vulnerable. Strategists were well aware that Washington could not easily defend the camp against a determined British attack. If Howe had moved his eighteen thousand men in full force against the Continentals, Valley Forge must certainly have fallen.

Washington had no sure avenue of escape. The high hills abruptly rising from the Valley Creek gave excellent defense against a redcoat advance, but equally they made retreat impossible. The Schuylkill barrier, crossed by a flimsy bridge, prevented quick withdrawal to the east. Two thousand British troops, posted on the high ground across the river, could have controlled both bridge and Fatland ford; two thousand other troops, placed in the narrow defile to the north, would have barred retreat to safety. The rest of Howe's troop, advancing from Philadelphia to attack the front and west flank, might thus pen Washington within the limits of the camp. In the weakened state of the Continental army, there could be but little doubt concerning the outcome of such an attack in force.

To guard against an onslaught, Washington well understood that constant vigilance was highly necessary. His scouting service, alert picket lines, mobile light horsemen, secret agents, all were called upon to play an active part in giving warning of a possible attack. Efficient outposts, acting as his eyes and ears, were urgent requisites if Valley Forge were to be kept safe against surprise.

The tallest trees which stood upon the highest knolls were used as sentry posts. High in the branches of the great white oaks, platforms were erected where sentinels might stand to watch for an approaching enemy. Necessarily, the signal codes were simple, but, by shouts and by dispatch of couriers, word of coming danger could be sent. A line of signal trees, chiefly oaks but one of them the seventy-foot chestnut near the Spread Eagle, extended across the Great Valley, up and down the South Valley hill, to Signal hill, an outpost near Devon, seven miles away from Valley Forge. From this last oak, in favorable weather, a sentinel standing in a half-barrel fastened in the treetop might watch over many miles of open country.

The signal trees were but a makeshift expedient; the real reliance for gathering intelligence was upon a mobile force of scouts. Detachments of troops, mounted wherever possible, kept watch over all possible approaches to Valley Forge. These scouts ranged far from the camp, covering a radius of more than twenty miles. The British were not able to move in force from their Philadelphia camp without running the risk that these scouts would report their movements to the rebels.

James Potter's frontiersmen, guarding the western bank of the Schuylkill, patrolled the Welsh country between Valley Forge and the Middle Ferry. Again and again his pickets, tiring of the passive role of waiting for Howe's attack, raided the British outposts; twice they destroyed the crude bridges flung across the river by Howe's engineers. To Potter's unbounded pride, the militiamen kept the British regulars confined to Philadelphia. Howe dared not send small forage parties beyond the British lines lest Potter's scouts capture the detachments.

Only by sending out the major portion of his army could Howe gather an adequate supply of forage for his cavalry. On one such expedition, the lines of the redcoats stretched three miles along the roads; yet, when the Britishers turned back toward Philadelphia, escorting a thousand tons of hay, the hopelessly outnumbered American scouts rushed recklessly from their hiding places in the woods to attack the rear. It was a reckless exploit, but the foolhardy onslaught was successful. A few of Potter's scouts recovered thirteen wagonloads of food from the strong British column.

Potter's pickets won the most spectacular successes, but they were not invariably efficient. Frequently the British Rangers slipped through the rebel lines. Occasionally, Dragoons penetrated far into the Welsh country, sometimes to within a few scant miles of Valley Forge. In one such episode, Captain Henry Lee, later to be known as "Light Horse Harry" was surprised at Signal Hill near the last sentinel oak.

With fourteen Virginians, Lee was guarding the Valley Forge approach. By a blazing fire, fighting off the crisp January cold on the eve of his twenty-second birthday, Lee heard hoofbeats on the lawn of his ancient farmhouse quarters.

Looking hurriedly out the window, he saw two hundred Dragoons milling about the grounds. The house was surrounded. One of his companions, who had flung open the door to see the cause of the commotion, was so sabered that he could not thereafter fight. Lee's men forced the door shut again, barricaded the doorway as best they could, and seized their guns. The wounded man ran upstairs, threw open a window looking toward Valley Forge, and, pretending to see help advancing, set up a loud cheer and beckoned with his bloody hand. While the British were distracted, another American rode at full speed through the British lines to fetch assistance.

Before the reinforcements arrived, young Major Banastre Tarleton demanded Lee's surrender, threatening to burn the house unless the rebels came out peacefully. The little blond captain, freckle-faced and slight, was not dismayed. "Who but a fool ever threatened to burn a stone house?" he asked.

Tarleton made a final effort to take the house by crawling through a window. A private, seeing him scrambling over the sill, snapped a musket within a foot of Tarleton's head. The gun missed fire. Tarleton pushed himself away from danger, then, smiling, coolly addressed his assailant, "This time, my lad, you missed."

The Dragoons were beaten. They rode off, destroying unprotected farmhouses on their way and capturing four American foragers. The official British loss was four men killed and as many wounded, but tradition insists that twelve British dead are buried in the corner of the old Welsh graveyard near Devon. The Americans lost two dead and four prisoners. Washington sent Lee a letter of congratulation, and thanked him in the general orders. Lee was promoted to the rank of major and each of his comrades received a commission as a reward for bravery.

As a rule, the Americans were busier in raiding the enemy than in repelling surprise attacks. Rebel outposts, stationed far from the encampment, kept the British safely bottled within Philadelphia. On the east bank of the Schuylkill, Americans stationed sentries less than four miles from the center of the town. From these advanced positions the raiders could make sudden unexpected swoops upon the British lines. Thus the rebels kept the redcoats in a constant state of apprehension.

On Christmas Day, for instance, Colonel John Bull led two thousand Pennsylvania militiamen far into Philadelphia "to wish the redcoats a Merry Christmas." He celebrated that snowy day by bombarding the town at such close range that cannon balls were falling close by old Christ Church where the British officers were attending service. When, alarmed by the closeness of the rebels, they rushed out to prepare their men for resistance, Bull successfully withdrew with the loss of but a single man.

Not every outpost was as successful as were those where Potter, Lee, and Bull commanded. Luckless John Lacey, who plunged neck-deep into all the hot waters of Revolutionary times, suffered half a year of almost continuous misfortune.

Pleased with his recent appointment as a brigadier general, Lacey went into his home country near Hatboro to prevent food supplies from being sent to Howe's men in Philadelphia. His assignment was to patrol the strongly rebel region and to warn Washington against surprise attack on Valley Forge. He had few men, but the residents were his friends.

The task seemed easy. The territory lying directly north of Philadelphia was one of the most staunchly patriotic sections of the state. Known for half a century as a nonconformist center, famous for its educated citizenry—it was here that William Tennent had opened his "Log College," which was the spiritual ancestor of Princeton—Lacey's area should have been the easiest region for a rebel general to patrol.

Undoubtedly his force was insufficient for the wide sector under his command. With fewer than fifty men, he was commanded to control more than five hundred square miles of open country. Many of the soldiers, moreover, were nearing the end of their enlistment terms and were giving more thought to leaving the army than to keeping an assiduous patrol. Some were unarmed; others were without sufficient clothing. The morale was poor. British gold, distributed through secret agents, induced a few of Lacey's men to relax their vigilance.

Not only did food continue to seep through to Philadelphia, but Lacey found great difficulty in defending his territory. His first serious setback brought him into renewed conflict with his former nemesis, General Wayne. Mad Anthony, foraging far off in southern New Jersey, had commandeered a herd of a hundred and thirty fat cattle. Evading British scouts, Wayne's men had brought the animals, by a difficult fifty-mile circuitous detour, safely across the Delaware into the presumably friendly region where Lacey was on guard. Wayne's soldier-drover asked the general for an armed escort; Lacey, considering the county safe from danger, refused. Knowing that the Valley Forge camp was virtually bare of food, he ordered the drover to push on immediately without a guard.

Word reached the British that the herd was on its way. A strong force of Dragoons, disguised as countrymen, slipped north to intercept the animals. Riding by day through the forests bordering the Skippack road, camping at night in the woods, they caught the cattle barely eleven miles from Valley Forge.

Then they boldly took to the open roads. Too far east from the camp for the Valley Forge pickets to learn what had occurred, too far west for Lacey's small force to become aware of the capture, the disguised Dragoons drove the sorely needed

243

food away from the starving soldiers at the camp. By careful maneuvering, the British guided the animals along roads midway between the various American outposts. The cattle, thinned by their exhausting travels, came into Philadelphia. They arrived, by unhappy mischance, on Washington's birthday. It was a bitter jest on Washington's hungry men.

So far as Washington was capable of anger, he lost his temper at the catastrophe. He demanded explanations from his outposts. He insisted on knowing why the roads had been left unguarded. He pointed out to Lacey that word of the loss had come to Valley Forge through Philadelphia before Lacey had deigned to report the affair. He commanded Lacey to inform him why the guard had been refused.

Lacey's reply was far from the perfect answer. "Had I suspected the least danger, I should have sent what men I had," Lacey wrote. The reply continued with a rebuke to Washington for expecting Lacey to patrol so wide a territory with so few soldiers. Then Lacey wrote a sheaf of letters to half a dozen brother generals, charging each of them with partial responsibility for the loss of the cattle.

When Lacey had more time to gather his thoughts, he laid the blame upon his soldiers. The shift of responsibility was to be a usual defense for Lacey in his troubles. He blamed Armstrong and Potter for sending him raw recruits and unarmed men but then proceeded to condemn himself by inadvertently declaring that he had himself sent away his guns and stores to distant Allentown. He had so few men, he pathetically remarked to Potter, that he had been expecting to be left alone as the sole defender of the wide region between the Schuylkill and the Delaware.

The defense was unconvincing, but there seemed to be no ground for ordering a court-martial. Washington commanded

Wayne to come back toward Valley Forge, driving before him any cattle he might find and bringing all the horses and the wagons that remained within the Lacey territory. For these, the "well-affected" would receive certificates for which, Wayne hoped, "they may at one day receive compensation." Any forage which could not be carried in the wagons was to be destroyed lest it fall into British hands. "They are," thought Washington, "in more want of forage than of anything else."

Lacey, as usual, misunderstood the directions passed on to him through Wayne from Washington. Smarting under the rebuke for losing the hundred and thirty fat cattle, Lacey called a conference with Brigadier General Lachlan McIntosh at Spring-House Tavern.

The conferees were much alike. Lacey, always the victim of unfortunate circumstance, invariably the victim of his innocent trust in others, met with a Georgian who considered himself the butt of political enemies. McIntosh less than a year before had killed Button Gwinnett, Signer of the Declaration of Independence, in a duel. In all his misfortunes thereafter McIntosh suspected that he was the victim of implacable enemies seeking to avenge the Signer's death.

The two unfortunates evolved a plan to punish traitors who would not cooperate with them in starving the British out of Philadelphia. From the Spring-House they dispatched a letter to George Washington, advising him that they proposed to devastate a fifteen-mile swath between the rivers. Thus, the two generals believed, the British foragers would be compelled to cross a scorched earth strip from which they could derive no help. American light horsemen, dashing through the man-made desert, could readily cut off any wagon trains bound for Philadelphia. Then, "to know the peoples' minds with respect to moving," Lacey set reports afloat of his intention to lay waste the countryside by April 1.

There was an immediate response. Lacey's old associates and neighbors poured complaints upon him, charging him with unheard-of barbarism. Washington promptly disapproved of the suggestion. He wrote from Valley Forge peremptorily forbidding the devastation and expressing his horror and amazement. Lacey was compelled to cancel the arrangements.

His troubles were not over. Receiving reinforcements, he ordered them to take up a stronger position. His men refused to follow his instructions. Instead of marching briskly and in order, they moved, one clear, cool, Sunday evening, in a careless, lazy fashion. Piling their guns upon the wagons, some strolled leisurely; others dozed on the piles of baggage as they jounced along the country road. None kept watch. Lacey failed to say why he did not insist on stricter discipline.

Suddenly they were attacked. Two Dragoon troops, riding out from Philadelphia, fell upon the stragglers. Twelve Americans were killed; six were taken prisoner; the rest fled into the woods. The British took back two wagons loaded with the Lacey baggage.

The worst was still to come. Lacey's four hundred militiamen were again surprised early May Day morning. Camped in the woods at Crooked Billet, the present town of Hatboro, in what was supposedly a strong position, the Americans had failed to post proper guards. Lacey's militiamen were again disobedient. He had ordered his patrols to take their stations at three o'clock in the morning; they failed to leave their beds until almost three hours later.

Meanwhile Major J. G. Simcoe's swift-stepping, green-uniformed Queen's Rangers, a raiding group of American

Tories, cut across the fields in pincerlike formation to hide within the rebel lines. Had the Lacey guards obeyed their orders, the maneuver would have been impossible; but the Rangers, meeting no patrols, came within two hundred yards of Lacey's sleeping camp before their presence was discovered.

The Paoli Massacre was repeated. Firing just sufficient shots to signal the advance to another detachment of royalist troops, the Rangers fell upon the camp with bayonets. Twenty men were killed. Lacey leaped from his bed in his nightdress, snatched up his clothes and ran for his horse. Still unclad, holding his uniform in his hand, he rode across country to a distant woods where the men could be re-formed. His baggage was abandoned. The Rangers did not lose a man.

Just as ugly rumors had spread after Paoli, so local gossip charged the British with atrocities after the Battle of the Crooked Billet. Wounded Americans, Lacey reported, had crept into a strawstack to escape the British. Tories denounced the refugees to the enemy. Then, said Lacey, the Rangers fired the stack, bayoneting the men as they attempted to escape. The tale depends entirely upon the Lacey letters, and at the time the massacre is supposed to have occurred Lacey had already ridden far from the scene.

A further story, for which there seems to be more trustworthy evidence, relates that at the time the buckwheat straw was set afire, the British rounded up civilians whom they suspected of rebel partisanship. There were in the neighborhood two Captain van Buskirks, one a rebel, the other an enthusiastic Tory. Hearing a spectator addressed as Captain van Buskirk, the Ranger leader asked the man if that was his name. The Tory Captain, expecting to be thanked for his services to the King, admitted that he was Captain van Buskirk. He was at once arrested, though he protested his

247

loyalty. The pro-rebel neighbors kept silent while he was bound for transport to the city. The jailing at Philadelphia, it is said, converted the Tory to the patriotic cause.

On their way back to Philadelphia, the jubilant Rangers, who prided themselves on their nickname "Blood-Hounds of the Revolution," pillaged the countryside of whatever was portable.

Lacey was court-martialed for his negligence in the Crooked Billet disaster, but he convinced the court that the surprise was due to the disobedience of his troops. Had his orders been carried out, he showed, the attack could not have been successful.

Realizing that additional outposts were essential to plug up the holes through which the captured cattle had been passed into Philadelphia and to guard against future surprise attacks, Washington belatedly sent new forces to protect approach to Valley Forge. Lafayette, newly returned from his unfortunate Canadian expedition, was detailed to take two thousand men to watch the roads along the eastern Schuylkill River shore.

He took up a strong position at Barren Hill, close to what is now the Philadelphia city line. One flank rested on the heights of a steep bluff overlooking the river; the far flank commanded the Bethlehem and Skippack roads from Philadelphia. Fifty Oneida Indians were sent two miles southward, into what is now Roxborough, to warn of any British move along the Ridge road. Lafayette himself held the center, near the Reverend Michael Schlatter's old stone church at Barren Hill.

Schlatter, Swiss-born missionary soldier who, in 1754, had been the first Pennsylvania superintendent of schools, had set up here a thriving settlement. Sunday after Sunday, he had thundered from the pulpit his condemnation of the Tories. Most of his male parishioners had joined the local militia bands and were away when Lafayette arrived, but the women remained to support Schlatter's war activities. It was regarded by them as a very special mark of favor for the bustling pastor, scurrying in his usual fashion up the aisle toward the pulpit, absent-mindedly to stop short and, without a word, raise the short starched apron of one of the ladies to clean his glasses. Then, without a word of thanks, he would drop the apron, nervously fit the glasses to his eyes, and hurry to the pulpit to preach one of his denunciatory sermons.

Schlatter, however, was now in British hands, lying in Walnut Street jail in Philadelphia as a punishment for his rebelliousness. Most of the women had made a regular practice of riding into town to take him food. Among them was his daughter, the athletic, almost masculine, fourteen-year-old Rachel, youngest of the nine Schlatter children.

Lafayette made use of the opportunity. He sent Rachel to call upon her father and to bring back word of what the British troops were doing. Rachel reported that she had seen a force of redcoat cavalry on the highway to the east of Barren Hill. Lafayette, believing that the girl had confused British Dragoons with some of the red-coated Pennsylvania militiamen whom he had sent to watch the eastern roads, paid slight attention to the warning.

The warning was, however, based on fact. The British were on the march to capture Lafayette. Howe had learned of Lafayette's position. A plan to fall upon the rebel force was hurriedly executed. General James Grant, with more than five thousand men, was sent by a roundabout route to a place where he might cut off the American retreat to Valley Forge. Muffling the wheels of the artillery, moving in the early morning hours, Grant quietly advanced through Frankford, in the far northeastern part of Philadelphia, around the northern boundary of the city to Lafayette's rear. Grey, the victor at Paoli, marched with equal silence by another, more direct, route to prevent Lafayette's escape toward the east. Howe and Clinton, with a huge force, marched by the Ridge road through the Falls of Schuylkill, to attack Lafayette's advance positions.

The plan was perfect. Superior British forces blocked the Americans on three sides; the high wooded bluff and the river prevented flight on the only possible outlet. Had the British generals been efficient in the execution of the strategy, Howe would have made good his boast that Lafayette would soon be prisoner.

Grant, however, was too slow on his long march. Dawn began to break. A rebel sympathizer, James Stoy, awoke to see the British marching and, slowly strolling out of the British sight into a near-by woods, rushed through forests and across open fields to warn the rebels. He was exhausted before he reached the Barren Hill positions, but he waked a friend, Rudolph Bartle, who took up the task.

Lafayette thus learned that Rachel's warning had been true, and that the British were close by. He did not know that his left flank, set to guard the Bethlehem and Skippack roads, had retreated at the first sight of Grey's redcoats. No warning had been sent by the militiamen that the British were near. Soon after, he discovered that his Oneida Indians, having caught their first glimpse of Howe's resplendent British Dragoons, were so terrified by the glittering crimson and gold uniforms that they broke and fled. After one volley, the Oneidas warwhooped and dashed for the Schuylkill. The Dragoons, almost equally terrified by their first sight of Indians, were too

250

amazed to fire a shot. They watched the Oneidas splashing to safety across the Schuylkill.

Lafayette had time to perfect his lines before the British columns converged upon him. Sending a small detachment to oppose Grant, he ordered them to fire briskly and to give an impression that they were a much larger force. While Grant halted in perplexity, calling a council to determine what strategy to use against this supposed attack by the entire Lafayette force, the rebels retreated through the woods by a "depressed road" under cover of high hills to the river. A small force stationed behind the old stone wall at Schlatter's church, held off Howe's advance until the main body of the army was safely on its way to Matson's Ford, at what is now Conshohocken. The Americans lost ten killed and thirty prisoners at Barren Hill, but they crossed the river without losing a man. The British report describing the rebel fording of the stream says that the Americans dotted the Schuylkill like the "corks of a seine."

Lafayette remained on the west bank of the Schuylkill until the British force returned to Philadelphia. Then he returned to take up his old position at Schlatter's church. The outpost remained here until certain news arrived that the British were intending to depart from Philadelphia.

For the remaining weeks of the encampment, Washington felt sure that no British advance could be made upon Valley Forge without giving ample warning. He had heard the guns of the Barren Hill engagement and had drawn his army into battle formation. The troops were prepared to march to Lafayette's relief had the engagement been long continued. The British believed, indeed, that Washington had come close enough to Barren Hill to watch the fighting through his telescope.

CHAPTER TWENTY-TWO

Breaking Camp

THE worst privations were now passed. Spring brought abundant food; the roads, no longer snow-bound, dried out and let the army wagons roll; the commissariat, under Greene's efficient care, poured needed supplies into camp. The spirits of the men revived.

Even yet the army was irregularly uniformed. Smallwood's gray-clad Marylanders, the Delaware Blues, and Pulaski's gay Light Horse wore uniforms sufficiently diverse to make them seem like soldiers of entirely different armies. Some of the detachments wore clothes exactly like the British uniforms. Pennsylvanians, indeed, had fired upon fellow Continentals, thinking them an enemy force; Connecticut troopers had engaged in sharp civil war because men from the same state could not recognize their comrades.

Some of the confusion came because the army had been dressed in captured clothing. A British brig, sent from England with scarlet and blue cloth for three thousand British soldiers, had been captured in the river below Wilmington and its cargo had been forwarded by wide roundabout detours to the camp at Valley Forge. With the captured cargo came a despondent British captain.

BREAKING CAMP

An hour before the capture, this Captain Nicholas had been boasting of his luck. "His Majesty," he had been saying, "has made me commander of a fine ship; I need never fight. I have nothing to do but transport gentlemen and ladies of the first rank. I have a fine stock of provisions aboard, hens, turkeys, geese, pigs, ducks, wine and cider. I have a good interest at home, and, what is above all, an agreeable family. I am not troubled in my mind. In short, I've nothing to make me uneasy, and I believe that I am the happiest man in the world."

The jubilation had been short-lived. Rebel privateers, evading the British naval patrol, caught his brig at a river bend while it was tacking against the wind, and, sending boatloads of supposed fishermen against the ship, took the vessel unawares. Captain Nicholas had lost his cargo and his luxuries.

Hats, shirts, shoes and stockings, boots and spurs were included in the prize, together with four thousand gold-and-silver epaulets. There was sufficient clothing in the cargo to care for all the Continental officers and, in addition, to help out many of the less fortunate private soldiers.

The Americans were delighted at their capture but, even in their happiness, they were torn by petty differences. The pride of rank remained. The colonels and the majors sought to secure for themselves and their immediate associates the benefits of the prize. They drew up a petition asking Washington to allot the cloth to "regimental officers only." The petition definitely stated that "commissaries, bull-drivers, etc." ought to be deprived of any benefit. Washington, while unwilling to brand any of his force as undeserving, gave first choice of material to the officers and men on active duty.

The capture, even of so large a quantity of cloth, did not end all need. Only a fourth of the soldiers could be cared for, and even these were not completely equipped during all the weeks of winter. The uniforms, though made of excellent thick material, could not stand the severities to which they were subjected. Constant use of coats in snow and rainy weather, by cabin comrades who lent their uniforms to those whose turn it was to go on watch, wore out good cloth more rapidly than could have been anticipated. Long before the winter was over the men were again in need of clothing. The same cry for clothing continued throughout the war.

In this emergency, as in so many other crises, the French alliance proved its worth. With the French definitely aiding the Americans, sea lanes were more open to the rebels. Supply ships, under the convoy of French frigates, brought cargoes of clothing, munitions, and medicines for the Continental troops. The shipments, to be sure, were necessarily landed at out-of-the-way ports and had to be transported by indirect roads to avoid the British, but the flow of goods came steadily and in abundant quantity.

Now that the men were adequately clothed, dapper General Anthony Wayne insisted that the army must spruce up in its appearance. For more than a year, he had complained that the troops had been careless, frowzy, and unkempt. Clothing, he had repeatedly pointed out, might lack uniformity and might be of poor quality, but "the soldier may always shave his beard, appear with clean hands and face, and, in general, have an air of neatness." During the period of privation, when "the whole army was sick and crawling with vermin," he had been unable to keep his men immaculate but, with the return of warm spring weather, and with brand-new uniforms, he demanded cleanliness.

As soon as his men were well equipped with clothes, Wayne ordered that barbers be appointed in each company to cut the hair of every soldier, and that tailors be assigned to keep the clothing in condition. Needles and thread were issued so that each man might mend his uniform.

His next step was to command his men to strip for a river swim. Each soldier in Wayne's division was ordered to go into the Schuylkill for a regular Friday bath. Corporals and sergeants stood upon the bank with watches, timing the troops to see that no man came out of the water until his allotted ten minutes had expired. Though lilac buds had swelled in mid-March and though peepers had sounded from the lowland marshes for many weeks before the bath commands were issued, the water was still cold. The soldiers complained that the stream was "near as cold as mid-winter," but Wayne insisted that the baths continue.

As an example to the remainder of the army, Wayne's clean division, new-clothed, fresh-shaved and with well powdered hair, paraded through the encampment. Farmers and frontiersmen of other commands, unaccustomed to the niceties, jeered at Wayne's macaronis, but soon learned that they, too, had orders to follow the Pennsylvanians into the river. The days of raggedness and dirt were over.

Steuben's iron discipline was now showing its results. The men complained that he was treating them as though they were Germans, and some murmured that Steuben was himself no better than a Hessian; but, for the first time in the history of the Revolution, the American orders were implicitly obeyed. Sentries were not now sleeping at their posts; watch was rigorously kept; army guns and uniforms were no longer bartered.

Better guns were available, after the conclusion of the French alliance. When the Revolution first broke out, each volunteer had brought his own village-made flintlock. These required great care; each night, the soldiers were obliged to clean their guns with oil, to polish the long barrels with buckskin, and to wax the wooden stocks. Long marches in bad weather had prevented these precautions against rust and deterioration. Guns had broken, and, since almost all the weapons had been handmade by local gunsmiths, new parts were difficult to find. In consequence, many of the men had been armed with clubs, or with "spontoons." Now that the French Alliance provided a steady flow of munitions, new French guns became available.

Standard flintlocks replaced the homemade muskets. No longer was it necessary for the troops to spend their evenings molding lead bullets of various sizes to fit different guns. Cartridges could be made in quantity for use in all the guns of any company. Although the novelty of the flint gun induced the troops to snap the lock too frequently in play, so that the sixty-round capacity of a good flint was prematurely exhausted, the waste of flints was soon stopped when Greene recommended that unnecessary snappings be punished by two days' confinement in the guardhouse on bread and water.

Long before the spring was over, Washington's army had been drilled, equipped, and formed into an efficient force. The old practice of shifting at will from one regiment to another had been stopped; the careless granting of furloughs to go home on unrestricted leaves of absence had been ended; the hiring of other soldiers to perform the necessary camp duties had been rigorously forbidden. Steuben had built Washington's disorganized army into an efficient band of trained men quite equal to European professionals.

The spirit of the camp had changed. Instead of being diverse units from rival states, each jealous of the others, and each suspicious that the foreigners would steal away American liberty, the troops were firmly bound to the common Continental cause. Virginians who, in February, had refused to take an oath of allegiance to the Continental Congress until they were assured by their political advisers that the oath did not reduce their state to servitude, now stood shoulder to shoulder with the New Englanders whom they once had suspected. Pennsylvanians who had meditated a secession from the other commonwealths now realized that every other former colony was a friend and not an enemy. The army had become, in truth, the "band of brothers" which Washington had sought to form.

Nor were they longer on the defensive. Du Portail's elaborate system of fortifications which he believed had made the camp impregnable against attack seemed not so necessary in the balmy spring as in the wintry February when the defensive works had been begun. The generals, especially the hotheaded group which looked on Wayne as leader, planned to force a fight upon the city-entrenched British.

The men were so restored in health that even the little stone hospital in the midst of the encampment ground, built for Letitia Penn in 1707, was no longer filled with the sick. This last hospital, now cleared of patients, was cleaned and was used as a camp school to give the rudiments of the "three R's" to soldiers anxious to improve their leisure time. Lessons continued daily through the remaining weeks of the Valley Forge encampment.

The men were looking forward to a resumption of the war. Rumors penetrated to the camp that the British were stirring at Philadelphia, and that the redcoats would soon leave the city. The destination was unknown, though Washington's strategists suspected that the enemy would withdraw from Philadelphia to New York to concentrate the British forces and to reunite the invading army for a new attack in force. In the event that such withdrawal should occur, the Americans planned to make a rapid movement across Pennsylvania to meet the British in northern New Jersey. The Valley Forge encampment waited eagerly for news that Philadelphia was evacuated.

Not until mid-June, however, did the British stir from their winter quarters. Washington's men, anxious and alert at Valley Forge, dared not make direct attack upon the well fortified British camp; nor was it possible to approach the city by assault upon the Middle Ferry. To do so, the strategists knew, would give the English an easy escape through the fertile northern part of Philadelphia and might jeopardize the valuable iron-making regions. Washington could do nothing until the British had completely withdrawn from Pennsylvania into the flat New Jersey plains. The Continentals waited until that moment should arrive.

Some British regiments left the town on June 3, but two weeks more went by before all the tents were struck and the garrison marched south into the Neck, that portion of Philadelphia where the Schuylkill empties into the Delaware. Exactly a month after the gay *Meschianza,* the remaining redcoat troops were ferried over the Delaware.

Through his spies, Washington had long known that evacuation was contemplated. As soon as the British heavy artillery had been set across the Delaware, American scouting parties had ventured far beyond the site of the burned Rising Sun almost to the British abatis. Scarcely had the first British grenadiers been embarked upon the boats to take them over the river before rebel horsemen were within the city. American troopers rode up to the wharves to take quick shots at the last boatloads of retreating redcoats.

BREAKING CAMP

Within two hours of the enemy departure the news came to Valley Forge. Almost immediately the drums were sounded recalling men to their regimental posts. The "grass-guard" which watched the horses at pasture was called in; the pickets were brought back from the crossroads posts which they had watched so efficiently ever since the establishment of the camp; the trenches were abandoned. Little packing was required, for the men had been ordered days before to be prepared to march. Before noon on June 19, the day that the British left Philadelphia, the first American detachments were crossing Sullivan's bridge.

The well drilled, beautifully aligned army which marched in carefully formed columns through the Fatlands toward spook-ridden Whitpain and Welsh Gwynedd, to Doyle's tavern and Coryell's ferry on the Delaware was a vastly different army from that which had stumbled through the snows six months before. Steuben had done his work well. The despondent men of whom Washington had said, in December, "Unless some great and capital change suddenly takes place . . . this army must starve, dissolve, or disperse," had grown into a coherent, proud, high-spirited, and eager force of patriots. Not only was there a professional appearance to their sparkling bayonets, properly angled on their shoulders, but there was an alert spring to their easy, natural step, "about half way betwixt slow and quick," as the soldiers moved ahead to the beating of drums and to the piping of shrill fifes.

They sang now as they marched, but the dirgelike "Lamentation over Boston," closely copying with its "By the waters of Watertown we sat down and wept" the wording of the Psalms, was not now their hymn on this triumphal march. Eccentric William Billings' "Chester" set the key for these

259

confident troopers as they hurried to intercept the retreating enemy. Thousands of voices chanted:

> Let tyrants shake their iron rods
> And Slavery clank her galling chains;
> We fear them not, we trust in God;
> New England's God forever reigns.

Billings was blind and slovenly, the Massachusetts men admitted; he was crooked and deformed; his arm was withered, and one eye was blind; but crow-voiced William Billings could inspire an army with his songs.

The rollicking "Liberty Song" and the lusty, salty "Nothing Like Grog," which the troops had learned from privateersmen, rang out over the low hills over which the men were marching. Schoolmaster Andrew Law's soft, slow "Bunker Hill" and the tripping, dancelike "Washington Lyric" lent variation to the soldier's chorus. Never before had Continental soldiers sung so gayly nor so spontaneously as on their march away from Valley Forge.

Ten days later, they met the retreating British army at the battle of Monmouth. Ten thousand fighters rushed to battle shouting the inspiriting

> Come, join hand in hand,
> Brave Americans all;
> And rouse your whole band
> At Liberty's call.

It was the same catchy song that had set the Sons of Liberty on fire at Dorchester in the first days of the war. The loud chorus was a proof that the once dispirited Continental army had regained its confidence.

CHAPTER TWENTY-THREE

The Two-Man Army

HISTORY writing moves in cycles. In distant days the deeds of heroes were granted chief acclaim. An era followed, wherein the men of muscle were subordinate to kings, generals, and statesmen. The change unquestionably brought sounder history, but it has cost readers the acquaintance of thousands of exciting personalities who raged and swore and won their ends by violence. Then came, in turn, the sour debunkers, the hard materialists, the soft social historians, until again the movie-struck scenarist restored to a central interest the swaggering swashbuckler.

Such a gay and reckless desperado was Big Jim Fitzpatrick, first among the tavern athletes of the Revolutionary times. He owned no culture and no subtlety, he had no ethics and no sense of shame; he was an elemental creature of low sensibility. Moved entirely by his passions and reflexes, Big Jim was an abysmal brute. An Irish immigrant bound out to serve his passage cost at John Passmore's blacksmith shop, he fascinated gentler folk by his amazing feats of strength. Passmore's ten small daughters and his two young sons were captivated by the redemptioner's mighty muscles.

Those swelling biceps, developed by apprenticeship at Passmore's anvil, called forth no envy, however, from the stodgy, peaceful neighbors. Quakers much preferred the contemplation of the spirit to rivalries at wrestling. Adolescent boys might for a time admire the feats of strength, demure Quaker misses might thrill at sight of brawn; but these strayings from the ideal discipline were readily corrected. The quiet devastation of a First Day disapproval or, if matters came to so extreme a pass, the testimony of formal Quarterly assembly, would put an end to all such worldly matters.

Today, of course, Big Jim Fitzpatrick would be happier. The neighborhood in which he lived is still a Quaker settlement, but the occupations offer greater opportunity to men of might. Steel mills and quarries, heavy metal industries, the pasturage of blooded stock, the schooling of thoroughbreds for famous eastern Pennsylvania hunts, assure an outlet for pent-up energies.

The Revolutionary years were far less glamorous. Shoeing Quaker horses had but slight appeal. There was no athletic relaxation. The good old Irish games were frowned upon; wrestling was disapproved; Saturday carouses were forbidden flatly. When, therefore, the newborn Commonwealth of Pennsylvania called for men to sign up for the state militia, Jim dropped his hammer and responded promptly.

Patriotic sentiment had no bearing on the matter. Either the rebel cause or that of the Tories would have served if only the army offered hand-to-hand encounters, continued excitement, and, above all, an abundance of rich, red meat at every meal. The Quakers, Fitz believed, were not addicted to the pleasures of the table.

Military life seemed perfect. The long march overland to join the militia was enjoyable. Fitz reveled in new adventures, among companions who were frankly envious of his tremendous strength. He and his friends laughed heartily at the strange Welsh folks who lived along the Philadelphia road; they roared at the undeserved quip that the name of the miry, unpaved capital was really "Filthy-dirty"; they were delighted when frightened housewives thought that these "long-faced" recruits were Hessian soldiers. Friendly taverns were met at almost every mile where innkeepers gave to volunteers a plentiful amount of good hard cider. Tavern owners dared not refuse the boon, for those who failed in generosity might be denounced as Tories. Discipline was lax upon this march, lest the volunteers desert before they came to camp.

Once safely in the army, Jim found that military life was not all loot and laughter. He did not seriously object to early rising, nor to constant drill and simple routine tasks. These were duties which he expected, and which he could do well. But when the officers turned stern and barked quick orders which he must immediately obey under penalty of lashings from a rawhide whip, when he was made to live by clockwork and to dwell in what he thought a prisonlike condition, when striplings younger and far feebler than himself were set above him as his masters, Jim Fitzpatrick was dismayed. This was not the liberty which he had pictured; this was no better than his blacksmith's life. Fitz was disillusioned. The food at Passmore's home was heartier and more abundant, more regular in its arrival.

Disgusted at the army, Fitz and his close satellite, Mordecai Dougherty, swam the Hudson River and started to walk back toward Valley Forge. At the first farmhouse they ate a big meal, drank their fill of cider, and, before they left, dressed themselves in farm-hand jeans. Henceforth, they considered themselves free civilians.

The two deserters were simple souls. In all innocence, they headed straight for Passmore's blacksmith shop, believing that their change of heart was sufficient excuse for abandoning the army. They were indignant when the Pennsylvania authorities arrested them for desertion.

If, however, the fugitives were naive, the military authorities were stupid. The army needed men; Fitz and Mordecai were well built fighters. At Philadelphia's Walnut Street jail, the prison keepers offered freedom to the strong boys on condition that they report to regimental headquarters on the Hudson.

Promises meant little to Big Fitz. His mind grasped no abstractions. If the keepers were willing to let him leave the crowded, filthy, almost airless jail, he and Mordecai would swear any promises that might be asked.

Happily, they went back to Passmore. But the soldiers were not finished with the parole breakers. Militiamen were not so numerous that a likely volunteer could easily be spared; nor was it prudent to allow recruits to quit at pleasure. The army sought Jim Fitz.

This time the officers failed to find the deserters. Passmore had sent the boys to distant fields to make hay. No one gave information where the parole breakers might be found. The searching party gave up and returned to Philadelphia with word that the two deserters had escaped.

No moron strong boy who had twice deserted and had fooled the prison keepers could be expected to keep silent. Hard cider loosed Jim Fitz's tongue. The loungers at the crossroads tavern, eager at first to hear of these Ulysses-like adventures, grew bored with repetitions and indignant at the elaborations that the story steadily received. They were jealous of the Fitz exploits, and they were resentful that Chellie, the tavern siren, listened so eagerly to the handsome Irishman's inventions. Once the sweetheart of all the small community, Chellie was now the willing slave of Hero Jim Fitzpatrick.

In time, perhaps, Fitz might have been betrayed by his jealous tavern associates, as their last step toward recovering the affections of the errant Chellie; but sheer accident forestalled the need for treachery. Two wandering soldiers, stopping for a hasty mug of hot rum, happened to overhear a secondhand narration of the Fitzpatrick exploits. Aware that rewards were given to those who caught deserters, the newcomers listened carefully, learned that Jim Fitz was mowing one of Passmore's fields, and set out for the capture.

Jim, caught unawares, looked up from his scything to see two fully armed soldiers covering him with loaded guns. Realizing that he could not fight his way to freedom, he surrendered. The soldiers commanded that he march ahead of them to army headquarters. Fitz agreed to go.

"But let me go home first," said he, "to get my uniform. It isn't far out of our way. It won't take long. If I've got to go back to the army I'll have to have my clothes."

The captors were, at first, inclined to refuse. Then the recollection that special bounties were paid for the recovery of army property persuaded them that the request was reasonable. Fitz marched ahead, scythe over his shoulder, while his two captors followed with leveled bayonets. In this order Chellie saw them come to Fitz's isolated shanty. Fitz marched straight past the girl, quickly winking as he went by; then, opening the door, he reached suddenly to the wall, seized a rifle, threw it to his shoulder and threatened to fire unless the soldiers cleared out. When they left in haste, Fitz grinned, smacked Chellie briskly, and returned to his scything. He continued to work the farm as though nothing had happened. The two brave captors evidently made no report to their superiors, for Fitz was not thereafter bothered.

His warlike fever flared again when Howe arrived at Elkton. In hope, probably, that allegiance to the British would grant freedom to plunder, Fitz marched with the British, fought against the Americans at Brandywine, followed Howe through eastern Pennsylvania and entered Philadelphia triumphantly. One of his first calls was at the Walnut Street prison, but he was disappointed to discover that his friends the keepers were no longer in residence.

Jim's military experience had not been extensive, but after service in two opposing armies it seemed to him and to the faithful Chellie only proper that he should receive promotion. From the time of his "capture" of Philadelphia the big blacksmith assumed the rank of captain. Henceforth, as commander of an army of one man, Lieutenant Mordecai, the self-appointed Captain Fitz swaggered through the streets of a city which he, together with Cornwallis and Howe, had captured for the Crown.

The British generals were loath to recognize the title of their colleague, but they were wholly willing to make use of his services. Britain had need of such as Jim Fitzpatrick. The army was nearly blind for want of an efficient secret service. No redcoat could go forth among the Pennsylvania farmers to bring in adequate reports; few Quaker citizens could be relied upon to gather helpful information. Fitz, well acquainted with the local customs, could perform an effective service as spy and provisioner.

There was profit in such enterprise. For some weeks after the capture of the capital, the English were besieged. Rebel fleets and forts cut off the city from the sea; Potter's militiamen blocked communication with the countryside. Scattered riders could hurry into town with a few pounds of flour or a bit of meat, but no pack train sufficient for the feeding of ten thousand troops and thirty thousand civilians could break through the rebel lines. So long as the Delaware was blocked, the Englishmen were short of supplies.

Food costs shot skyward. Good beef, normally selling at ten cents a pound, now cost the army sixty cents. Civilians paid much more, especially if they gave paper money. Flour prices tripled almost immediately upon the occupation and, as the supplies in warehouses were exhausted, went even higher. A chicken cost ten shillings; brown sugar sold at six shillings a pound; chocolate, the favorite Philadelphia breakfast drink, fetched five shillings.

Rich pay in hard British gold awaited the smugglers of supplies. The rewards were irresistible to those who held their purses dearer than their principles. Small-minded men who were willing to betray their friends for gain, drove off the livestock from the fields of patriot Americans. Sometimes the marauders were well known; more often the denouncers secretly disclosed hidden stores to British raiding parties.

In such enterprise Captain Fitz was in his element. His private army, Lieutenant Mordecai and private Chellie, robbed hen roosts, mills, and barnyards. Their raids upon the Whigs were so frequent and so profitable that, even after the Delaware was opened, Fitz carried on the commandeering for his private gain.

To give him advance information, Chellie took service in a patriot house where she could gain the confidence of rebel leaders. Learning when new supplies were expected, she told Captain Fitz about the plans; and she shared in the profits of his ambushing. She gave him warning, too, when posses were prepared to hunt him down. Thus it was possible for Fitz, pursued by angry rebels, to escape.

Fitz dramatized himself as a daring desperado. On one occasion fifty well armed men set out for his capture. They roamed the hills for hours but, finding no trace of their man, gave up the chase at nightfall. Wearied of the futile effort, they stopped at a tavern for refreshment. Food and rest and warmth and drink restored their spirit. The talk grew louder and more confident. Daringly they boasted of their determination to kill the criminal. Each man sighed that he had had no opportunity to meet with Fitz in hand-to-hand encounter.

The door swung open. All eyes turned to greet the newcomer. A rifle stared them back. Captain Fitz was swaggering. "Keep your seats," he called. "I'll shoot the man who moves." Then, striding to the bar, he called for rum, toasted the company, drank down the liquor, smashed the glass against the wall, walked backward to the door, courteously took leave of his friends, wheeled, and disappeared into the dark.

Soon after, another party of some twenty hunters searched the hills for Fitz. The men spread out in a long line through the woods, determined to sweep the area. The man upon the left wing saw a stranger step into the open.

"Can I assist you?" asked the stranger.

"I am looking for a man," the hunter answered.

"For whom?"

"For Fitz, damn him!"

"For Fitz? That's lucky. I know where he is. Come with me, and I will show you to his cave."

The gullible man hunter followed his new-found friend. Fitz led him beyond the sight of other trackers, put a pistol to the searcher's forehead, tied him to a tree, gagged him, and then flogged him with a length of heavy grapevine. "Now go, and tell your friends that you have smoked out Captain Fitz," the desperado mocked.

Certainly the former blacksmith was not devoid of courage. His daring was worthy of a better cause and of a better fate. Despairing of taking him by force, the Pennsylvania Supreme Executive Council tried to trap him by a purse of gold. Captain Fitz, learning that a price was put upon his head, deliberately marched down in broad daylight from the hills. Armed with two pistols and a dagger, he strode through the village streets. Although many of the men had muskets in their hands, they opened the way for him to Taylor's tavern. There Fitz called for rum, drank down an ironic toast to "King Cong," the Tory nickname for the Congress, banged down his glass and walked away unharmed.

But the big blacksmith was betrayed. Chellie was bribed. Word was sent to Captain Fitz that Captain Robert McAfee had been supplied with two hundred and fifty pounds in gold for payment of militiamen. Chellie added that McAfee would be alone that night, and that the specie could be stolen with but little danger. She did not add that round about the house a ring of rebels would be waiting to catch Fitz in their trap.

Fitz trusted Chellie. He arrived at night, found McAfee at home with two other men, and demanded the money. McAfee denied that he had any cash. Fitz searched the room in vain while the three men waited for their opportunity. In the midst of the excitement a woman of the McAfee household came downstairs. The courtly desperado did not forget his manners.

"I'm sorry to have disturbed you, ma'am," he said. "I hope that you are well. No harm will come to anyone tonight."

The search was fruitless. Fitz was about to leave when he

spied a pair of McAfee's new shoes. He picked them up to carry them away, then, changing his mind, he laid his pistol on the table while he tried them on.

It was McAfee's opportunity. Quickly the militia captain swung around, threw himself on Captain Fitz, and with the aid of his two friends pinioned the bandit. McAfee then went outdoors to call the ambush party. It had not until then dared approach the house.

Even so, Fitz almost effected an escape. While the captors were waiting the arrival of the rebel soldiers, a boy and a girl, moved by curiosity, entered the McAfee house. Fitz was lying bound on the floor and the girl, leaning over him, smoothed his hair and caressed him. Then, saying that Fitz was cold, she threw a blanket over him and, under cover of the blanket, she loosed his bonds. Fitz, however, could not get away before the American troops arrived.

Twice during his trial, Fitz broke away to freedom; and, when placed in irons following his recapture, he twice filed through his chains. He was, however, convicted of burglary, treason, and desertion, and was condemned to death. A month after his capture, Jim Fitz was hanged. Lieutenant Mordecai was never seen again.

Captain McAfee gained the thousand dollars reward offered for his capture. He used the money to buy an interest in the old Syng mansion at St. George's, where he again established a tavern.

Chellie indignantly complained that she had been cheated of her rightful reward. Insisting that she alone had been responsible for the capture, she refused the offer of half the head money. For months thereafter she wandered about, lamenting that she had been unforgivably tricked.

"Jim had his faults," she said, "but Jim was honest."

CHAPTER TWENTY-FOUR

Hessians Return

SOON after the American evacuation, the Hessians returned to Valley Forge. This time, however, they did not come as conquerors to raid the farms and to destroy the mills; they came unwillingly, under guard, as prisoners.

Sickly and sallow, they came with bitter complaints of ill treatment and abuse. Burgoyne had surrendered them at Saratoga under the express convention that they should be repatriated; but, though Canadians, Tories, and even Indians had been permitted to go home, they had been singled out for punishment. For a year these Convention Troops, so called because of the Burgoyne agreement, had been interned. Then, because no troopships had come to take them back to Germany, they were ordered to leave their camp in Massachusetts and go south to winter quarters.

The march was started in December, 1778. The Americans, hoping that the Convention Troops would dwindle through desertion and so save the United States the cost of feeding captives, were lax in guarding the prisoners. The Hessians, ragged and bedraggled after their year's internment, strolled southward almost as they pleased. Not knowing English, fearful that the patriotic farmers would attack them, trained to implicit obedience, they plodded straight ahead through New England, New York, and New Jersey.

In Pennsylvania, it was hoped, the Convention Troops would desert. Ragged, homesick Hessians, hearing the familiar syllables of their fatherland, envying the well stocked farms of their compatriots, seeing the huge barns "nearly as large as common country churches," looking hungrily upon the fat geese, hobbled by the curious foot-long cross sticks fastened round their necks to prevent their flying, would, the Americans believed, be induced to run away. In Pennsylvania German country, the guards deliberately lagged far behind the marching columns, leaving the Hessians unwatched almost all day long, affording every opportunity for the prisoners to stray.

In regions so far removed from Valley Forge that there had been no ravages of war, the German residents were willing to be friendly. Buxom Pennsylvania girls, flaxen-haired and red-cheeked, stared hard at the brass-capped, heavily mustachioed Hessians. But when the marchers tried to talk to them, the strange Pennsylvania German dialect proved difficult to understand. The homes of Hessians had been close to the Palatinate from whence the ancestors of these Pennsylvanians had come; but in the course of half a century the language in America had been corrupted.

The few British prisoners were more puzzled than the Hessian troopers. English, they discovered, could not be understood at all in upstate Pennsylvania; pure German such as had been taught in British schools was quite unintelligible to these strange farmers; Latin, which some desperate British officers tried to speak as an alternative, was much less understood. The British, in despair, fell back upon the belief that

Pennsylvania Germans were stupid folk "incapable of human understanding."

Though the people in remote upstate Pennsylvania German districts were friendly enough, even to the point of offering their daughters as wives to Hessians who would remain behind, the Convention Troopers feared to stay. The Hessians did not like America. They complained that in everything the United States was inferior to Germany. The food, they said, had little nourishment; the animals were half-grown specimens; though American geese, they grudgingly admitted, were as good as German fowl, the taste was no better; the much-praised American wild game, the Hessians thought, was just ordinary meat.

The prisoners feared even the friendly Pennsylvania Germans. "I have never," wrote one astonished Hessian, "seen so many madmen in my life." Heavy stands of timber and the numerous running brooks, the Hessians thought, were not only unhealthy but weakening to the American intelligence. The highly changeable climate, with its extremes of heat and cold, seemed unendurable to the mercenaries.

Tales of the fearsome wild animals frightened the gullible Convention Troops. They feared the snakes, particularly the rattlers—which, they were told, were sixteen feet long with doglike heads capable of biting off a human leg. The Hessians were assured that rattlesnakes had the power of charming human beings to a point where men were too paralyzed to move. A rattlesnake "perched in a tree" could, the Hessians believed, catch a man's eye and so deprive him of the power of motion that the man would stand stock-still until he toppled over dead.

The summer fireflies had already proved an unending source of wonder. Great dots of greenish light flickering over

273

New York pastures had caused the Hessians to credit tales of ghostly elves. Unaccustomed to such sights in Germany, the Hessians had believed that fireflies were portents of disaster. Sentries on guard with Burgoyne's army had frequently mistaken the insects for the lights of an approaching American army. In Pennsylvania pasture land, they were told, the spooks were far more numerous than in the Hudson valley.

Few of Burgoyne's three thousand men stayed, then, in the friendly upstate German settlements. In spite of the loose watch kept over them, in spite of all the open encouragement given them to run away, the docile Hessians clung together. Almost without a guard, the prisoners trudged along through unknown country toward their winter quarters in the distant south.

As the wandering mercenaries drew closer to the regions where battles had been fought, the welcomes faded. Close to Valley Forge, the Pennsylvania Germans showed intense hatred of their captured kin. Farmers refused to give them shelter; housewives fled at their approach; food was difficult to find. Burgoyne's men were being punished for the excesses committed by the Knyphausen marauders.

Six months after the evacuation, and precisely a year after Washington's arrival at the wintry camp, the Hessians filed across Sullivan's log bridge into the encampment grounds. Major General Friedrich Riedesel, traveling with his wife and his "hungry family of children," billeted his men in the "three thousand sheds" left by the Americans. The camp, which he said looked "like a badly built town," was, the few residents informed him, now called Washington.

For several days, the Hessians lived at the encampment. As further incentive to desert, the German officers were allowed

274

to travel down to Philadelphia to see the capital and observe for themselves the prosperity and the high morale of the American civilians. British officers were, however, refused permission to accompany their German friends. They spent their time in inspecting the supposedly "insuperable camp" and in criticizing their late commander Howe for not assaulting the encampment upon its right flank and upon the wide-flung front. They came to the conclusion that Howe had suffered, like Burgoyne, for want of an efficient intelligence service to give him adequate and accurate reports.

"The Americans have a decided superiority over us," the captured British reasoned. "Our post and situations, nay even our secret marches, with their intentions, are made known to General Washington by the innumerable spies and secret enemies who came into our camp under the specious character of Loyalists; it is quite the reverse with him; every man who enters his camp is known to some one or another as his army is composed of troops from every province."

For the first time, the Riedesels, accompanying their Hessian troops in their own well springed light carriage at their own expense, felt the violent hostility of those who had suffered from the war. The women of Valley Forge, who Frau Riedesel said were "not as good looking nor of as pretty form as those of New England," flatly refused at first to sell food to the Hessians.

"Starve! You shall be made to suffer," said one housewife. "You shall not have a morsel. You are of our blood, but you sell yourselves for British gold. You came to fight us, to kill us, and to waste our goods and possessions. Now you are our prisoners; it is our turn to torment you."

The anger of Valley Forge was, however, directed against soldiers. The women and children accompanying the officers of the Hessian regiments could not be looked upon as enemies. When pretty little three-year-old Caroline Riedesel went up to the housewife to take her by the hand and to say in English, "Good woman, I am very hungry," the stern refusals disappeared. The woman took small Caroline into the kitchen, where the man of the house was eating, and handed her an egg.

"I have two sisters," said Caroline.

The woman was touched. "I am just as angry as ever," she insisted, "but I cannot withstand the child." She gave Caroline two more eggs, offered Frau Riedesel milk and bread and allowed her to make tea.

"The woman eyed the tea longingly," the Riedesel diary reports, "For the Americans love it very much, but they had resolved to drink it no longer, as the famous duty on tea had occasioned the war."

Frau Riedesel was invited to share the family meal. "I found the husband gnawing a pig's tail," she said, "while his wife, to my great satisfaction, brought out from the cellar a basket of potatoes. When she came back, he reached out to her his tidbit. She ate some of it and gave it back to him in a little while, and then he again began to feast on it. I saw this mutual entertainment with amazement and disgust, but he believed hunger made me begrudge it of him, and he reached out to me the already gnawed tail. What should I do? Throw it away and not only anger his feelings, but lose my beloved basket of potatoes? I accordingly took it, pretended to eat it, and quietly threw it into the fire. They gave me the potatoes, and I made a good supper off them, with excellent butter."

After leaving Valley Forge, the Riedesels were quartered at the home of Ezekiel Howell, whose name the Riedesels unfortunately twisted into Howe. "I thought I was paying a compliment," she wrote, "when I asked him if he was a relative of the English general."

"God forbid!" he answered, much affronted by the question. "He is not worthy of the honor."

Frau Riedesel was shocked, too, at the fourteen-year-old Howell daughter, "pretty but of a wicked disposition," who looked into the coals of a glowing fire and cried out, "Oh, if I only had the King of England here, with what satisfaction I could cut his body to pieces, tear out his heart, dissect it, put it on these coals and consume it!"

"I looked at her with horror," wrote the Hessian diarist, "and said, 'I am almost ashamed to belong to a sex that is capable of taking such pleasure.' " Though Frau Riedesel confessed that she had never been able to forget "this detestible girl," the Riedesels were later so reconciled to the United States that they stayed in the country after the conclusion of the peace, and named their fourth daughter "America."

Burgoyne's Hessians, knowing little of the lootings that had turned Pennsylvania against their fellow countrymen of Knyphausen's regiments, were astonished at the reception. Misled by the friendliness of remote regions which had not been ravaged by the war, they were taken by surprise at the vindictiveness of the Great Valley region.

On Christmas Eve, the great jubilation time of Germans, the farmers' hatred toward the mercenary Hessians reached its climax. The march had been halted early to allow the men to search the woods for pine trees to be set up in the temporary camp; pathetic little decorations were prepared to hang upon the branches of the impromptu Christmas trees; the Hessians made ready to celebrate their great feast day by songs and gayety. To their amazement, the farm folk of the Great Valley refused to grant accommodation to the troops.

The Quaker farmers were opposed to making sport on Christmas Day, the Scotch-Irishmen into whose territory the Hessians were advancing proved to be intolerant of any action that would bring pleasure into the mercenaries' lives; even the German settlers seemed unwilling to forget the devastations of the war.

"Our hopes of being received in a hospitable manner by our countrymen were cruelly deceived," the diarist wrote. "They behaved altogether very mean to us. We were ashamed of being Germans, because we had never met so much meanness in one spot from our countrymen. It really does no credit to the character of these Germans that our countrymen were the only ones who treated us mean and tried at the same time to get something out of us and to cheat us. They were also very rude."

The Hessians spent Christmas Eve camping in the woods, but they made the best of their misfortunes. Some of Knyphausen's men, captured by the Americans and sentenced to hard labor in the iron mines and at the furnaces, joined the party of the Convention Troops. They came with the bass viol from the near-by church, and, with the horns and fiddles of the Burgoyne men, danced and sang in the clearings. Scandalized farmers, angry because the church musical instrument was used for a secular purpose, protested vigorously and called on the American guards to stop the Hessian noise. The church viol was taken away from the prisoners, but the singing and dancing continued.

Some of the people of the neighborhood of the Christmas Eve encampment sold liquor to the mercenaries and, later

278

in the evening, the simple harmless gayety turned into rioting.

"It was as if the abyss had opened and all the furies with Mephistopheles and Zitzleputzli had come among the Hessians," a shocked clergyman wrote. "They made themselves outrageously drunk and then the women began to fight; after them the men, who had taken sides with the women, and finally the fight became general. The guard was called, but as soon as they left the fight was resumed and continued well into the night."

The iron regions west of Valley Forge at the head of the Great Valley had suffered previously from the jubilations of the Hessian captives quartered at the mines. Often there had been more prisoners of war than there had been armed patriots to keep the peace. The iron centers had sometimes been fearful that prisoners, allowed to roam freely from their camps, might organize to capture the powder mills and destroy the Continental munition stores. Complaints had frequently been made that the prisoners had not been disarmed, and that they had been allowed to frequent the taverns where they drank themselves into a state of riotous disorder. The law-enforcing agents had been reduced to the humiliation of asking Hessians to cease carrying guns and to request them voluntarily to return to their encampments at eight o'clock at night. The sudden arrival of more than two thousand additional Hessian prisoners, inadequately guarded, had been far more of a burden than the inland towns had anticipated would be put upon them.

After the Christmas Eve jubilation, the Convention Troops resumed their long march through Lancaster, York, and Hanover to Maryland and Virginia. During much of the time they were unguarded; often they had not even guides. Under irregular leadership they wandered onward for a month until they eventually arrived at Charlottesville, Virginia. In spite of every inducement to desert, only four hundred men were missing. The rest had marched more than seven hundred miles, sleeping in barns, in haystacks, and in open fields.

The brief visit of the Convention Troops was the Great Valley's last direct experience of war. The combatants were well away from the vicinity of Valley Forge. After the Monmouth engagement, Washington had gone toward the vicinity of West Point; Sullivan was campaigning against Britain's Indian allies of western New York; other American leaders were repelling invasion in the South. Eastern Pennsylvania remained comparatively peaceful.

Prosperity slowly returned. Great Valley farmers tilled their fields and hauled their produce into Philadelphia; drovers once again shouted their herds of cattle down the rugged, narrow roads; broad-faced innkeepers again smiled welcome. Once again, the cattlemen boisterously cracked their whips against the scarred oak tavern doors when the market price of beef was high; again they sulked in sullen silence on the few occasions when the slaughterhouses paid too small a price. Life along the highways had returned to normal.

Valley Forge shared in the return of prosperity. Colonel Dewees' ironworks and powder mills were restored to make munitions for the troops; millers rebuilt their ruined flour mills. The larger huts that had been set up for the army officers became the homes of workers in the blacksmith shops, the forges, and the factories. Although the great majority of soldier huts soon sank into ruinous condition and the trenches and parade grounds were ill kept and overgrown with weeds and brush, the small crossroads settlement at Valley Forge was thriving in the year following Washington's departure.

CHAPTER TWENTY-FIVE

Wine, Silk, and Radicals

WITHIN a year after the departure of the troops, the camp site was in ruins. High waters, rushing down the Schuylkill in early January, lifted the split-log floorboards from Sullivan's bridge. Ice floes crashed against the piers, sweeping three supports away, leaving the others badly shattered. The bridge has never been restored.

The camp huts were but slightly longer-lived. Neighbor farmers took the slabs for fuel, or dragged away good logs to repair their buildings. Tall grass grew where troops had drilled; seedling trees flourished on the hills; wild grape and blackberry, poison ivy and honeysuckle helped create a matted tangle of vegetation.

The desolation was, however, only on the hills. Along the creek, and for a little distance on the road, industrial activity partially revived. Isaac Potts and Colonel William Dewees joined forces to restore the forge that British troops had burned; the gristmill was rebuilt; farmers in the lowlands slowly put their lands into cultivation. Valley Forge did not immediately recover from the injuries inflicted by the British, but the little settlement was still alive.

A homesick Frenchman's dream envisioned a new industry

that might, with better luck, have yielded vast returns. Peter Legaux, surgeon, scientist and lawyer, politician and colonial governor, planned to flood the Schuylkill valley with home-grown Burgundy, champagne, and claret. Had he enjoyed the help of but a dozen of his fellow countrymen, the Pennsylvania vintages might well have rivaled those of southern France.

Fleeing from his governor's palace in seething Martinique upon the discovery of a poison plot against his life, Legaux came to Pennsylvania in 1786. Safe in the Quaker commonwealth, he packed up his jeweled decorations and his glittering court uniforms, returned them to Louis XVI with the explanation that "in democratic America all these things are useless and unbecoming." Then, drawing all his wealth from France, he set up a vineyard where, like the Romans, he might grow grapevines on the trunks of native oaks.

There was a double purpose in the Legaux program. The first, and possibly the more important, was to make his farm the presidential home if not, indeed, the site of the permanent White House. Legaux was active in the movement to persuade Congress to accept a block of land near Valley Forge as the seat of government for the United States. When, however, political bargainings transferred the capital to the Potomac, Legaux's suggestions were declined.

His vintages were more acceptable. Hoping to change American tastes away from the crude rum and cider of colonial times, Legaux planned to sell thousands of gallons of native wines at prices not to exceed two dollars per gallon. His port was poor and his Madeira was indifferent; but, from sweet, black South African grapes, he pressed a Constantia of which connoisseurs approved. It was, according to the contemporary experts, "of the same quality and flavor as the celebrated Tokay." Rich Pennsylvania merchants, whose once well filled cellars could not be replenished because of foreign wars, found the native vintages an admirable substitute.

Legaux, however, was both a poor business man and an inefficient manager. Lacking financial genius, lacking skilled labor, and lacking experience in fighting plant diseases, he went bankrupt. Ten years after his establishment of the Mount Joy vineyards, Legaux was sold out by the sheriff. His southeastern Pennsylvania hills, admirably adapted for vineyards, reverted to farm land and to forest. The fox grape spread luxuriantly where once aristocratic foreign vines had grown.

The dense underbrush that sprang up when Valley Forge reverted to a tangled wilderness sheltered innumerable birds. More than a hundred varieties, ranging from the cardinals and blue jays that stay all winter to the migrant orioles, vireos, and warblers, found the woods a sanctuary. The bright red berries of the dogwoods, the pale yellow buckwheat, the plentiful supplies of acorns and beechnuts drew countless swarms of birds.

Chief among the yearly visitors was the splendidly adorned passenger pigeon, whose purplish crimson plumage, flecked with golden-green and blue, covered the oaks with a fluttering shimmer of iridescent color. In mild seasons when the North was suffering from excessive cold, the pigeon flocks were unbelievably numerous.

On such occasions, hunters spread their nets over fields of ripening grain. Four or five live pigeons were fastened to a movable stick which could, by the pulling of a string, be alternately raised and lowered. Thus the decoy wings were fluttered to produce the effect of birds alighting on the buckwheat fields. The wild passenger pigeons, deceived by the decoys, came down to feed and, by a quick drawing of the nets, were trapped by the dozens. Wagonloads of birds, so gathered, were hauled to Philadelphia to be sold for not more than a cent apiece.

Not all the residents of the Valley Forge community were, however, ruthless hunters. Across the river in the Fatlands, where Washington had talked scientific farming with inventive James Vaux, lived the most humanitarian of American bird lovers. Slender John James Audubon, still in his teens, roamed in his satin pumps and silken breeches through the bird-filled woods to sketch strange specimens and to study bird migrations.

Here, too, young Audubon courted Lucy Bakewell, his neighbor and his companion in his search for birds. The old brownstone Audubon mansion, bought by Captain Jean Audubon, French slave dealer and colonial planter, four years after John James Audubon was born, sat amid fields of flowers. Close by was William Bakewell's home, built by a homesick fox-hunting Englishman who picked the Fatlands as the most attractive site that he had ever seen in the United States. Settling here in the spring of 1804, about the time that Audubon was beginning his bird observations, Bakewell and his pretty daughter made fast friends with the Audubons.

Others than the Bakewells and the Audubons appreciated the great beauty of the Fatland region. William Penn had picked it as the site for a great manor where he hoped to settle down; John Penn, his Anglican and Tory grandson, had chosen the place for his own residence, though the Revolution had upset his plans; methodical Joseph Priestley fled here to escape the distractions of banquet-loving Philadelphia. The Fatlands opposite Valley Forge had seen, too, the birth of American science, for here David Rittenhouse had labored with his astronomy and his mathematics.

Possibly the rigid scientific atmosphere of Fatlands in the days of Jefferson was too didactic for the young and charming Lucy Bakewell. Her stern father, brought up in the household of a bachelor country-squire uncle, subscribed to Spartan philosophies. Each morning the brood of children was immersed in the great stone pump trough; each day the entire family, including dignified Professor Priestley when he was a Fatland guest, took two hours of supervised exercise. No time was wasted in light reading, for one morning when Bakewell found his Lucy weeping over the moralistic fictions of Maria Edgeworth's *Simple Susan,* he threw the book into the fire. Bakewell preferred to have his children browse in his well stocked scientific library or to experiment in the chemical laboratory that was a feature of his Fatlands home. The Bakewells were a clever but a sober folk.

For such a girl as Lucy, the gay and blithesome Audubon offered glamorous release. They roamed together to identify the birds; they explored the grottoes in the hillsides; they hunted out the revolutionary cannon balls spilled in the mire when Washington's ammunition wagons had upset in what they called the "bullet field." Soon after Lucy's mother died, Audubon and Lucy were engaged. After a brief period during which Audubon unsuccessfully tried to manage the lead mines on his father's property, the newly married couple moved away from Valley Forge to try their fortunes in in the West.

For fifteen years, the Valley Forge community lived uneventfully. The Fatlands and the Great Valley acres were well tilled, for these returned rich crops, but the less fertile hills remained almost untouched; the forests were allowed to grow thick with weed trees and underbrush. The site of the entrenchments became almost undiscoverable.

Enthusiasm at Valley Forge turned toward plans for canal construction. Old surveys made by Franklin, Rittenhouse, and Provost William Smith were drawn from dusty pigeon-holes to show that the Schuylkill might easily be connected with the Susquehanna and even with the Great Lakes. Valley Forge saw visions of steamboats puffing up a widened and deepened Valley Creek toward a dredged Brandywine and thus to Harrisburg and the West. "The suggestion is not so extravagant as some imagine," a leading editor asserted. "As sure as there is a Sun in the firmament the thing will and *shall* be accomplished." The coming of the Pennsylvania Railroad, however, doomed the canal scheme, though diehards insisted that Baltimore commercial interests had used corrupt methods to kill the canalization project.

A Schuylkill canal was more successful. For many years after its completion, in 1825, the waterway from Philadelphia past Valley Forge to Pottsville was an active common carrier. Its boatmen, driving their mules along the path that lay between Washington's Headquarters and the river, chanted robust new ballads as they passed. Waiting their turn at the locks just below the site of the encampment, or loading limestone at the near-by wharves, the rough Irish canallers lent color to the Valley Forge scene. Some terrified the community by their rowdy drinking at the riverside inns; some were suspected of bringing cholera epidemics; still others were frowned upon for their bloody cudgel battles. Their disease and dirt and drunkenness were influential arguments for replacing canal traffic by swifter, more convenient railway service.

The canallers were, however, patriotic. To their efforts were due the first markings of the site of Sullivan's bridge. Canal

286

workers, camped at Valley Forge while they awaited the thawing of the river, put up a commemorative stone to show where the bridge had been erected. When the spring freshets almost immediately washed away the marker, a larger and better built monument was set up by the boatmen. This stone, in turn, was broken by ice and floating logs, but the stump of the memorial long remained as the only marker at the site of Sullivan's bridge.

Meanwhile, strangers had come to rouse the peaceful Valley Forge community. Seldom have new arrivals been so violently at odds with the established residents as were the enthusiastic theorists who came, in 1824, to establish a Utopia.

The period was one of social readjustment. The profound changes of the Industrial Revolution were inspiring radical ideas. Both in Europe and in America, philosophers were re-examining the fundamental principles upon which society was founded. Old theories were being cast aside as antiquated and unfair; new speculations were winning wide acceptance.

Little of this intellectual ferment had reached isolated Valley Forge. Great Valley farmers could understand and could appreciate a Revolution which turned upon questions of taxation and of self-government; they knew of difficulties due to suppression of political and economic freedom; but they were only casually concerned with matters of broad social relationships. The problems of wage slavery and of city crowding, of free philosophical speculation and of the cultivation of the arts, meant little to the hard-working rural community.

When, therefore, a group of radicals, advocating "villages of self-supporting cooperation," arrived to take up residence at Valley Forge, the farmers were puzzled but welcoming. Robert Owen, fifty-year-old British cotton manufacturer and well regarded philanthropist, who headed the group, promised to bring unbounded prosperity to Valley Forge. Rich William Maclure, long-time president of Philadelphia's Academy of Natural Sciences, announced that the entire library and museum of that famous institution would be at once transferred to Valley Forge. James Jones, benevolent and affluent farmer who had come from his homestead near the battle field of Brandywine, vouched for the good faith of his two comrades.

Washington's Headquarters were selected as the capitol of Owen's Friendly Association of Valley Forge. Land on both sides of the creek, close to the Headquarters, was purchased for the site of a perfect community where "select persons of choice spirits" might live in a Utopian commonwealth without the customary restraints of law and order.

The welcome ceased abruptly when the Owenites announced their program. From the front room of the Headquarters, where Washington had had his offices, Owen issued a radical challenge to all that Valley Forge held dear. "America," he said, "is founded on hypocrisy and corruption. The whole world is a mass of absurdity and folly. This state of society is not worth supporting." He demanded that existing systems of trade, commerce, education, government, and religion be immediately overhauled. Owen pleaded for equality of men and women; he asked that children be made wards of the state; he suggested that men might do the cooking, and that no one should be required to do unpleasant work. Then he shocked Valley Forge by seeming to attack the soldiers of the Revolution.

"The very name 'soldier' is a disgrace to human nature," Owen told his neighbors. "The honor which is attached to the profession is fallacious."

WINE, SILK, AND RADICALS

To the conventionally minded Pennsylvanians, the arguments of the Owenite agitators seemed treasonable. The farmers were infuriated. Some looked upon his scheme as a British plot to destroy the independence of America; others were convinced that he and his Friendly Association favored aristocratic rule, and that they hated American democracy; all were convinced that Owen and his clan were morally and politically dangerous. The issuance of labor money, in competition to the currency of the United States, seemed proof of criminal intent. The more charitable, hearing Owen say, "Were we to open our minds freely, many of us would be put into the lunatic asylum," believed that the small community was entirely crazy.

The Reverend William Latta, pastor for half a century of the Great Valley Presbyterian Church, a student, a scholar, and one of the pillars of the faith, did not believe in compromise. He instigated a vigilante movement to expel the undesirables. Owen was forced to move away, together with Maclure. The Owenite community was transferred to New Harmony, Indiana.

James Jones alone was allowed to stay, since Jones insisted that Owen had misled him. Jones, persuaded of Owen's cooperative arguments, had been the Valley Forge Friendly Association's financial manager, and with his own money he had bought the Headquarters. Now that Owen and Maclure had left, Jones remained at Valley Forge. His descendants continued to occupy the Headquarters.

Two years later, the campground had reverted to a wild and wooded state, without a trace of the careful agriculture that the cooperative Owenites had tried to introduce. Much of the level ground had been allowed to grow in weeds; the hills, where the Valley Forge Friendly Association had made little progress, were covered with trees "as universal and as towering, though not so thick of trunk, as any forest elsewhere." Dense underbrush covered the remains of trenches and of breastworks. At one extremity of the camp, a high redoubt was traceable; but even here chestnut trees were growing in the moats, and deep fox holes indicated that no human beings had frequented the vicinity.

The town, however, near the thriving ash tree at the crossroads, was more prosperous. A new forge and a slitting mill had started, a gristmill and a paper works were operating by the creek, a gun factory and a cotton mill were offering employment. Stone tenements, built in rows along the main highway, were crowded by mill workers.

The silkworm craze, backed by the Pennsylvania Legislature, then caused the residents to dream of untold wealth. Native mulberry trees, it was believed, could be transmuted into threads of gold.

None in the Valley Forge community had ever seen the fearsome poverty of Chinese silk farms; nor had they lived in Asiatic hovels where every inch of available space was packed with trays of silkworms. None had ever been subjected to the unending watchful labor that silkworm culture necessarily involves. Few thought of these conditions; it was quite enough that twenty cents a pound in bounty would be paid for home-grown cocoons, and that good reeled silk would sell for fifty cents a pound. No one stopped to estimate how many worms would be required to yield a pound of silk. The entire community was caught by the fad.

The craze was feverish. Scrubby mulberry trees growing wild upon the hills were dug up for sale. Seven dollars was paid for a good tree; silkworms were worth more than their weight in gold. But as soon as the first "crop" was gathered and men saw how slight was the return that could be secured the mania calmed down. The bubble had completely burst.

Scarcely had the canal fever subsided and the silkworm craze abated when more exciting episodes occurred. Valley Forge had been devouring sensational pamphlets wherein William Miller, a Massachusetts clergyman, predicted the imminence of the Judgment Day. However, little credence was placed in the writings until a fierce tornado, sweeping down the valley, ripped the roof from the grand new Methodist "synagogue" at Valley Forge. Fear spread quickly, especially when more spectacular phenomena followed close upon the storm.

Early in the morning of November 13, 1833, the skies exploded. From a focal center in the constellation Leo, bright streams of burning stars shot forth in all directions. During four full hours, long trails of fire flamed across the skies. No sleep was possible while two hundred thousand brilliant meteors presented an alarming spectacle. Many were convinced that the end of the world had come.

Midweek prayer meetings that night were jammed with terrified Great Valley residents. Dr. Latta, then in his thirty-fourth year of service, earnestly argued, from his most convincing Princeton scholarship, that the remarkable meteoric display was merely a scientific phenomenon; but the populace was unconvinced. The Millerites triumphantly enrolled an awed and worried throng. Not until the fatal year of 1843 had passed, with its impressive series of hilltop meetings where white-robed "angels" waited for the world to end, could Valley Forge be reassured.

Almost immediately a second pamphlet series captivated the community's imagination. From Philadelphia, Theophilus Ransom Gates and Hannah Williamson, his chief votary, were publishing "Battle-Axe and the Weapons of War" to expound the principles of freethinking communism. "Issued only as often as the writer has anything which he believes it right for him to communicate," the pamphlets stressed the right of everyone to live in mutual goodwill, harmony, and peace, in what the "Battle-axes" believed "a holy community." By the Gates principles, all goods were to be held in common, but "from a principle of holiness, not a beast principle, and unto the Lord, not from a selfish feeling."

Certain of the beliefs necessary for the assurance of immortality were peculiar. Marriage was not to be permanent, said Gates. "Men and women had better change their partners twenty times over, under the best regulations they can make with each other, so as at length to have one with whom they can live in harmony, unity, and peace." Falling in love, the Battle-axes believed, was "an enchantment of the Devil." To show that heaven was close at hand, Gates fastened wings of light shingles to his arms and leaped from the roof of his house that he might then fly upwards to the sky. The experiment failed, but Gates explained the lack of success by declaring that too many skeptics had been present. His baptismal rites consisted of a weekly march of all the Battle-axes, naked and in single file, through a pool of water to the log house where he had his headquarters.

Dr. Latta warred more successfully against this abomination than against the Millerite fear. He succeeded in keeping the worst excesses of the Battle-axe from finding a strong foothold in the Great Valley. It did, however, gain converts in the secluded hill regions to the north. Close to "Hell's Hinges," near the Warwick furnaces, the Battle-axes won numerous followers. An isolated valley was converted into a Battle-axe Republic.

WINE, SILK, AND RADICALS

The Battle-axes flourished for more than six years in the "Hell's Hinges" community. Then the outraged neighbors, angered because a Battle-axe had deserted his wife and six children in favor of a younger mate, called on the community to disperse. When the Battle-axes refused, legal action was brought. Several of the Gates converts were jailed on immorality charges. The community finally dissolved in 1846 following the death of the founder.

Valley Forge, meanwhile, was becoming a popular rostrum for political orations. Black Dan Webster set the fashion by campaigning here for William Henry Harrison in 1840. His speech helped gain the slender popular margin whereby the hard-cider hero of Tippecanoe won the Presidential election. Four years later Henry Clay made history here by inviting women, for the first time in American political history, to attend a major party gathering. The Clay rally was noteworthy, too, because the precedent was set that Presidential candidates, after the conclusion of their speeches, should preside over a gigantic ox roast for the refreshment of their guests. Such feasts were regularly held during the Scott, Taylor, and Buchanan campaigns.

Just before the Civil War, Valley Forge fell into another period of decay. Not even low wages could enable the mills to compete with industries in the city, where labor was more plentiful and markets were more readily available. The massive buildings were abandoned; the windows grew cobwebbed; vines festooned themselves over the gray and weather-beaten walls. A tall brick stack leaned perilously toward the main highway to Philadelphia. Scores of Irish immigrants, brought to Valley Forge for mill labor, moved away.

Temporarily, the Civil War restored prosperity and led, indeed, to the construction of flimsy new factories to fill war orders; but the boom was short. After Appomattox, Valley Forge again subsided. The moss-grown dam, holding back the half-mile of broad, quiet lake, saw no new industry appear. The camp site was again as quiet as it had been during the weeks after the army's leaving.

CHAPTER TWENTY-SIX

The Monument to Glory

TWO Civil War nurses of the Valley Forge community, Mary Thropp Cone and Anna Morris Holstein, inspired the movement for the preservation of the encampment grounds. In a series of persuasive poems, Mrs. Cone pleaded for a national memorial to the sufferings of Washington's army. Mrs. Holstein, after Mrs. Cone had left Valley Forge to accompany her husband on his consular mission to Brazil, furthered the suggestion.

Through Mrs. Holstein's instigation, other Valley Forge residents took up the idea. Colonel Theodore W. Bean, I. Heston Todd, and Isaac W. Smith, landowners and local historians of the vicinity, formed in 1877 a Centennial and Memorial Association "to secure to the nation Washington's Headquarters at Valley Forge as a national memorial for all time."

The time was peculiarly propitious for success. The recent Centennial Exposition at Philadelphia had awakened widespread interest in Revolutionary history. Slender, nervous, vivacious Henry Armitt Brown, young Philadelphia lawyer, was stirring patriotic sentiment by a series of eloquent commemorative speeches. The Grand Army of the Republic and the newly formed Sons of the Revolution were drawing attention to the need for giving proper care to places of historic importance. The Centennial and Memorial Association found slight difficulty in popularizing the idea of a memorial at Valley Forge.

Certainly there was need for concerted action to save the campgrounds. For many years, the hills had been unkempt. The slopes were covered by dense growths of underbrush; the trees were overgrown with cat brier and wild grape; not for more than a decade had horsemen been able to ride through the woods. Only by walking on the mounds of the inner line entrenchments was access possible to the interior of the encampment. The Star Redoubt was nothing but a steep, cone-shaped hill. So much earth had washed from the embankments that the rifle pits were almost level with the ground. In a corner of Fort Washington, an oak stump three feet in diameter testified to long neglect.

Little had been done to preserve the historic relics. To be sure, the Headquarters, where Mrs. Hannah Ogden, daughter of James Jones, resided, was still in good repair, though "modernized" from the condition of Revolutionary days; but no care had been taken of other important buildings. Some of the former quarters had been razed; those that remained were dilapidated or in ruins. Near the site of the old forge a row of crumbling tenements, relics of the prosperous mill days, looked "like the old Spanish quarter of St. Augustine or like an alley side of an Italian town." The old bake-ovens at the cross-roads were filled with debris and were buried under rubbish.

Such were the conditions on June 19, 1878, when the Centennial and Memorial Association sponsored military, religious, and historical observances to commemorate the hundredth anniversary of the evacuation of the camp. A throng of sixty thousand people, coming mostly by carriage, crowded the Parade Ground to listen to Brown's memorial address.

The day was filled with difficulties. Heavy rain beat down upon the crowded listeners. Hundreds of carriages were mired in the wet, slippery mud. Thieves, rambling through the orchard where the horses were tied, "carried off shawls, whips, blankets, and everything else that was portable." One culprit, caught red-handed, narrowly escaped lynching. The angry crowd had fastened a rope about his neck and was in the act of hanging him when a policeman arrived.

The little railroad station, predecessor of the present colonial-style building, was overwhelmed by fifteen thousand patrons. In the excitement, hundreds of the visitors boarded wrong trains. One company of the National Guard was shuttled back and forth on one wrong train after another until, twelve hours after they had started their return, they found themselves again at Valley Forge. Eventually, they marched fifteen miles back to their armory through the rain and mud.

In spite of the unfortunate circumstances, the Valley Forge Centennial was outstandingly successful. Henry Armitt Brown's magnificent oration, tracing the privations of the Revolutionary army, pleading for a rebirth of virtue, courage, self-sacrifice, unfailing patriotism, and unceasing vigilance for justice, was ranked by listeners among the rhetorical masterpieces of the century. The crowd's applause for the address was so loud that it was heard five miles away in Phoenixville.

Among the many listeners swayed by Brown's eloquence was a fellow lawyer Francis M. Brooke, a descendant of Mad Anthony Wayne. "Valley Forge" Brooke, as he was later to be known, devoted thereafter much of his time and money to furthering Mrs. Cone's suggestion of making the camp site a permanent memorial.

VALLEY FORGE

Two independent movements thus began for the preservation of Valley Forge. While the Centennial and Memorial Association, aided by the Pennsylvania Camps of the Patriotic Order Sons of America, purchased the Washington Headquarters from Mrs. Ogden as the nucleus of what they hoped would be a national park, Brooke sought to persuade Pennsylvania to take over the encampment as a state reservation. He lobbied unceasingly at Harrisburg.

Brooke's energy resulted in the creation, on Memorial Day, 1893, of the Valley Forge Park Commission. The ten members of the Park Commission, of which Brooke was chairman, were granted $25,000 with which to buy two hundred and fifty acres of land, including Forts Washington and Huntingdon, as the nucleus of a state park. Because the Headquarters were already well cared for by Mrs. Holstein as Regent of the Centennial and Memorial Association, that building was expressly exempted from the Park Commission's jurisdiction. Five thousand dollars had already been granted to the Association by the State to restore the Headquarters to the condition in which it had been during Washington's residence.

Difficulties faced the Commissioners almost at the outset of their work. Real-estate speculators, buying options on the land, sought to sell the site to the State at inflated valuations. Ground assessed at $17,000 was now held at six times that amount. Condemnation proceedings dragged slowly through the courts. The Commission's task of developing the run-down tracts was delayed for more than ten years. The initial appropriation of $25,000 for land purchase had, eventually, to be quadrupled.

Some of the disputes were astonishing. The heirs of a Continental colonel demanded that all development cease until the United States paid four million dollars rent for Washington's use of land. Their ancestor, they said, had owned part of the camp site, but he had never been indemnified for the damage done to the ground, nor for the trees which the troops had cut for firewood. The claim was disallowed, both by the Park Commission and by Congress, on the ground that no historic record showed that the ancestor had ever owned the land.

Personal jealousies within the Park Commission membership caused other difficulty. I. Heston Todd, one of the founders of the Centennial and Memorial Association and a member of the first Commission, objected to what he termed the Tsarism of "Valley Forge" Brooke. Anticipating that the Park Commission was about to condemn his land, where Rhode Island's Lieutenant John Waterman and six hundred other New Englanders were buried, Todd sought to keep the graves from Chairman Brooke's control. In 1896 he offered the land outright to Rhode Island, together with a ten-foot strip of ground linking the grave sites with the public road, if that State would annex the ground. When Rhode Island replied that Pennsylvania could not thus be deprived of its sovereignty, Todd sought an agreement whereby, "so long as Brooke is alive and presiding, the Park Commission shall have nothing to do with it." This, too, proved impossible to arrange, and so Todd, anxious to keep Brooke "from waving his dictatorial finger under the shade of my own vine and fig tree," deeded the land to the New England Chapter of the Daughters of the Revolution.

After ownership had been finally vested in the patriotic society, the Rhode Island Legislature passed an appropriation to aid the erection of a memorial obelisk to John Waterman and to his comrades who died at Valley Forge. The fifty-foot granite shaft marks the only identified grave within the limits of the Park.

More complications came when the Commissioners sought to condemn land owned by William Stephens, descendant of the Stephens family in whose houses Varnum, Weedon, and Huntingdon had been quartered. Stephens, priding himself that he was the sixth in direct descent to till lands deeded to his family by William Penn, resisted condemnation proceedings. For eleven years, the "Rebel of Valley Forge" fought the case in the courts, until, in 1929, the Park Commission was upheld.

Despite these difficulties, the progress of the Park was noteworthy. Additional acreage was bought, and in 1905 the Legislature authorized the purchase of the Washington Headquarters from the Centennial and Memorial Association. For the mansion, bought by the Association in 1879 for $6,000, and for the stone barn and the camp spring later added to the Association's holdings, the Park Commission paid more than eighteen thousand dollars. Much of the seeming excess was, however, balanced by the transfer to the Park Commission of contributions made to the Association for the permanent maintenance of the Headquarters.

Meanwhile, the various states were building monuments in memory of their soldiers. Soon after the establishment of the Park, Pennsylvania erected two tall granite columns, topped by bronze eagles, as a memorial to her troops camped in the surrounding fields. Maine's less ornate marker, commanding a fine view of the hills where her soldiers, then included in Massachusetts regiments, were encamped, soon followed. Massachusetts built an impressive granite exedra, or low semicircular seat, with a pillar bearing the state's coat of arms and the names of her chief officers. Delaware's stone overlooking the site of Sullivan's bridge, the tall New Jersey column in the midst of the Dogwood Grove, and a memorial to the unknown dead were also added to the Park's monuments.

Two statues merit particular attention. One, to Major-General Steuben, cast in bronze by J. Otto Schweizer, was the gift in 1915 of the National German-American Alliance in honor of the great drillmaster. The other, a magnificent equestrian statue of Anthony Wayne, created by Henry Kirke Bush-Brown and donated by Pennsylvania in 1908, looks over the rolling country toward the house where Wayne was quartered. The Wayne statue, the Park's finest sculpture, dominates the landscape.

Suggestions that Valley Forge be transferred to the United States as a national park have been frequently made, but, except for a very early offer in 1787 by Pennsylvania that the region might be used as a Federal District, the Commonwealth has refused to consider any loss of its control.

The movement to make Valley Forge a national park was particularly strong about 1900, when various local historical societies, the Valley Forge chapter of the Daughters of the American Revolution, and a few former members of the Valley Forge Park Commission sought a $200,000 appropriation from Congress for the purchase of the land. The bill, introduced by Senator Boies Penrose, never emerged from committee. Similar efforts, by the Valley Forge National Park Association two years later, although backed by a trainload of Philadelphians seeking to lobby in Washington for the purchase, similarly failed. A third effort, asking $500,000 appropriation, followed the visit of President Theodore Roosevelt, but this was buried in committee.

Attention then turned toward securing from Congress

an appropriation to erect a memorial arch to commemorate the encampment. Again difficulties arose. After the passage by Congress, in 1910, of a bill to grant $100,000 for the purpose, controversy raged concerning the type of arch to be erected and the location on which the monument should be built. Paul Cret's design of a Roman marble arch, similar to the Arch of Titus, seemed to many inappropriate; to others the severe classic lines seemed peculiarly well adopted to the cultural ideas current during Revolutionary times. The placing of the arch so far from the Headquarters, on an eminence which was not the highest in the Park, was opposed by critics, including the original sponsor of the Congressional bill. Like many others, he preferred a location closer to the railway station and to the house where Washington had lived. Still other criticism suggested that there should be no arch whatever, but rather a wide bridge flung across the Schuylkill on the site of Sullivan's wartime bridge. The Merion Chapter of the Daughters of the American Revolution reiterated the old demand that the whole area be made a national park.

The placing of the arch high on a hill visible for many miles, with smooth green fields sloping away from it in all directions, was, as it happens, an admirable decision. Between the period when the War Department began construction, in 1910, and the completion of the monument, in 1917, a transportation revolution had occurred. Prior to the World War, virtually every visitor who came to the campgrounds arrived by train, or by the trolley line which then connected Valley Forge with northern points; following the War, almost every visitor came by motor car. The change in vehicle gave to the arch an accessibility which would not have been possible under old traveling conditions.

THE MONUMENT TO GLORY

The arch serves as a mighty monument to those who suffered here. Carved upon its walls is Washington's famous tribute to the fortitude of the troops:

"Naked and starving as they are, we cannot enough admire the incomparable patience and fidelity of the soldiery."

Within the arch, on the right, is a bronze tablet bearing the Arms of the United States and below it the names of George Washington as Commander-in-chief, and of his eight major generals, De Kalb, Greene, Lafayette, Lee, Mifflin, Steuben, Stirling, and Sullivan. The names of seventeen brigadier generals appear within the arch.

The inner wall of the left side of the arch bears a portion of the famous 1878 centennial speech by Henry Armitt Brown:

"And here, in this place of sacrifice, in this vale of humiliation, in this valley of the shadow of that death out of which the life of America rose regenerate and free, let us believe with an abiding faith that to them Union will seem as dear and Liberty as sweet and Progress as glorious as they were to our fathers and are to you and me, and that the institutions which have made us happy, preserved by the virtue of our children, shall bless the remotest generation of the time to come."

Even at the time of the dedication, on Evacuation Day, 1917, strong efforts were being made to revive the idea of a national park. A local newspaper, running a series of prize essays on the desirability of putting the reservation under Federal control, observed the occasion by printing a strong editorial opposing the idea that Valley Forge should be the property of a single state.

The dedication ceremonies, in which Speaker Champ Clark of the House of Representatives, for the Federal Government, presented the arch to the Commonwealth of Pennsylvania, were exceedingly impressive. Memories of Valley Forge, mingled with the strong patriotic emotions stirred by the recent declaration of war against Germany, caused the speakers to stress the American devotion to liberty, freedom, and democracy. Valley Forge was a sounding board from which the high American principles resounded to all the nations then at war.

The success of the Valley Forge Park Commission, and of its independent colleague, the Washington Memorial Chapel, in furthering the best care of the encampment grounds and of the cause for which Valley Forge has stood, effectively put an end to further suggestions that the campground be transferred to the national government. Only on one other occasion, in 1928, when Senator George Wharton Pepper asked that, if the War Department planned to establish cavalry quarters in the East, Valley Forge be chosen as the site, has any further mention of the plan been made.

Freed from the fear that the campground might be taken from the Commonwealth by national decree, the Valley Forge Park Commission has been able to devote its efforts to proper restoration of the Park to Revolutionary conditions. The famous Dogwood Grove was an early accomplishment, augmented by the planting of such native shrubs as spicebush and shadberry, laurel and azalea. Great pains have been taken to ascertain the type of buildings, furnishings, uniforms, flags, and equipment used by Washington's men, and either obtain originals or reproduce them in exact replica. The Park Commission has furthered exhaustive research in the interest of authentic history.

Valley Forge Park is not, however, solely a historic memorial; for more than half a century fervent efforts have been made to stress the encampment's spiritual significance. Ever since 1885 when the Reverend James Guthrie fell on his knees to vow that a great national church should be erected on the site of Valley Forge, the urge has been strong to establish a religious center here. Guthrie's campaign failed because funds were contributed in only small amounts, but the idea of a Valley Forge shrine haunted the imaginations of patriotic churchmen.

The idea gained new strength in 1901, when the Reverend W. Herbert Burk of Norristown took his choir boys on a picnic to Valley Forge. Their eager questions as to the meaning of the encampment induced him to make a special study of Revolutionary history. On Washington's Birthday, 1903, he preached a stirring sermon on the religious character of Washington, so rousing his parishioners that they immediately began campaigns to raise funds for the creation of a Valley Forge chapel.

The idea rapidly matured. I. Heston Todd, aroused by Burk's eloquence to a renewed interest in the preservation of the park, donated ground for the erection of "a wayside chapel where the American patriot might kneel in quest of courage." The Patriotic Order Sons of America lent its Valley Forge building for the first meeting of a Washington Memorial Chapel Association. Work rapidly progressed. Less than four months after the Washington Birthday sermon, on the one hundred and twenty-fifth anniversary of the evacuation of the camp, the cornerstone of the present great chapel was laid.

Dr. Burk's plan swiftly widened. The round little rector looked upon Valley Forge as the logical site for an inspiring American memorial to patriotism, honor, and religion. His pink face glowed beneath his carefully parted white hair as he talked excitedly about the possibilities of creating a twenty-million-dollar cathedral worthy of the title "The American Westminster." In thousands of meetings throughout the nation, Dr. Burk popularized the idea that Valley Forge should become the shrine of patriotism. So extensive was his vision, and so successful his steps toward the realization of his dream, that in 1928 Dr. Burk was granted the Philadelphia Award of $10,000 for "service calculated to advance the best and larger interests of Philadelphia, its suburbs, or vicinity."

The Washington Memorial Chapel, designed by Milton B. Medary, Jr., has been described by Christopher Morley as "this amazing poem in stone, endless in lovingly elaborated beauty, as perfect, as unique as 'The Eve of St. Agnes,' as rich in color and as thrilling in meaning." Erected as the result of a successful fund-raising campaign headed by Charles Custis Harrison, provost of the University of Pennsylvania, and Thomas J. Garland, bishop suffragan of the diocese of Pennsylvania, the great chapel, a memorial to Washington, was dedicated in 1916. From that time onward, the chapel has been the dominating architectural feature of the Park.

Within the gray Gothic bulk of the Washington Memorial Chapel are numerous artistic triumphs. Huge stained-glass windows, tinted chiefly red and blue, offer a pictorial record of American love of country and of devotion to religion. Nicola D'Ascenzo's magnificent glass commemorates the periods of discovery, settlement, expansion, revolution, patriotism, democracy, and union. The windows also set forth the services of Hamilton, Greene, Wayne, Paul Jones, Jefferson, Franklin, and Morris to the cause of freedom. Over the monolithic ten-ton limestone altar is a window given by the Colonial Dames of Pennsylvania in honor of Martha Washington, while over the door a tall, three-paneled window glo-

BRIGADIER GENERAL ANTHONY WAYNE

*Photograph, by Dr. William A. Jaquette, of bronze statue
by Henry Kirke Bush-Brown*

CLOISTER OF THE COLONIES

(*Courtesy Mrs. W. Herbert Burk and Washington Memorial Chapel*)

riously sets forth the life of Washington in thirty-six beautiful scenes.

Each portion of the Washington Memorial Chapel has been dedicated to the memory of persons, institutions, or events connected with historic national crises. Much of the ornamental iron work was done through the artistry of Samuel Yellin, a winner, in 1925, of the Philadelphia Award for his artistic craftsmanship. The Chapel is embellished by an admirable statue, "Valley Forge," by which the sculptor, Franklin Simmons, represents Washington as anxiously, determinedly, but confidently, he bears the burdens of the war. A Gilbert Stuart portrait of George Washington, once owned by Washington Irving, hangs upon a wall.

In addition to the Washington Memorial Chapel, Dr. Burk's vast dream envisaged a Valley Forge Museum of American History, opened on Washington's birthday, 1909, a Valley Forge Historical Society, founded on Evacuation Day, 1919, and a Washington Memorial National Carillon of a graded series of bells, one for each state, with a forty-ninth bell to represent the United States. This carillon, played as part of the regular Sunday services held in honor of each of the states by turn, and played also at hourly intervals throughout the week, is audible over a wide stretch of the surrounding country. The chimes were first played on Independence Day, 1926.

The Valley Forge Museum of American History possesses authenticated Washington relics of inestimable value. Two silver camp cups, made for the Commander-in-chief just before the battle of Brandywine, and each engraved with his initial, are preserved here. The cups are those used by Washington and his staff at the daily three o'clock dinners to toast "in humble toddy" the Continental cause. They accompanied

Washington throughout the remainder of the Revolution and remained in the possession of Washington's heirs until Dr. Burk secured them for the Museum. Washington's private medicine chest is also exhibited here.

A faded flag of light blue silk, with thirteen six-pointed yellowish white stars appliquéd upon it in the double cross pattern of the British Union Jack, is a particularly prized possession. The Valley Forge Museum believes that this is the original Headquarters flag of the Commander-in-chief, and that it was flown daily during the Revolution over Washington's residence. Historians of the Valley Forge Park Commission, while admitting that the banner is undoubtedly an authenticated record of the encampment, hold that the flag was more probably a regimental standard. Their own researches, based largely upon a Charles Wilson Peale painting, indicate that Washington's personal flag had its stars arranged in circular form. The Peale design is that flown over the Headquarters at the present time.

The Museum takes its greatest pride, however, in its possession of the faded gray marquee used by Washington as his office and his sleeping quarters during the first week of the encampment. The oblong tent, made of heavy homespun linen, with scalloped edges bound with red twilled wool, was one of two made for the Commander-in-chief's private use. First pitched on Dorchester Heights in Boston, it accompanied Washington during most of his Revolutionary campaigns. Held up by two supporting poles, and braced by twenty guy-ropes, fastened by wooden buttons inside the marquee, the tent, twenty-five feet long, twelve feet wide and five and one-half feet tall at its highest point, was Washington's only shelter during the six snowy days when the army first came to Valley Forge. Behind the webbing that hung from iron hooks at the far end of the tent, Washington slept and prayed for victory; in the larger fore part of the marquee, he issued his orders for the welfare of his men. Set up under a gum tree on the brow of a hill, about a mile south of the present site of the Washington Memorial Chapel, the marquee was the administrative center for the Revolutionary army.

Prior to its acquisition by the Valley Forge Museum, the marquee had a curious history. George Washington Parke Custis, Washington's protégé, left it to his daughter Mary Custis, wife of General Robert E. Lee. During the Civil War the tent was seized by Federal forces and was taken to Washington to be exhibited. Then, after President McKinley ordered the return of Lee's personal property to the rightful owners, Mary Custis Lee, daughter of the General, sold the tent to Dr. Burk. The purchase price of $5,000 was contributed by Miss Lee to the Confederate Old Ladies' Home.

Parallel organizations, dedicated to the commemoration of the same historic events, find difficulty in avoiding duplication of effort, but the Valley Forge Park Commission and the great enterprises begun by Dr. Burk have, in spite of minor divergences, worked harmoniously for the best interests of Valley Forge. Still a third cooperative agency, the University of Pennsylvania, has joined with them, in recent years, for the promotion of their common aim.

By the generosity of Henry L. Woolman, owner of the former Du Portail and Lafayette quarters, a large tract of land has been donated to the university as the site for a small experimental college to offer progressive education to a selected student group.

The plan is, however, not new. Shortly after the Revolutionary War, the trustees of the University of Pennsylvania were considering the removal of the institution to the vicinity of

Valley Forge. The project failed when, in a new charter granted in 1791, a special clause provided that the university must, at all times, be located within the city of Philadelphia. The scheme for founding a new small college, thus avoiding the charter prohibition, is scheduled for completion as a feature of the university's two hundredth anniversary in 1940.

In recent years, the philosophy underlying the Park management has altered somewhat from the original conception. Once regarded wholly as a reservation to preserve the historic campground, the Park is now considered as possessing a broader, more modern, and more socially significant character. To safeguard near-by forests, and to secure watersheds against contamination, to preserve the Park against corruption by undignified commercial interests, and to include all possible areas whose historic past is important, the Valley Forge Park Commission has now embarked upon a plan to extend the reservation by more than double the present area. The shift from a purely historic concept to one with a wider, social interest is typical of the change which has occurred in general social thought.

More recent plans envisage the transformation of the reservation into a more accurate replica of the campground as it existed in Washington's time. The rebuilding of Revolutionary huts arranged along company streets, the restoration of entrenchments wherever it is possible to do so without destroying the authentic relics of the 1777–1778 embankments, the installation of proper cannon to replace the late-model guns now used, and other activities to restore the grounds to a condition more nearly approximating Revolutionary times, are now desired by the Park Commission.

Material for such a restoration is, of course, available. The entire terrain has been closely studied by historians and engineers; documentary sources have been consulted; maps drawn by both Americans and Frenchmen at the camp have been carefully checked against other drawings supposedly made by British secret agents; excavations at the camp-grounds have disclosed valuable information.

Much yet remains, however, to be discovered. The outer-line entrenchments cannot be accurately located; the hut sites, except in a comparatively few cases, cannot be con-clusively placed. Great care would be required lest the present parklike character of the reservation be transformed into less attractive expositionlike surroundings.

The success of the Williamsburg restoration, however, where the undesirable characteristics have been completely subordinated to careful replica of colonial conditions, seems to many friends of Valley Forge to prove that restoration as a model settlement can readily be secured.

CHAPTER TWENTY-SEVEN

Errors and Delusions

Because complete scholarly investigation into Valley Forge Park history has been so unaccountably delayed, because no full-length volume based on first-hand data has ever been compiled, and because no book of personal reminiscence has been available, strange legends have grown up concerning the events at Valley Forge. No other American area of such historic importance has been so sadly misunderstood.

Thousands among the annual visitors come under the impression that the campgrounds were the scene of battle; some think, indeed, that it was here that Washington made his famous crossing of the Delaware; many, accepting the fictions of popular novelists, believe that Valley Forge was the theater for sensational plots against the life of Washington.

The favorite yarn revolves about the legend that Washington visited the home of Jacob Manheim, a nonexistent Tory farmer, to ask for lodging. Mary Manheim, daughter of the farmer, and a rebel sympathizer, showed the General to her own large room instead of to the less desirable one to which her father had assigned him. She took the bedroom in which Washington was supposed to sleep. During the night, Manheim, according to the wholly fictitious story, plunged a knife into the figure sleeping in the room where Washington was supposed to lie. Astonished in the morning at the appearance of the General's "ghost," Manheim rushed upstairs to find his daughter dead.

The story stems from George Lippard's sensational mid-century series of lectures on "Washington and His Generals," whose extraordinary popularity gave wide acceptance to Lippard's imaginary history. Few of his listeners challenged the plausible bogus history which Lippard presented; none inquired to learn if such a person as Jacob Manheim had ever really existed, nor to ask why it might have been necessary for Washington to seek a lodging. The myth was cut from the whole cloth, with not a shadow of evidence in its support.

Bogus history similarly states that Tories plotted at the near-by King of Prussia Inn to capture Washington, that Howe sought to bribe the American commander by offering him the post of viceroy, and that Washington suffered so severely from the cold and hunger that he fled to seek comfort among the Pennsylvania Germans.

None of these wild tales is correct; nor, in all likelihood, is the pleasant story true of how George Washington, finding a shivering west Massachusetts boy standing sentry duty on the great square stone doorstep of the Headquarters, sent the soldier inside for breakfast while he himself stood guard. The action might have been in keeping with the character of Washington, but the anecdote was invented by a New York newspaperman in 1829, half a century after the encampment.

A more elaborate tale, that of the Washington prayer under a great oak in the snow, is true in principle, but erroneous as to its locale. According to the usual belief, certified by the United States Post Office Department in issuing a commemorative stamp, Isaac Potts, son of John Potts the ironmaster, while walking in the woods heard Washington at prayer. The General was interceding "to the Ruler of the Universe" for his beloved country. "With tones of gratitude that labored for adequate expression, he adored that exuberant goodness which, from the depths of obscurity, had exalted him to the head of a great nation, and that nation fighting at fearful odds for all the world holds dear. He utterly disclaimed all ability of his own for this arduous conflict; he wept at the thought of that irretrievable ruin which his mistakes might bring upon his country, and with the patriot's pathos spreading the interests of unborn millions before the eye of Eternal Mercy, he implored the aid of that arm which guides the starry host."

The story is beautiful in theme, patriotic in character, exact in detail, and in complete accord with the character of Washington, if not with his literary style; but, unhappily, the incident on which the tale is based did not occur at Valley Forge. Potts told the story in his old age to a daughter, Ruth Ann Potts, who wrote her reminiscences some years later. The event did occur, it is now known, though not in so elaborate a speech, near White Plains, New York, earlier in 1777. Potts himself was not at Valley Forge during the latter part of December when, he said, he stumbled upon Washington at prayer.

A similar legend, backed by slight actual proof, relates that Washington was baptized at Valley Forge by immersion in the Schuylkill; but, although forty witnesses were allegedly present at the ceremony, no other evidence appears to have been offered than the testimony of an aged minister who, in late life, remembered a story told him by his great-grandfather. Few historians accept the incident at face value, although the story excited considerable interest when it was first told, in 1907.

Equally unhistoric tales are current concerning the camp-grounds and the Headquarters. Because an outdoor cellar entrance leads down a flight of stone steps into a dark, brick cavern, rumors spread that a subterranean passage runs from the Headquarters to the Schuylkill River. Through this underground exit, so the false rumor says, Washington received secret stores of food from the river bank; through it, too, he planned to escape in case of danger.

The truth of the story is that the cave was not dug until more than half a century after Washington departed from Valley Forge, that there is no secret passageway, and that the excavation was intended as a root cellar for the storage of provisions during hot summer months.

Another legend tells of the secret hiding places cut in the wide window seats in Washington's first-floor office at Headquarters, for important private documents. Such a storage place exists, but no special secrecy could have been intended, for the joinery is so loose-fitting and so apparent even to a casual observer that the openings could not have escaped a searcher.

Much of the misconception concerning the encampment events is traceable to the imagination of "Captain" Peter M. Emery, an early caretaker of the Headquarters. Ready-tongued and resourceful, but none too well versed in Revolutionary lore, Captain Emery invented plausible replies to puzzling questions asked by visitors. These answers, presumably authentic because given by a responsible official, were remembered by the inquisitors and were passed on as truth. Thus the one-time shoe closet became a hiding place for papers; the root cellar was turned into a secret passage; the distant spring along Valley Creek Road was entitled Washington's Spring; cellars in all buildings surviving since Revolutionary days were glibly described as jails in which prisoners were kept. To Captain Emery is also due the confusion concerning the locations of the original Mount Joy forges.

No fewer than four separate sites are pointed out as the places from which Valley Forge was named. Emery was unaware that, during the pre-Revolutionary era, a forge was not merely a blacksmithy but included also a complete iron-making unit. The Mount Joy Forge was a bloomery, where pig iron was converted into foot-long iron billets, a finery, where cast iron was turned into wrought iron, a chafery for drawing billets into bars, and a slitting mill for manufacturing nails and other finished products from the bars. Thus, the four forge "sites" indicated places where different branches of the iron industry were carried on.

The main building of the original Mount Joy, or Valley, Forge stood in pre-Revolutionary times close to the crossroads near the Headquarters. Workmen excavating at this site, under the skilled direction of Jerome Sheas in 1929, found charred timbers twelve feet below the surface of the ground. The remains of an ancient breast wheel, connected with the shaft of a trip hammer, the ruins of a sluice and of a wheel pit, the remains of heavy oak planks, and a section of a four-foot-high stone wall indicated that the forge burned by the British had stood here.

Upstream, under seven feet of Valley Creek silt, the remains of a bloomery were found. A huge undershot water wheel, measuring more than fifteen feet in diameter, once revolved here on heavy oak channels. Sections of a second stone wall indicated that an old forge building more than thirty-two feet square must have stood here in Revolutionary days. Near by were oaken slabs of an old flume, part of a hearth, and ironwork inscribed with "Andover." Andover Furnace, from which the ironwork must have come, was in southern New Jersey. So carefully had the original foundations been laid that even after the passage of more than a century and a half the beds for the machinery were accurately level.

The relics, after being carefully measured and photographed, were treated with preservatives and were reset in their original position. The Valley Forge Park Commission now plans to restore the upper forge to illustrate the iron-making process used in Revolutionary days.

Misconception has been common, too, concerning the equipment. Although the furniture at Headquarters is of authentic pre-Revolutionary manufacture, and although it corresponds in exact detail to the furnishings inventoried by Deborah Hewes, none of the furniture was actually used by Washington at Valley Forge. Notwithstanding this, souvenir hunters often ravaged the property prior to its acquisition by the State. Stone was chipped from the Headquarters, wood was carved away, small relics were stolen; even two trees were cut down by curio seekers.

None of the cannon now at Valley Forge were with the army during the encampment, though three of the guns saw Revolutionary service and one was captured by the Americans at Yorktown. The other artillery pieces are modern copies of Revolutionary guns. Here too, however, vandals have been active, for attempts have been made to carry off small parts of the artillery. The modern cannon balls, cast to simulate the Revolutionary munitions, were so frequently pilfered that the Park Commission was obliged to bolt down the hollow imitations and to set them firmly in concrete for safety.

It is difficult, however, to disabuse the credulous or to protect them against impostors. A Grand Army post in Philadelphia, thanking Hannah Ogden, a former owner of the Headquarters, for selling to it Washington's favorite ladder-back chair, was astonished to learn that it had bought from an unauthorized "agent" a discarded nineteenth century piece. A curious, symbolic "throne," built of gnarled laurel limbs and twisted roots, with a body shaped to represent the campground, and with a Continental flag inlaid upon the back with parti-colored wood and star-headed nails, long traveled through the United States under the pretense that it was a Revolutionary relic exhibited for the benefit of the Valley Forge authorities. Not even museums have been exempt from error, the Valley Forge Park Commission believes, in accepting unverified "relics" of the encampment.

Stranger legends have been circulated. Near Gulph Mills, on the road where Washington's men made their bloody march, a huge rock, now bearing a tablet in commemoration of the week's encampment there, is popularly supposed to have been split off from the hilltop by a bolt of lightning. Folklore relates that the phenomenon occurred on the same night as the Paoli Massacre, and that neighbors were thus warned of danger. A companion story, in a guidebook sponsored by the Pennsylvania Historical Commission, vouches for the untrue statement that Washington stood upon the near-by Hanging Rock to review his troops at a time when blinding snow would have made a review impossible even if Washington could have climbed the steep slopes of the rock.

Tradition states also that each year on September 20, the anniversary of the Paoli Massacre, General Anthony Wayne rides again, from his tomb at Radnor, to visit his former camp at Valley Forge. The "ghost," it is alleged, has thus ridden his favorite steed "Nancy" for more than a century. Oddly enough, Wayne never revisits the Paoli encampment.

The myth received a fillip in 1933, when a young Philadelphia reporter, "beaten" on a number of news items, conspired with a friend to create a story which he could have exclusively. The friend donned a three-cornered hat, mounted a horse smeared with phosphorescent paint, and rode at midnight through the neighborhood. The reporter, calling a number of other friends to witness the phenomenon, prepared a startling story which his paper published. On the following night, the friend rode again, in a different locality, and thus continued during several successive evenings. Highway police were called upon to patrol the roads against the ghostly visitor, but, after the reporter had drained the story dry of interest, the rides were ended. The myth, however, lived on, although Wayne has not since ridden.

Washington and Lafayette, as well as Wayne, are popularly supposed to have returned as ghosts to Valley Forge. The former's spirit has been seen at midnight at the Washington Spring which the Commander actually rarely saw in life. Lafayette, uneasy because at the time of his triumphal return to the United States in 1825 he had no time to visit Valley Forge, restlessly walked up and down his old quarters at the western end of camp. The spirit vanished, it is said, when the old Negro woman to whom his presence was visible, politely asked him to be seated. Lafayette did so, but, after resting for a few moments, disappeared never to return. Still another ghost, identified as that of "Lord" Stirling, called at his old residence, where he and Parson Currie had enjoyed long metaphysical debates, but was not visible. Steps were heard ascending and descending the staircase; the door flew open and would not stay closed until the steps had finished; then, when the steps had died away, the door could finally be closed.

Yet another ghostly visitor is that which appears but once a year, at sunrise Christmas morning. He stands in the rifle pits of the Pennsylvania line, close to the Wayne statue. He wears a ragged Continental uniform and he carries a small drum. As the first sunrays gleam on Christmas morning he raises the drumsticks, sounds the reveille, and vanishes until another year.

The belief was long prevalent that where American blood was shed in the greatest profusion an abundance of wild thyme sprang up spontaneously. Near Brandywine there is, moreover, a legend that when the Americans were pursued by British forces a redcoat officer stopped at a blacksmith's shop to command the smith to shoe his horse. This the blacksmith, a fervent rebel, refused to do; but, threatened by the officer, he pretended to comply. Watching for an opportunity, the blacksmith struck the officer with a hammer. Then, dragging the dead body to a well, he threw it into the water. Many persons, according to the unpublished memoir of Bayard Taylor, have seen the blacksmith perform the daring act over and over again in the dead silence of midnight.

The folk ghosts of Valley Forge have long been famous. From earliest Colonial times, when superstitious settlers mistook as specters the frequent wisps of fog that rose at night from off the creek, stories of supernatural visitors have gained wide currency. A headless horseman, riding a white ghostly mount, is said to haunt the valley; a roaming spirit which leaps to the saddle of a stranger riding late along the roads is still gospel among the unsophisticated. Some may be but shadows, others merely scraps of fog; but, in former days at least, all were credited with superhuman power.

The restored Welsh farmhouse, where Varnum had his quarters, was particularly psychic. An old witch doctor from the credulous Flourtown settlement, where everyone believed in magic, once made his headquarters here. On one occasion, shortly after the Revolution, this *Hexenmeister* put his sign with chalk upon the rafters. Ailing folk from far up the Great Valley, farmers whose cattle were suffering from strange diseases, unfortunates whose luck was bad, young girls afflicted with an unrequited love, rode down to Valley Forge to seek relief. The Varnum house had power, because of its hex sign, to cancel out the spells imposed by wicked conjurers. These quarters of "The Light of the Camp" possessed a more potent magic than any other house within a range of many miles of Valley Forge.

CHAPTER TWENTY-EIGHT

Stranger in Black

ON a hot Monday afternoon in late July, 1787, Edward Woodman, North Carolinian veteran, was plowing the fields of his father-in-law, Abijah Stephens, when a dignified elderly gentleman, dressed in plain black, rode up the highway from Trout Run. Pulling his horse to a stop and throwing the reins to his Negro attendant, the gentleman strode across the fields to talk with the plowman.

Woodman told the stranger the names of the farmers residing in the neighborhood, gave details of the farming methods used and of the grains and vegetables raised, explained, while the grave gentleman in black methodically wrote down the data in a memorandum book, the best ways to till the soil, the average quantities raised, and other information interesting to a farmer. The plowman apologized for not being able to give more complete answers to the stranger's questions, explaining that he had settled at Valley Forge since the Revolution, and had not been trained as a farmer.

His statement that he had been a Revolutionary soldier, and that he had been encamped here with his Tarheel regiment, gave a new turn to the conversation. The stranger said that

he, too, had been in the army, and that he had also been encamped here. He had come from Philadelphia to visit the
place, to see the old encampment which had been the scene
of so much suffering and distress, and to see how far the inhabitants were recovering from the losses they had sustained.
His name, the stranger said, was George Washington.

Woodman was profuse in his apologies for not having recognized his old Commander, now the President of the United
States. Washington's costume and appearance, Woodman
hastily explained, were so changed that he had been unable
to identify the visitor.

Washington answered that to see the people happy and content, the fields recovering from the desolation they had experienced, and old comrades in arms peacefully engaged in the
most useful of all employments afforded him more real satisfaction than all the servile homage that could be paid to his
person or his station. He asked Woodman's name, noted it in
his memorandum book, and regretted that pressing engagements made it necessary for him to return to Philadelphia that
night. He wished that he might spare the time to call upon
some of his old friends at their houses. He walked back to the
road, mounted his horse, and rode off to the south.

The incident records the only visit made by Washington
to Valley Forge following the encampment. He had come with
Gouverneur Morris, Pennsylvania's Federalist delegate to the
Constitutional Convention, during a recess in the sessions of
that body. While Morris remained near Muhlenberg's old
quarters to fish in Trout Run, Washington had ridden on to
inspect the old cantonment ground.

The Washington visit was the first of the long series of pil-
grimages made in later years to the "wide hollow in the rugged
hill beside the curving Schuylkill" where the spirit of America

323

was preserved. For more than a century and a half, the camp-ground has been a patriotic shrine to honor the men who made the nation.

Valley Forge marked the turning point of the Revolution. The men who came to its wind-swept, snow-clad acres in stormy December, 1777, were battered, hungry, sick, and in distress. Abandoned, as they thought, by the civilians of the Continental Congress, deserted, as it seemed, by their own states, the ragged, barefoot volunteers huddled helplessly about their smoky green-wood fires. Defeated at Brandywine, at Paoli, and at Germantown, they had not lost their confidence nor weakened in their morale until the smooth-tongued statesmen had seemed to turn against the army's leaders. The fearful winter, despite its tragic hardships, had taught them that their courage, fortitude, patience, and unstinted fealty to ideals would bring them to eventual victory. A disciplined, resourceful, and heartened army marched away from Valley Forge.

The lesson of Valley Forge must not be lost. The Continental troops who came as unrelated, virtually independent groups from separate states went forth a welded national army. Their Spartan endurance of distress and disaster had taught them the need for a federated union of free men, enlightened and politically equal, if their ideals of liberty, democracy, and the pursuit in peace of happiness were to be realized. They had staked their lives, their fortunes, and indeed their honor, in the furtherance of these great aims; they had displayed a fortitude unexampled in the history of mankind in the face of physical suffering and spiritual anguish. They had set a pattern for the world to follow.

"Defects in the Commissary's Department, contingences of Weather and other Temporary impediments have subjected and may again subject us to a deficiency for a few days," wrote Washington in his general orders; "but soldiers, American soldiers, will dispise the meanness of repineing at such trifling strokes of adversity. Trifling indeed when compared with the transcendent prize which will undoubtedly crown their patience and persevearance, Glory and Freedom, Peace and Plenty to themselves and the community, the Admiration of the world, the love of their Country and the gratitude of Posterity."

These blessings were secured at Valley Forge. Peace, wealth, and undreamed-of power followed the victory which Valley Forge prepared. The foundation of a great nation, made possible at Valley Forge in time of trouble, in days of sorrow and perplexity, wrought revolution not only for the thirteen struggling states but for the oppressed peoples of the world. The doubt, distress, and danger, the cold and hunger, the suffering and want of Valley Forge were sacrifices for the welfare of the newborn nation. The unfailing patriotism of the soldiers, their unceasing vigilance, their courage and devotion were bright examples for a world to follow.

No such inheritance can be kept safe without continued watchfulness. In the first days of the American Republic, John Philpot Curran, Irish statesman and warrior for freedom, pointed out the deathless truth that eternal vigilance is the price of liberty. "It is the common fate of the indolent," he said, "to see their rights become a prey to the active. The condition under which God hath given liberty to man is eternal vigilance; which condition if he break, servitude is at once the consequence of his crime and the punishment of his guilt." Honor to the memory of the sufferers of Valley Forge is best expressed by zealously serving the ideals for which they labored.

VALLEY FORGE

For, as Henry Armitt Brown so eloquently phrased it in his moving centennial address, "a country is benefited by great actions only so long as her children are able to repeat them." The heroes of the winter at Valley Forge created and established a nation of ideals; they patiently endured unspeakable suffering to set up a government where justice and humanity might rule; they gave, through their incredible ordeal, a goal toward which the struggling folk of every land might themselves aspire. But they could not guarantee that their heroic sacrifices would for all time assure the safekeeping of their legacy.

The ancient deeds are now secure; the new times are uncertain. Citizens of later generations, marveling at the achievements of their spiritual forefathers, bless the memory of Valley Forge; but they must, in their turn, be watchful to perpetuate the gains wrested at such cost. The age in which we live is but a link in the endless, eternal chain of time; new devotions and fresh sacrifices are required if the heroism of the Revolutionary age is not to be cast away. Vigilance and devotion, endless self-sacrifice and willingness to endure privation for the common good are as necessary in our modern days as in the snowy winter of the Washington encampment.

As everlasting symbol of that need, a peaceful park now stands at Valley Forge. Its dogwood trees, gleaming white in the crystal sunlight of spring days, stretch out their limbs like suppliant palms, upturned, to beg that passers-by accept the vow to keep the nation great. Its sturdy forest wall of eternally burgeoning trees, its firm but friendly hills, its long, inviting, lush green lawn bear now no signs of suffering and death. Yet they recall to every patriot American, to every lover of freedom and democracy throughout the world, that beauty springs from sacrifice, that peace was dearly bought, and that the

326

heroism of George Washington and his devoted men can never be forgotten while America still lives.

"Where stands Valley Forge," said Governor Martin Brumbaugh at the dedication of the arch, "there stand the hopes, the aspirations, the glories of the human kind."

INDEX

INDEX

Brinton, Crazy Johnny, 223

Bristol, 144

Brooke, Francis M., 297 ff.

Brown, Henry Armitt, 295, 297, 303, 326

Brown, Joseph, 38

Bull, Col. John, 242

Burgoyne, Gen. John, 69, 101, 118, 120, 132, 271, 274, 277

Burk, Rev. W. Herbert, 305–309

Burlington, 184, 218

Bush-Brown, Henry Kirke, 301

Bushnell, David, 219

Cadwalader, Brigadier-General John, 223

Camp Hill, 131

Camps. *See* Pennypacker's Mill, Pottsgrove, Towamensing, Whitemarsh, Whitpain, Worcester

Canal, 286 f.

Carlisle, Abraham, 210

Carroll, Charles, of Carrollton, 124

Catherine the Great, 186

Centennial and Memorial Association of Valley Forge, 295 f., 298–300

Center Square, 125 f.

Chadds Ford, 35 f., 41

Chapel, Washington Memorial, 155, 304–307, 309

Chesapeake Bay, 30, 55, 58, 138

Chester, 41, 112

Chester Creek, 13

Chestnut Hill, 123, 144

Chew, Chief Justice Benjamin, 107

Chew House, 107–109

Cheyney, Squire Thomas, 37 f.

Choiseul, Étienne François, 206

Cincinnati, Order of, 186

Clark, Champ, 303

Clay, Henry, 293

Clinton, Governor George, 170

Clinton, Gen. Sir Henry, 221, 222, 250

Clothing, 26, 63, 66, 91, 97 ff., 114, 124, 129, 131, 133 f., 142, 163, 167, 170, 206 f., 210, 252, 253 f.

Clouds, Battle of. *See* Battles

Cold, 114, 119, 124 f., 129, 131, 133 f., 137, 144 f., 147, 163, 233, 255

Colonial Dames of America, 306

Commissary, 134, 153, 252

Cone, Mrs. Mary Thropp, 295

Congress, 30, 46, 50, 115 f., 124, 129–134, 142, 147 f., 150, 153, 163, 164, 167, 168 f., 193 f., 229, 257, 324

Congressional Board of War, 218

Connecticut, 142, 156, 158, 164, 189, 218, 252

Conshohocken, 16, 141, 251

Convention Troops, 271–280

Conway, Brigadier Gen. Thomas, 132 f., 155, 158, 167

Cooch's Bridge, Battle of, 34 f.

Cornwallis, Earl, 36 f., 43, 59 ff., 102, 108 f., 145 f., 209 f., 266

Coryell's Ferry, 259

Council, Pennsylvania Supreme Executive. *See* Pennsylvania

Court-martial, 61, 130, 198, 203, 244, 248

Coventry, 35, 41, 51, 62, 67, 71 f., 74, 138, 227

Cox, Martha, 60 f.

Craig, Capt. John, 142 f.

Crammond, Major John, 211

Creeks. *See* Brandywine, Chester, French Manatawney, Perkiomen, Pickering, Skippack, Valley, Wissahickon

Cret, Paul, 302

Crooked Billet, Battle of, 246 ff.

Crooked Hills, 91, 94

Cunningham, Capt. William, 212 ff.

Currie, Parson William, 160 f., 319

Dana, Francis, 167 f.

Darby, 122, 240

Darragh, Ensign Daniel, 142

Darragh, Lydia, 142

D'Ascenzo, Nicola, 306

Daughters of the American Revolution, 301 f.

330

INDEX

INDEX

INDEX

INDEX

INDEX

INDEX

75, 80–83, 85, 88–91, 104 ff., 109 f., 115, 119 f., 122–125, 131 f., 133 ff., 138–145, 148, 150 f., 154, 156 ff., 160 f., 166, 170, 176 f., 182, 186, 190, 192 ff., 199 ff., 202 f., 207, 213–216, 218, 220, 223, 225, 227 ff., 233 ff., 241, 244 f., 251, 253, 256 ff., 280, 302, 322 f.

Washington, Martha, 231 f.

Waterman, Lieut. John, 299

Wayne, Brigadier Gen. Anthony, 38, 43, 45–49, 51, 57, 62, 65 f., 67, 74, 76 f., 80–83, 89–91, 102, 104, 106, 109, 123 f., 129 f., 134 f., 138 ff., 156 f., 164, 170 f., 174, 182, 189, 194 ff., 215, 227 f., 243, 245, 254 f., 257, 297, 301, 318 f.

Waynesborough, 76, 81, 83

Webster, Daniel, 293

Weedon, Brigadier Gen. George, 156 f., 199, 300

Weikel, Rev. John H., 116 f., 121

Welsh, 10, 12 ff., 17 ff., 21, 23, 45, 92, 239, 259, 263

Wentz, Peter, 102, 119 ff.

Wheeler, Richard, 165

Whig, 21 f., 43, 67, 75, 79, 115, 139, 160

Whitefield, George, 93

Whitemarsh, 123, 130 f., 134 f., 142 f., 145

Whitpain, 125, 128 ff., 259

Wilkinson, James, 132

Wilmington, 31, 57 f., 62, 102, 122, 138, 252

Wissahickon Creek, 92, 123, 129

Witchcraft, 16 f., 105, 128 f., 321

Witherspoon, Major James, 108

Witherspoon, Rev. John, 108

Witt, Christopher, 128

Woodford, Brigadier Gen. William, 158

Woodman, Edward, 322 f.

Woolman, Henry L., 309

Worcester, 117 f.

Yellin, Samuel, 307

Yellow Springs, 52, 141, 160, 182, 184

York, 130 f., 209, 226, 279

Zedwitz, Herman, 216

Zinzendorf, Count Nicholas Ludwig, 93

Date Due